New Southern Cooking

New SOUTHERN COOKING

Nathalie Dupree

ALFRED ✿ A. ✿ KNOPF

NEW ✦ YORK ✦ 1988

Copyright © 1986 by Nathalie Dupree
Illustrations copyright © 1986 by Karen Barbour

Grateful acknowledgment is made to the following
for permission to reprint previously published material:

Irena Chalmers: "Cream of Carrot Soup"
reprinted from *Cooking of the South* by Nathalie Dupree,
published in The Great American Cooking Schools series
by Irena Chalmers Cookbooks, Inc.

Doubleday & Company, Inc.: "Peach-Pecan Pie" from *Southern Cookbook,*
by Grace Hartley. Copyright © 1976 by Grace Hartley.

Library of Congress Cataloging-in-Publication Data

Dupree, Nathalie.
New Southern cooking.

Bibliography: p.
Includes index.
1. Cookery, American—Southern style.   I. Title.
TX715.D8924   1986   641.5975   86-18564
ISBN 0-394-55818-9

Manufactured in the United States of America
Published December 17, 1986
Reprinted Twice
Fourth Printing, November 1988

*To the women who influenced my cooking;
to my mother, Jean "Van," and Kate;
and to Ted*

Contents

Acknowledgments

I owe a debt of gratitude to so many people—without them this book and the "New Southern Cooking" television series couldn't have become a reality.

Thank you to Judith Jones, who pulled this book out of the fire, encouraging me to finish it. I shall always be grateful. Her painstaking interest in the design has made this the beautiful book it is. Toula Polygalaktos, also at Alfred A. Knopf, has devoted many hours and much energy to it, with care and good humor. Sue Hunter, my collaborator, put in a great deal of effort as well—thanks for your patience.

My beloved friend Kate Almand has worked for me since 1972, starting at my restaurant in Social Circle, Georgia, then coming on to Rich's Cooking School with me. She arrives at my door at 7:30 each morning. She's at the television studio when I'm there, or at home with me, testing these recipes. One of thirteen children, she is the best traditional Southern cook I know, and contributed many of the solidly traditional recipes in this book. I'm very grateful for her friendship and support. To Kay Calvert, who has worked with me since my first class at Rich's—thanks for never complaining.

The other teachers and assistants at Rich's Cooking School contributed enormously in developing recipes over the years, encouraging me and helping define Southern cooking, and the students brought me more riches.

The "food group," a group of Atlantans with whom I cooked monthly over a period of time (Jim and Gwen Bentley, Tom and Susan Puett, Dick Williams and Rebecca Chase, Anne Byrne, Jean Thwaite and Walter Thwaite, and Betty Talmadge), was another source of recipes. Cicero Garner is one of the true gourmands of the South, and he and his wife Laurie have given me so many ideas. All sorts of recipes were developed because Tom went trout fishing, Jimmy picked turnip greens, or Cicero's uncle gave us a baby goat. Thanks to Beth and Billy McKinnon, who shared their vast knowledge of Savannah and New Orleans cuisine.

Bernard Clayton, Merle Ellis, Bert Greene, Paul Prudhomme, and Philip Schultz helped immeasurably by giving me their support and advice on both the television series and the book.

Without Ted Pedas, Lloyd Montgomery, Cynthia Stevens Cartledge, and Beverly Molander there would have been no series. The crew and the cooks for the television series, led by Forsythia Chang, did a wonderful job. Many thanks for working such long hours and for remaining cheerful and devoted.

My family and my former husband, David Dupree, helped considerably just by calling and checking on my progress, as well as spending long hours with me at the studio. I'm grateful to them all. A special thanks to the White Lily Foods Company, which underwrote the television production of "New Southern Cooking"; Georgia Public Television; and Amanda Brown Olmstead and Associates.

I don't know where anyone who has prospered in their love of good food in America would be without Julia Child, and we all owe her a debt of gratitude.

The cooking magazines of today have greatly influenced the growth of new Southern cooking: *The Cook's Magazine, The Pleasures of Cooking, Food & Wine, Bon Appétit,* and *Gourmet.* My articles in *Atlanta* magazine and *Brown's Guide to Georgia* were sources for many of these recipes.

Many other people—those who contributed recipes or spent hours talking with me about the origin of Southern cooking, where it is today, where it was yesterday, where it will be tomorrow—and the friends who helped type, edit, and test these recipes, all mean a great deal to me. And then there are the ones that just encouraged me to write and be the best I could be: Dick Acheson, Barbara Bacon, Anne Poland Berg, Fred Brown, Faith Brunson, Eilenne Smythe Buchanan, Irena Chalmers, Phyllis S. Cherry, Ginger Converse, Evelyn Cook, Shirley Corriher, Bart Duncan, Weida Duncan, Celeste Dupree, Susan Eckstein, Diana Everett, Martha Fiveash, Peggy Foreman, Alma Freedman, Anne Galbraith, Charles Gandy, Kay Goldstein, Elise Griffin, Muriel Hancock, Dotta Hansell, Leila Hansell, Lee Hopper, the London Cordon Bleu, Kay Messenger, Chuck (Gordon) Meyer, Col. Walter Meyer, Victoria (Vicky) Mooney, Audrey Odegardt, Barbara

Persons, Alice Phillips, Pat Portal, Victoria Proctor, Kelli Questrom, Grace Reeves, Bill Rice, Susan Rice, Barbara Robinson, Trigg Robinson, Carmen Sanders, Jean Sparks, Margaret Anne Sparks, Bobbi Sturgis, Marion Sullivan, Martha Summerour, Dean Terry, Candy Thrasher, Judith Tuggle, Flora Undercofler, Jean Van den Berg, LuLen Walker, Roxanna Young, and Conrad Zimmerman.

Introduction

Since we say, Once a Southerner, always a Southerner, I'd like to invite you into my home, and the homes of my friends, and make you a Southerner for a time. Life in the South stamps you, and you'll be richer for it. We don't know a stranger here. Having company in our homes is a natural way of life to us. And that always means sharing what we eat.

The seed for this book is my nationwide television series "New Southern Cooking with Nathalie Dupree." We called it that because we felt people wanted to learn about the kind of cooking that is being done *today* in the South. So I selected all the dishes I love the most—the ones I have served to my friends and loved ones at home many times over the past years. Although they are all dishes that are easily prepared, I made a point of stopping to explain techniques that many new young Southerners (and Northerners, too) might not understand because they didn't learn cooking at Mama's knee as people did in past generations (Mama may have been too busy, or she may not have even come from the South). I included, of course, some of our traditional recipes—but as I would make them today. And, when I was through with the series of twenty-six programs, I found I had many, many more recipes—my own accumulation of more than thirty-five years of living and eating in the South.

Before you eat with me, let me stop here for those of you who may not know what I mean by the South and let you know who we are. We are a vast region, larger than Europe, loosely defined by those states that seceded from the Union in the nineteenth century. At that time we were predominantly British people, who settled the rice and cotton and tobacco plantations and grew their crops with the labor of African slaves. People from many nationalities and cultures traded vigorously with us—among them French, Spanish, West Indian, Dutch, German, and Chinese. Some came to settle and then moved on, while others came and stayed. They all left influences on our cooking—curries, ginger, soy sauce, spices, along with the foods of the Africans—okra, eggplant, peanuts, and more.

The poverty and humiliation resulting from the War Between the States and the Great Depression fixed us in time. Our desire to preserve, hold on to, and remain set in our ways is reflected in our politics and customs and in the soul food that became a trademark and mainstay of Southern cooking. Much of it came from former slaves who were our cooks. This kind of down-home cooking gives us a feeling of security when the rains don't come or when the mill closes, today as much as yesterday.

The spiciness and diversity of Creole and Cajun foods and the Spanish and Mexican foods of Texas and Florida are powerful cuisines reaching into our region, but are not in the mainstream of Southern cooking. We're not an island, however, and you will find that my favorites from these styles of cooking have insinuated themselves into this book—Chili, Acadian Peppered Shrimp, Boiled Crawfish, and Orange and Lemon Garlic Pork.

The meals served fifteen years ago in the South evolved from the kinds of meals we ate one hundred years ago. Although since the Second World War we have had an influx of people from many countries, the real amalgamation is only just beginning. We have been slow to alter our ways, and the gradual changes that have occurred reflect a difference in the way we live, not the current food fads from other parts of the United States. We have not been willing to relinquish those foods that satisfy our yearnings for days gone by, but we are willing to accept the new, and enjoy a little tweak of fun at our traditional favorites. Our lifestyles are different from those of our parents. We like grilling more, our houses are air-conditioned, we eat later, we want to be thin and healthy, so we cut back on fats and salt.* Our kitchens have all the modern conveniences—food processors, microwaves, freezers, indoor/outdoor grills—today, the help we have is not hired, it's *in* our homes!

In these pages I give you recipes for the legendary favorites like barbecue, Brunswick stew, grits, turnip greens, poke sallet, Hopping John, and biscuits. And interspersed are some of my new ideas—luscious grits cooked in cream and cheese,

---

*For this reason you will not see specific amounts of salt called for in this book, but constant urgings to taste before seasoning. I only give set amounts in cases where the salt is definitely important to the final recipe.

an effervescent butterbean and champagne soup that sizzles as you serve it, an unusual lasagne made with turnip-green pasta and sausage meat (if you can have spinach pasta, why can't you have turnip-green?), crisp grilled duck married to muscadine preserves, and a feather-light lemon and peach mousse. What they have in common is that the principal ingredients for both the time-honored and new-fangled recipes come from our gardens, our coastal waters, and our farms.

Some of the foods from the eighteenth century—recorded by Martha Washington, Thomas Jefferson, his niece Mary Randolph, and others—seem to have disappeared over the years and are now surfacing again—caveach, gazpacho, game, duck, mussels, sturgeon, fresh herbs, curries, even puff pastry—and I have borrowed from that early heritage, helping to restore some of these treasures to our tables. Before pasta became the rage in America there was the Southern noodle! The fun of new Southern cooking is to take the old and the new and put them together with creative zest. I've tried to arrange menus that blend the two, and in the menu section you'll find lots of ideas for you to work with.

Don't be afraid to mix and match. We're the same people we always were; we've just come into our own now, and our cooking reflects that independence.

Southern cooking is primarily home cooking, not chef's art. It certainly "ain't nouvelle" or precious. It's just good food, fit for savoring, not simply pretty to look at. The foods of the South for generations were meant to nourish hardworking families as they came together at mealtimes. Foods were always served "family-style" in big bowls at the table. I've never had a plated meal in a Southern home, except in the kitchen when you could go back to the pot for refills. Perhaps that's a poor people's way to avoid looking stingy. We wanted to make a show of abundance and served a number of vegetables. Sometimes the only meat in our daily fare would be the fatback cooked in the vegetables because that's all that was on hand. When I was a child, you could look into the kitchen window of each house and know what was cooking in every pot, because it was all the same.

So our gardens, backyards, and farms have dictated what we ate and still do. Our long, hot summers have enabled us to eat fresh produce for much of the year—vine-ripened lush tomatoes, okra, squash, greens, peas and beans, hot peppers and sweet peppers, fresh corn, the sweetest peaches in the world, and our own nut, the pecan. When we weren't eating from the garden, only a limited number of foods were available from the grocery store in our small towns. So we bought enough Vidalia onions to last all winter long and hung them in stockings, a knot between one onion and the next, to keep them cool. We put up conserves and preserves, canned beans, dried beans and peas, salted and preserved meats and fish, and kept a country ham on the cool larder shelf. These are the things we combined to make a meal.

We've only recently started "entertaining" at home—what we did before was have "company" over. The country home cook never had a dinner party in her life.

But her table was always full of family, people from church, a stranger in town. She cooked for a crowd, then sat down to eat in the same gingham dress she had worn all day. How many did a dish serve? Well, you made a "mess" (a quantity) of, say, peas, and they stretched to feed the crowd. You brought a big, tall cake to the church supper, and there was always enough to feed everyone.

Making you a Southerner makes you a cousin. Sometimes I think we're all related. While traveling in the South as director of Rich's Cooking School in Atlanta—to Birmingham, Columbia, Savannah, and Memphis—and while filming the location inserts for my television show, I was often invited into the homes of strangers. They would invite their closest friends and we'd all share a meal. I rarely left without a regional cookbook, full of names of new cousins, and their recipes.

Perhaps that is why we always credit recipes here in the South. A recipe is always named for the person who gave it to you, no matter how long you've been making it, because the whole extended family knows she made it before you did. I live in dread that I've not acknowledged a book or a friend, much less a relative. I hope I've covered them all, either in the Acknowledgments or in the Bibliography in the back of the book.

New Southern cooking is, then, a melding of foods and styles of cooking. Sometimes the food is for family, sometimes for company, which is nearly family, and sometimes for "entertaining." In the spirit of Southern hospitality it pleases me to offer you these recipes. I hope you enjoy them.

New Southern Cooking

STARTERS
and
BRUNCHES

Asparagus Topped with Scallops

This is a pretty fix-ahead starter with the green and white colors of spring. I prefer thin asparagus and like it peeled since it's much easier to eat that way. The peanut oil adds a light, nutty flavor.

2 pounds thin asparagus, rinsed
2 tablespoons vegetable oil
1 medium onion or 2 or 3 shallots,
    chopped

1 pound bay or sea scallops

☆   ☆   ☆

Dressing:
2/3 cup vegetable oil
1/3 cup white wine vinegar
    or herb vinegar
1/4 cup cold-pressed virgin peanut oil
    (you can also use hazelnut or
    walnut oil)

Salt
Freshly ground black pepper
1 tablespoon chopped fresh herbs
    (optional)

Cut off the thick, woody ends of the asparagus. With a vegetable peeler, peel each stalk, beginning at the little offshoots near the tips. Place in a large pot or frying pan with enough boiling water to cover. (The tips can lean their heads slightly

Asparagus with Scallops, continued

out of the pan.) Cook, uncovered, briefly until just done and still crisp, about 3–5 minutes, then rinse in cold water to stop the cooking and set the color.

Make the salad dressing (see below). Toss the still-warm asparagus in some of the dressing. Set aside. Don't refrigerate unless necessary; the bright green color of the asparagus will change if you do.

Heat the 2 tablespoons oil in a large saucepan, add the onion or shallots, and cook until soft. Add the scallops and cook, covered, for 5 minutes. Remove and toss them while still warm in the remainder of the dressing. Chill. When ready to serve, place some of the asparagus on each plate, and top with the scallops and dressing.

To make the dressing, combine the vegetable oil and vinegar in a food processor or blender or in a bowl with a whisk. Taste and add peanut oil as desired for flavor. Season with salt and pepper and optional herbs.

Broiled Oysters with Georgetown Caviar

Serves 6

Upon returning to the South in 1971, I visited the parents of an old friend who lived in Hilton Head, South Carolina. Mrs. Hansell served me their "local caviar" on a bed of ice, with only crisp toast, chopped hard-boiled eggs, and chopped onions as accompaniments. I was stunned by its quality. In Georgetown, South Carolina, and several other places in the South, American black sturgeon caviar is processed and sold to a few select shops. Its existence as a fine caviar, rivaling Russian and Iranian, was a well-kept secret until recently. Any good caviar will do, but by no means should you use lumpfish or salmon roe.

3 dozen oysters in the shell
1 recipe White Butter Sauce (p. 301),
    replacing shallots with
    2 julienned leeks

6 ounces fresh Georgetown, beluga,
    sevruga, or oesetra caviar or, if
    unavailable, 6 ounces golden
    whitefish caviar

Clean the oysters and open each by inserting the end of an oyster knife between the shells near the hinge. Pry open and cut the muscle attaching the oyster to its shell. Place each oyster in the deeper half of its shell and arrange them all on a large baking sheet. Run under the broiler just until the edges curl. Serve 6 oysters on each plate and top with White Butter Sauce and caviar.

Grouper with Leeks, Herbs, and Butter Sauce

Serves 8 as starter, 4 as main course

Our Southern grouper, a species of sea bass, is particularly moist. It ranges in size, and makes lovely steaks as well as fillets.

4 leeks
4 tablespoons butter
2 pounds grouper fillet or other firm,
    fresh non-oily fish
3 tablespoons chopped fresh herb,
    preferably basil or
    lemon balm (optional)

1 recipe White Butter Sauce with
    Tomatoes and Herbs (using basil)
    or White Butter Sauce
    with Ginger (p. 301)

Cut and trim each leek at the root end and a little above the white portion. Clean thoroughly, halve lengthwise, and slice into 1 1/2-inch julienne strips. Melt the butter in a large non-aluminum frying pan. Add the leeks and cook until they are slightly soft, about 3–5 minutes. Measure the thickness of the fillets and place the fish on top of the leeks. Reduce the heat, cover, and cook until done, about 10 minutes per inch of thickness. Check and turn if necessary. Remove the fish to a warm platter and top with the leeks, herbs, and hot butter sauce.

Barbara Persons' Caveach of Marinated Shrimp and Scallops

Serves 16 as starter, 8 as main course

Variations of this dish abound from Mexico to the Eastern Shore. It's easy, fast, and tasty and is best made ahead, a day or two even, and served chilled. With the abundance of seafood along our coasts, we serve shrimp as much as possible. It's nearly an addiction for the average Southerner.

3 fresh limes, sliced
3 pounds raw large shrimp in shells
    (about 30–35 per pound)
1½ pounds raw scallops
    or shark pieces
Juice of 8–10 limes (1 cup)
Juice of 5–6 lemons (½ cup)
6 tablespoons chopped fresh parsley
1 tablespoon fresh thyme
1 tablespoon chopped fresh marjoram
1 tablespoon chopped fresh basil

1 medium red onion, diced
4 tablespoons finely chopped bell
    pepper, preferably a mixture of
    red and green
¾ cup vegetable oil
1 teaspoon Tabasco
2 tablespoons Creole Seasoning
    (p. 297), optional
Salt
Freshly ground black pepper
4 avocados, peeled and sliced

Bring a quantity of water to the boil in a large pot along with the sliced limes. Add the shrimp and poach just a few minutes, until tender and pink. Remove the shrimp and set aside, saving the water and discarding the limes. If you are using sea scallops, slice them horizontally. Bay scallops should be left whole. Shark should be cut into ½-inch cubes. Place the scallops or shark in a strainer and dip into the boiling water until just cooked, about 30 seconds. Remove and set aside. Peel the cooked shrimp and cut into thirds. Place in a bowl with the scallops or shark. Add the lime and lemon juices, cover, and marinate overnight, tossing occasionally.

Bring to room temperature, drain, and discard the juice. Add the parsley, thyme, marjoram, basil, onion, bell pepper, oil, and Tabasco, and toss lightly. Taste and add Creole Seasoning and/or a quantity of salt and pepper; it takes a great deal to bring out the flavor. Chill. To serve, arrange on scallop shells, placing a slice of avocado on each portion.

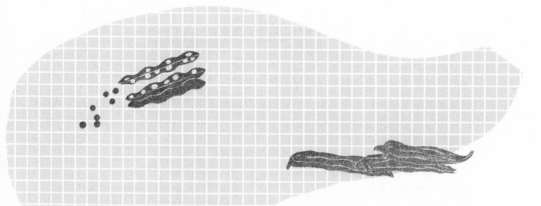

Acadian Peppered Shrimp

Serves 8

When Terry Thompson, one of Louisiana's most talented cooking teachers, first came to Rich's Cooking School, she had a fine background in Creole and Cajun cooking but no classical training. As the classes progressed, I would always taste a little of something different in all of Terry's food. Then one day I found a red-pepper shaker in her pocket! I had to hide it from her for the duration of the class so she could learn the way French food should really taste, free of Cajun influence. This recipe is adapted from a recipe of Terry's. She tells me that in New Orleans shrimp are often eaten unshelled, particularly if the shells are crisp and crunchy.

1 pound butter	5 cloves garlic, minced
1/2 cup lemon juice	1 bay leaf, crumbled
2 teaspoons chopped fresh basil	1/2 cup finely ground black pepper
1–2 teaspoons cayenne pepper	Salt

2 teaspoons chopped fresh oregano
   or marjoram
	4 pounds raw large shrimp in shells
	   (about 30–35 per pound)

Melt the butter in a large deep-sided frying pan or iron skillet over low heat. When melted, raise the heat, and add the remaining ingredients except the shrimp. Cook, stirring often, until browned to a rich mahogany color, about 10 minutes. Add the shrimp, stirring and turning to coat well with the seasoned butter. Cook until the shrimp have turned a rich deep pink, about 10 minutes. Serve the shrimp in their shells, peeling them at the table.

Coconut-Topped Shrimp

Serves 8

This is a great hors d'oeuvre for a party and can be multiplied to any quantity you like. It may be made ahead through the first broil, then topped with coconut and reheated from room temperature.

Freshly ground black pepper	1/8 teaspoon ground ginger
3 tablespoons soy sauce	1 pound raw peeled large shrimp
2 tablespoons oil	(about 30–35 per pound)
1 tablespoon finely chopped onion	1/2 cup grated coconut

In a bowl, combine the pepper, soy sauce, oil, onion, and ginger. Mix thoroughly with the shrimp and let marinate overnight. Preheat the broiler. Place the shrimp on a greased foil-lined broiler pan and broil about 3–4 inches from the heat for 4–5 minutes, turning once. When ready to serve, dip the shrimp in the marinade, sprinkle coconut over them, and return to the broiler just until the coconut is lightly browned, about 30 seconds. Serve at once.

Cold Shrimp Paste Spread

Makes 2 cups

This rich pink paste dates back in Georgia and South Carolina history. There are recipes for it in most coastal Southern cookbooks, like *Charleston Receipts* and *Two Hundred Years of Charleston Cooking*. It's smooth, buttery, and subtle, like a cold mousse or quenelle. Serve it on toast or with cold meats.

1 1/2 pounds large shrimp, cooked and peeled (about 30–35 per pound)	Freshly ground black pepper
	1/4 teaspoon thyme
3/4 pound butter, softened	1/2 teaspoon cayenne pepper
3/4 teaspoon salt	1 teaspoon freshly grated nutmeg

Chop the shrimp very fine in a food processor or blender. In a bowl, beat the butter until soft and white and add the shrimp, combining well. Add the seasonings and mix well. Refrigerate, covered, or freeze. Serve cold.

Hot or Cold Shrimp Paste
Makes 3 cups

This is the other of two famous shrimp pastes. Traditionally it is served cold on toast points or with cold meats, but I like to serve it hot as a rich starter, like a quenelle.

1 cup butter
1 pound large shrimp, cooked and
    peeled (about 30-35 per pound)

Freshly grated nutmeg
Salt
Freshly ground black pepper

Preheat the oven to 350 degrees. In a bowl, whisk the butter until soft and white. Chop the shrimp fine in a food processor or blender and add to the butter, beating the mixture well. Season to taste with nutmeg, salt, and pepper. Place in a buttered baking dish and bake 30 minutes or until the paste comes away from the sides of the dish and is light brown on top. Serve hot or refrigerate overnight, slice, and serve cold.

Hot and Spicy Shrimp
Serves 8 as starter, 4 as main course

Shrimp taste better when cooked in their shells because the fat under the shells preserves their flavor and tenderness. When the shells are crisp it is a pleasure to eat the shrimp with their shells on. This rich butter sauce cries out to be sopped up with crusty bread once the shrimp are gone.

Hot and Spicy Shrimp, continued

1 pound butter
1/4 cup peanut oil
3 cloves garlic, chopped
2 tablespoons rosemary
1 teaspoon chopped basil
1 teaspoon chopped thyme
1 teaspoon chopped oregano
1 small hot pepper, chopped,
    or 2 tablespoons ground
    cayenne pepper

2 teaspoons freshly ground
    black pepper
2 bay leaves, crumbled
1 tablespoon paprika
2 teaspoons lemon juice
2 pounds raw large shrimp
    in their shells
    (about 30–35 per pound)
Salt to taste

Melt the butter and oil in a flameproof baking dish. Add the garlic, herbs, peppers, bay leaves, paprika, and lemon juice, and bring to a boil. Turn the heat down and simmer 10 minutes, stirring frequently. Remove the dish from the heat and let the flavors marry at least 30 minutes. This hot butter sauce can be made a day in advance and refrigerated.

Preheat the oven to 450 degrees. Reheat the sauce, add the shrimp, and cook over medium heat until the shrimp just turn pink, then bake in the oven about 30 minutes more. Taste for seasoning, adding salt if necessary.

Hot and Spicy Deep-Fried Soft-Shell Crabs

Serves 4

I like to serve these as hors d'oeuvres, with their claws in the air and a sauce bowl of mayonnaise or White Butter Sauce in the center of the platter. Or I cut them in quarters and place them in a basket lined with a colorful cloth napkin. The egg batter makes a puffier crab, enhancing frozen crabs, which do not have as good a crunch otherwise. How much hot pepper you use is optional.

4–6 soft-shell crabs
2–3 tablespoons cayenne pepper or
    Creole Seasoning (p. 297)

2–3 tablespoons freshly ground black
    pepper
Salt

1 cup flour

2 eggs, beaten, or ½ cup
    evaporated milk

Fat or oil for deep frying

Cayenne pepper to taste

✿   ✿   ✿

Sauce:

1 recipe Mayonnaise (p. 306) or
    White Butter Sauce (p. 301)

Prepare the crabs as desired, quartered or whole (see p. 312). Mix the seasonings and pat a layer onto the crabs. Any excess seasoning should be added to the flour. Dip the crabs in the flour, then in the egg or milk, then again in the flour.

    Heat the fat or oil to 350 degrees and fry crabs until light brown and very crisp, about 5 minutes. It may be necessary to hold the crabs down if they bob up above the fat. Drain on a paper towel, and, if desired, sprinkle with more seasoning while hot. Serve right away.

Harold's Shad Roe

Serves 4

Harold was a porter on the Southern Railroad when my friend Marion was a child. When the railroad wanted to transfer him to New York, he chose instead to come and cook for Marion's mother. Harold taught Marion how to serve shad roe with ground pepper, lemon slices, and a covering of bacon. She, in turn, taught me.

1 shad roe

Salt

2 tablespoons vinegar

Freshly ground black pepper

4 tablespoons butter

1 tablespoon paprika

1 lemon, sliced

2 slices bacon, cooked crisp
    and crumbled

Cover the roe with water, to which a little salt and the vinegar have been added. Bring to the boil and simmer for about 10 minutes. Refresh with cold water to stop the cooking. Peel off as much of the membrane as you can and cut out the vein with the tip of a knife.

    Salt and pepper the roe and place in a baking dish. Melt the butter, add paprika, and pour over the roe. Broil, turning, until browned on both sides. Serve with lemon slices and bacon.

Steamed Farm-Grown Catfish

Serves 6 as a starter

Deen Terry, who grew up before catfish were farmed, is quite adamant about not using "caught" catfish. Caught catfish frequently have a muddy, nasty taste. Farmed catfish are fine and usually can be bought already in fillets. If you can't find catfish you may use any fish except salmon, mackerel, or bluefish.

Deen teaches Chinese cooking and uses this as a first course to a Chinese meal. It may be served cold as an appetizer. If you don't have a Chinese steamer, place a cake rack in the bottom of an electric frying pan. Pour the water in, keeping it below the level of the rack, and place the plate on the rack. Cover. Follow directions below. You may also cook this in the microwave, without using water, following your microwave directions for cooking fish.

I prefer this as a starter, although it may be used as a main dish.

**1¹/2 pounds fresh fillets of
   farm-grown catfish**

✿ ✿ ✿

Sauce:

1 teaspoon shredded fresh ginger root	1 tablespoon soy sauce
1 green onion, cut into very small pieces	1 tablespoon dry sherry
	1 teaspoon red pepper flakes
1 teaspoon fermented black beans	1 tablespoon peanut or corn oil

Place the fish on an oiled heatproof plate. To make the sauce, combine the remaining ingredients. Pour the sauce over the fish and place in a Chinese steamer. When the water boils, steam the fish 10 minutes for every inch of thickness. Reduce the time if the fish is less than 1 inch thick.

Marinated Beef

Serves 20

This can be used as a first course, or as an hors d'oeuvre for a cocktail party. I am a firm believer in always serving meat at cocktail parties. It helps keep my guests sober since they enjoy eating it so much. And it is usually less expensive than those little cubes of yellow cheese that no one wants to eat.

5–6 pounds tenderloin of beef,
   roasted rare
1 tablespoon chopped fresh rosemary
1 tablespoon chopped fresh basil
1 cup chopped shallots
Grated rind of 1 lemon
2 tablespoons Dijon mustard
Juice of 2 lemons

1 cup red wine vinegar
1 1/2 cups extra-virgin olive oil
   or virgin cold-pressed peanut oil
1 cup vegetable oil
Salt
Freshly ground black pepper
1/2 cup sun-dried tomatoes,
   sliced (optional)

Slice the tenderloin very thin and place in a deep dish. In a bowl combine the herbs, shallots, lemon rind, mustard, lemon juice, and vinegar, and blend with a whisk. Slowly add oil and continue to whisk rapidly. Season to taste with salt and pepper, then pour over the sliced tenderloin and marinate, chilled and covered, for 4 hours. Garnish with sun-dried tomatoes. Serve cold with the marinade.

Doren's Cocktail Meatballs

Serves 25

Doren Chisholm, who for years was the manager of Brennan's Restaurant in Atlanta when Paul Prudhomme was their executive chef, entertains with great style. This recipe of hers is always the hit of my cocktail parties. The meatballs freeze very well, for an indefinite amount of time. I defrost them in the microwave or overnight in the refrigerator, then reheat them for 15 minutes at 350 degrees before placing them in the sauce.

Doren's Cocktail Meatballs, continued

Meatballs:

3 pounds ground lean beef, ground
   together with 1 pound lean pork
3 cups quick rolled oats
1¾ cups milk
1 eight-ounce can chopped
   water chestnuts
5 tablespoons Worcestershire sauce
1 medium onion, finely chopped
5 cloves garlic, crushed with salt
   (see p. 315)

3 tablespoons Tabasco
6 tablespoons soy sauce
1 tablespoon cayenne pepper
1 tablespoon ginger, chopped
1 tablespoon oregano
1 tablespoon thyme
Salt
Freshly ground black pepper
8 tablespoons butter, for frying

✿   ✿   ✿

Sauce:

4 cups brown sugar
3 cups vinegar
4 tablespoons paprika
2 tablespoons salt

3 cups pineapple juice
4 tablespoons cold water
8 tablespoons cornstarch

To make the meatballs, in a large bowl combine the ground meat with the remaining ingredients except the butter, and mix well. Taste for seasoning by melting a little butter and frying a small amount of the mixture. Season with more salt and pepper if necessary and shape into 1-inch balls. Melt the butter in a heavy skillet and brown the meatballs in batches.

    To make the sauce, in a saucepan combine the brown sugar, vinegar, paprika, salt, and pineapple juice, and heat through. In a small dish, add 4 tablespoons cold water to the cornstarch and blend until smooth. Add some of the hot sauce to the cornstarch mixture, then pour back into the sauce. Cook until thick. Add the meatballs and heat thoroughly.

Pulled Pork and Sage Spread

Makes 1 ½ pints

There is a traditional French technique of pulling or shredding meat with two forks resulting in a kind of minced meat that is called rillettes. In France, as in the South, the long cooking of the meat with salted fat is a method of preserving and tenderizing. Some call this spread potted pork and it's cooked unattended nearly an hour or more, with most of the actual preparation time spent in cutting the meat to start and pulling or shredding it at the end. It keeps for a week or so in the refrigerator and freezes well. Serve with crusty bread and little sour pickles.

3 pounds pork from the back, loin,   1–2 teaspoons sage
    or ribs   1–2 teaspoons thyme
½ pound salt fatback, trimmed of rind   Salt
    and well rinsed   Freshly ground black pepper
6 cloves garlic, chopped

Cut the pork into finger-length strips and the fatback into 1/4-inch cubes. Place the fatback in a large pan. Cook over low heat until it renders some fat. Add the pork and enough water to cover the meat—about 1 cup. Partly cover the pan and cook over low heat for 45 minutes, without browning, stirring from time to time. Check to be sure there is enough water in the pan to prevent the pork from drying out and browning. When done, the meat should look white and be tender. Remove to a cutting board, saving the liquid and fat, and with 2 forks pull the meat into shreds, or shred in a food processor. Place in a bowl, taste for seasoning, and add most of the reserved liquid and fat to moisten and flavor. Mix in half the garlic, the sage, thyme, salt, and pepper. Taste again and add the rest of the garlic if desired. Place in pretty jars or pots, without packing too tightly. Cover with plastic wrap and refrigerate or freeze.

Pork and Peanut Hors d'Oeuvres

Serves 15

Pork and peanuts are staples in Southern cooking, as are hot peppers and onions. Small wonder we look to recipes like this one, adapted from the Indonesians, for

Pork and Peanut Hors d'Oeuvres, continued

modern ideas to combine the two. This is ideal to make ahead, freeze, and then broil or grill when ready to serve at your cocktail party.

Marinade:

1 cup shelled, roasted, and
  salted peanuts
1 bunch green onions, chopped to
  make 3/4 cup
Juice of 1 lemon
2 tablespoons honey
1/3 cup soy sauce

3 cloves garlic, chopped
1 tablespoon coriander seeds
2 tablespoons hot red peppers, fresh
  or dried
1/2 cup beef broth or bouillon
1/4 cup melted butter

✿   ✿   ✿

1 1/2 pounds lean pork,
  cut in 1-inch cubes

To make the marinade: Put the peanuts, onions, lemon juice, honey, soy sauce, garlic, coriander seeds, and peppers in a blender or food processor. Process until smooth, add the broth and melted butter, and process until well blended. Pour over the cut-up pork and marinate 8 hours or more in the refrigerator, covered.

Drain, reserving the marinade. Preheat a broiler or grill. Place the meat on a wire rack or on a barbecue grill 6 inches from the heat, in one layer. Broil or grill on one side until crisp and brown, about 5 minutes. Turn, brush with the marinade, and brown on the other side. Bring the remaining marinade to a good boil, turn down the heat, and simmer briefly. Serve the pork hot with toothpicks and the hot marinade.

Sautéed Pork Tenderloin

Serves 2 or 3

This was a traditional treat for farm families who had worked since dawn, killing and dressing hogs to put up (cure) for the winter (see p. 311). Mama would fry up the tenderloin, put pieces in the middle of biscuits, and have them ready for a late breakfast. Sautéed sliced tenderloin takes next to no time to cook and is delicious for breakfast, lunch, or dinner. It needs no sauce or garnish—it's perfect in its simplicity.

1 pork tenderloin	Salt
3 tablespoons butter	Freshly ground black pepper

Cut the tenderloin diagonally into 1/2-inch-thick slices. Melt the butter in a heavy skillet. Add the tenderloin and cook on both sides until done, about 2–3 minutes. Season with salt and pepper and put inside biscuits.

Liverell

Serves 16

Probably most non-Southerners have never heard of Liverell. Yet my friend Honey Hollingsworth said she first had it in 1910. Traditionally it was made in the fall, right after the first heavy frost, when the hogs were slaughtered, to make use of the liver. It's somewhere between a pâté and liver pudding and is particularly tasty when fried in butter or bacon grease and served for breakfast or a Sunday-night supper. The pork used should be as tender a cut as possible—a pork loin or ribs that are lean with very little bone. It freezes well.

For the Liverell:

2 1/2 pounds pork liver	Salt
1 1/2 pounds fresh pork	Freshly ground black pepper
1/4 teaspoon poultry seasoning	3 1/2 cups water
1/2 teaspoon crumbled sage	3 cups sifted corn meal

✿   ✿   ✿

To serve:

1 slice bacon per person, fried crisp, drippings saved	Fried sliced apples
	2–3 tablespoons butter or drippings

Rinse the liver and cut it and the pork into 1–2-inch chunks. Place in a large pot. Add the poultry seasoning, sage, salt and pepper to taste, and 3 cups water. Bring to a boil, reduce heat, and simmer, tightly covered, until the liquid has boiled down and the liver and pork are soft and mushy, about 3 hours. Check to be sure all bones are removed. Mash to a fine pulp, using either a potato masher followed by a blender, or a food processor. Return to the pot. On low heat slowly blend in the sifted corn meal. Take 1 tablespoon of the mixture and fry in a little butter or fat to check for taste and consistency. It should be crispy on the outside and softer on the inside. Add more corn meal and 1/2 cup water if necessary, making sure there is enough meal in the mixture to hold it together when frying and enough water to keep it soft inside.

Liverell, continued

Grease 2 loaf pans. Place a piece of wax paper on the bottom of each pan to facilitate removal. Put the pork-and-liver mixture in the pans and let cool. Refrigerate overnight until cold and firm. To freeze, slice the cold Liverell into 1/2–3/4-inch-thick slices. Freeze the slices flat individually, then remove to a freezer bag collectively and seal tightly.

To serve: Slice the loaves into 1/2–3/4-inch-thick slices, place in a hot frying pan with bacon drippings, and brown on both sides. Place 1 slice of bacon across the top of each serving of Liverell and serve with fried sliced apples. Sauté the apples, sliced in 1/4-inch-thick rounds, in butter or bacon drippings. These may be done ahead and kept warm.

Country Ham with Coca-Cola Red-Eye Gravy

Serves 2

Many Southerners make red-eye gravy with leftover black coffee or red wine, but I much prefer Coca-Cola.

2 1/4-inch-thick slices country ham
3 ounces Coca-Cola

Trim some of the fat off the ham slices and melt it in a large heated frying pan or skillet. Add the ham and fry slowly until the fatty edges are soft and brown. Turn and cook until lightly browned. Remove from the pan and keep warm. Add the Coca-Cola to the pan and bring to a quick boil. Place the ham on a plate or platter, and pour gravy over.

Ham with Hot Pepper Jelly and Apple Juice

Serves 4

Salty country ham is one of the South's indigenous and beloved foods. But, if you don't care for it, you may use any cured ham. If you are using a ham that doesn't have a fatty edge, as country ham does, you may have to add some fat.

4 slices ham
1/2 cup Hot Pepper Jelly (p. 303)
2 tablespoons apple juice

Trim some of the fat off the ham and melt it in a large heated skillet. Add the ham and fry until light brown. Turn and fry until browned on the other side. Remove. Add the Hot Pepper Jelly and apple juice to the pan. Heat until the jelly melts in the boiling juice and the sauce thickens. Pour over the ham and serve.

Hot Chicken Wings

Serves 2–6

These little wings make a good meal for two or are a great appetizer. Up North, they are called Buffalo wings and are served with celery and blue-cheese dressing. The little wing tips should be trimmed off to make neater pieces. But I cook them along with the wings and save them for myself. I call them the "cook's treat." You may fry or bake the wings, depending on dietary considerations.

2 1/2 pounds chicken wings,   **6 ounces Hot Sauce (p. 297)**
      12–15 individual wings   **or Tabasco**
Shortening or oil for frying (optional) **1/2 cup melted butter**

Hot Chicken Wings, continued

Cut the chicken wings in two at the joints. In a large frying pan or skillet, heat to 360 degrees enough fat to cover the chicken wings. Add the wings and fry until crisp, about 12–15 minutes.

To bake, preheat the oven to 450 degrees. Spread the chicken wings out on a baking sheet in one layer and bake 45 minutes.

To make the sauce, combine the Hot Sauce or Tabasco and melted butter and blend thoroughly. As soon as the chicken wings are cooked, douse with the sauce, and serve immediately.

Chicken Breast Nuggets with Soy Sauce

Serves 4

Soy sauce has been used in Southern cooking for a long time. In fact, there was a large population of Chinese living in Louisiana and Mississippi in the 1800s. In the 1870s a group of Chinese came to Augusta, Georgia, to build the canals there. Those Chinese who remained ran laundries or grocery stores. By 1930 there were 48 Chinese-owned grocery stores in Augusta, and by the mid-1950s the number had risen to 65. Today the grocery stores no longer abound, as the Chinese population has become more professionally oriented, but there is still a proliferation of Chinese restaurants. Here is a tasty blend of Chinese and Southern cooking.

1 three-pound chicken or **Freshly ground black pepper**
   3 whole chicken breasts **3 tablespoons soy sauce**
Salt **3 tablespoons butter, melted**

Cut chicken off the bones into chunks. Rub with salt and pepper. In a bowl, combine the soy sauce with the melted butter and dip the chunks in the mixture. Put them on skewers and grill over charcoal while basting with the soy sauce–butter mixture. They will take up to 10 minutes to cook over a hot fire.

Grilled Marinated Chicken Drumettes

Serves 20 as hors d'oeuvres

I have a weak spot for gingery, hot things, particularly at cocktail parties. These can be made ahead, frozen, and then crisped under the broiler at serving time. I prefer using both sections of the wing, but the single-boned piece, called the drumette, is nicer for a party. The other piece, with its two bones, is messier but tastier.

1 slice fresh ginger the size of
    a quarter, finely chopped
6 cloves garlic, finely chopped
3 fresh chilies or hot peppers,
    finely chopped
2 onions, finely chopped
2 cups finely chopped fresh parsley
1/2 cup fresh lemon juice
1 tablespoon paprika
1/4 cup vegetable oil

5 pounds chicken drumettes or
    chicken wings cut in two
    at the joints
1 tablespoon ground coriander seeds
1 tablespoon ground cumin seeds
1 tablespoon paprika
3 cups chicken stock
Salt
Freshly ground black pepper

Mix together the ginger, garlic, chili peppers, onions, parsley, lemon juice, and paprika in a food processor or blender. Heat the oil in a large pan. Add the chicken wings, fleshy side down, and brown on both sides. Remove. Add the coriander, cumin, and paprika to the pan and cook 1–2 minutes. Add the lemon-juice mixture. Bring to the boil and boil, stirring occasionally, for 5 minutes. Add the chicken stock and boil again.

    Return the chicken to the pan. Bring back to the boil, then turn down the heat, cover, and simmer 20 minutes. Taste for seasoning and add salt and pepper as desired. Remove the chicken from its sauce and set it aside to cool. You may refrigerate or freeze the chicken wings and sauce separately at this point.

    When ready to serve, prepare the grill or heat the broiler. Place a layer of chicken on the grill or on foil-lined baking sheets under the broiler. Brown in batches until crisp, about 5 minutes on each side. Remove and serve hot, without sauce.

Chicken Breast Hors d'Oeuvres

Serves 8

These should be fried just before serving, so they're good for kitchen parties or times when you have help in the kitchen.

4 chicken breast halves or
   1 whole chicken
1 teaspoon salt
1/2 teaspoon curry powder
2 teaspoons basil
2 teaspoons paprika

1/2 teaspoon ground coriander
3/4 cup all-purpose flour
1 egg, slightly beaten
1 cup grated coconut
Oil for frying

Cut the chicken off the bones into bite-size pieces and place in a bowl. Mix together the salt, curry powder, basil, paprika, and coriander. Sprinkle half of this mixture over the chicken, toss well to coat, and refrigerate overnight. Mix the rest of the seasoning mixture with the flour and set aside.

    Heat the oil to 360 degrees. Dip the chicken pieces in the flour, then in the egg. Roll in coconut. Deep-fry until golden brown. Serve with toothpicks.

Bacon Biscuits

Makes 140

Try these as an appetizer at a brunch. They're wonderful with bloody marys. The bite-size flavorful biscuits freeze easily after they are cooked, but they don't last too long in the freezer, a few weeks at most.

1 pound sliced bacon
3 tablespoons chopped
   fresh mushrooms

4 tablespoons chopped green peppers
1 1/2 cups all-purpose soft-wheat flour
   (see p. 314)

1 teaspoon salt
2 teaspoons baking powder
Freshly ground black pepper
1/2 teaspoon Dijon mustard

1 egg, beaten
1/2 cup milk
1/4 cup bacon drippings

Preheat the oven to 425 degrees. Fry the bacon until crisp, reserving the drippings. Drain on paper towels, then crumble into a bowl and mix with the mushrooms and peppers. In a separate bowl, sift together the flour, salt, and baking powder and add to the bacon and vegetables. Add black pepper, mustard, egg, milk, and bacon drippings, and mix all together with a fork. Grease 2 baking sheets. Drop the batter, 1/2 teaspoonful at a time, onto the baking sheets. Bake 6-8 minutes.

Cheese Straws

Makes 15-20

You'll find cheese straws in every freezer in the South, ready to be served at parties and impromptu gatherings.

1 cup all-purpose soft-wheat flour
    (see p. 314)
1 cup grated New York sharp
    Cheddar cheese

3/4 teaspoon salt
1/4 teaspoon cayenne pepper
1/4 cup butter
1 egg, beaten

Preheat the oven to 425 degrees. Mix together the flour, cheese, salt, and cayenne. Cut in the butter with a pastry blender or two forks until the mixture looks like corn meal. Add the beaten egg and stir. Knead until you can form a ball. If the dough seems dry, add a few drops of water. Place on a floured board and roll thin. Cut in finger-size strips and place on a lightly greased cookie sheet. Bake until lightly browned, 5-8 minutes.

Crispy Cheese Wafers

Serves 6

Prepared this way cheese will actually crisp like a cheese wafer. If you like eating the cheese that has melted on the pan from a grilled cheese sandwich, this recipe is for you. The "wafers" keep a long time in a covered jar and make a great snack, particularly for a long trip.

**1 pound Cheddar or Monterey
jack cheese**

Preheat the oven to 350 degrees. Cut the cheese into 1/16-inch-thick slices with a wire cheese slicer. Place on a nonstick baking sheet an inch apart for the cheese to spread. Bake for about 30 minutes or until the cheese stops bubbling. Baking time may vary depending on your oven. Remove with a nonstick spatula and cool on wax paper.

Ham Pinwheels

Makes 20 dozen

This recipe is adapted from one in a charming little book, *Recipes from the Old South,* by Martha L. Meade. It's a great finger food for a brunch or cocktail party and freezes well, baked or unbaked. Baked, it defrosts in the microwave as well as the oven.

Filling:

**1 pound cooked country or Smithfield
   ham, chopped**
1/2 cup butter, melted
1/2 cup mayonnaise

2/3 cup peanut butter
1 clove garlic, chopped
1 medium onion, chopped
Dash Tabasco

☆ ☆ ☆

Dough:
4 cups flour
1 teaspoon salt

2 tablespoons baking powder
1/2 cup shortening
1 1/2 cups milk

To make the filling, place the ham, butter, mayonnaise, peanut butter, garlic, onion, and Tabasco in a large bowl. Combine with a wooden spoon until evenly mixed. Divide into 4 equal parts. Set aside.

To make the dough, sift together the flour, salt, and baking powder. Cut in the shortening with 2 forks or a pastry cutter. Add enough milk to make a soft but rollable dough.

Preheat the oven to 425 degrees and grease 2 cookie sheets. Divide the dough into 4 equal pieces. Roll each piece out 24 by 8 inches and spread with one part of the filling. Roll up lengthwise, as you would a jelly roll. Cut the rolls in half and place on a flat surface in the freezer and chill until firm. Remove the chilled rolls from the freezer and slice into 1/4-inch-thick pinwheels. Place the pinwheels close together on the prepared cookie sheets and bake 8–10 minutes, until medium brown.

Sour Cream Brittlebread

Serves 10–12

This crisp, cracker-like bread is good just flavored with salt and sour cream. But add Creole Seasoning and you'll have a hot and spicy appetizer that will leave your guests begging for the recipe. Leave out the salt if you use the Creole Seasoning — it is salty in itself. It's nice to keep a big airtight cookie jar full of these for snacking.

2 3/4 cups all-purpose soft-wheat flour
   (p. 314)
1/4 cup sugar
1/2 teaspoon salt (optional)
1/2 teaspoon baking soda
1/2 cup butter

1 cup sour cream
2 tablespoons Creole Seasoning
   (p. 297), optional
1–2 tablespoons kosher salt
   for sprinkling

Preheat the oven to 400 degrees. Sift together the flour, sugar, salt, and baking soda into a bowl or food processor. Cut in the butter. Add the sour cream and Creole Seasoning, and mix to a soft dough. Roll out paper-thin on a floured board.

Sour Cream Brittlebread, continued

Cut into 1 1/2-inch squares. Sprinkle with kosher salt and place on an ungreased baking sheet. Bake for 5–8 minutes. Turn off the heat and allow the bread to crisp in the oven.

Grits Roll

Serves 6

I developed this recipe as the kick-off to a grits contest we held at Rich's for a school promotion. It later won $6,000 for someone else as "Appetizer of the Year" in another contest. It may be made ahead and reheated.

The roll:

1/2 cup plain yogurt
1/2 cup milk
1/4 cup quick grits
2/3 cup grated Cheddar cheese or
    1/3 cup Swiss and 1/3 cup
    Parmesan cheese, mixed

4 egg yolks
Salt
Freshly ground black pepper
6 egg whites

✿ ✿ ✿

The filling:

2 cups sliced fresh mushrooms
1/2 cup butter
1/2 cup sliced or chopped ham
    (optional)

1/2 cup flour
2 cups milk
1 cup grated Cheddar cheese

Preheat the oven to 350 degrees. Grease a 10 1/2-by-15 1/2-inch jelly roll pan, then grease a piece of wax paper or aluminum foil and line the pan.

    Heat the yogurt and milk to boiling. (It will look curdled.) Add the grits and cook according to package directions. Remove from heat. Add the cheese and the egg yolks, one at a time, then salt and pepper to taste. Beat the egg whites with a whisk or beater until they stand in firm peaks. Fold a spoonful of the egg whites into the grits mixture to soften. Then fold the whole mixture into the remaining egg whites. Do not overfold. When all the egg whites are folded in, spread the entire mixture onto the jelly roll pan. Smooth the top and bake until done, 20–25 minutes. The top should spring back lightly when it is touched, and a toothpick inserted into it should come out clean. Do not overcook or it will crack. When done, remove from the oven and turn the pan upside-down onto a piece of aluminum foil. Remove the pan and strip off the wax paper or foil.

For the filling, cook the mushrooms lightly in a small skillet with 4 tablespoons of the butter until they are tender. Add more butter if needed. Add the ham, if desired, and set aside. Melt the remaining 4 tablespoons of butter in a pan and stir in the flour. Add the milk and bring to the boil, stirring constantly until thickened. Add the mushroom mixture and blend thoroughly. Spread the mushroom filling over the baked grits, sprinkle with the cup of grated cheese and roll up like a jelly roll, beginning from a long side. Cut into slices and serve hot.

Grits and Turkey Casserole

Serves 4

This doubles easily, and is a wonderful dish to make when you have leftover turkey.

1 cup quick grits, cooked in
    4 cups turkey or chicken stock
2 cups cooked turkey or chicken,
    cut into small pieces
1 cup garlic-herb cheese (such as
    Boursin), Montrachet, or
    soft goat cheese

1/3 cup sliced sun-dried tomatoes
2 tablespoons chopped fresh basil
1 cup cooked chopped or sliced
    collards or turnip greens

Preheat the oven to 350 degrees. Cook the grits according to package directions, substituting turkey or chicken stock for the water. In a casserole mix together with the remaining ingredients and bake until heated through, about 20 minutes.

Crabmeat Casserole

Serves 4–6

This casserole is adapted from a recipe by Mrs. Jimmy Rae (Becky) in *Something Southern,* the Junior League cookbook of Americus, Georgia. My father-in-law was from Americus and loved this recipe. It's easily made a day ahead and reheated.

6 tablespoons butter
6 tablespoons flour
2 cups milk
1/4 cup dry Madeira
1 pound white lump crabmeat,
   shells and membrane removed

1 1/2 cups freshly grated
   Parmesan cheese
Dash salt
Freshly ground white pepper
1 teaspoon paprika
Juice of 1/2 lemon

✿ ✿ ✿

Toast cups:
4–6 slices white bread
2–4 tablespoons butter, melted

Preheat the oven to 350 degrees. Melt the butter in a heavy saucepan. Stir in the flour. When smooth, add the milk all at once. Turn up the heat and stir until the mixture comes to a boil and thickens. Stir in Madeira and the remaining ingredients, reserving 1/2 cup Parmesan. Pour into a greased casserole dish. Top with the 1/2 cup Parmesan. Bake until bubbly, about 20 minutes. Serve in the toast cups.

   To make the toast cups, grease 4–6 muffin cups. Mold the bread inside and brush with butter. Preheat the oven to 350 degrees. Bake a few minutes until brown.

Oyster Casserole

Serves 6–8

2 quarts oysters
8 tablespoons butter
3 whole green onions, chopped

1 green or red bell pepper, seeded
   and chopped
1/2 pound mushrooms, sliced

4 tablespoons flour
1 cup whipping cream
4 tablespoons freshly grated
    Parmesan cheese
Freshly grated nutmeg

1/2 teaspoon paprika
Salt
Freshly ground black pepper
1/2 cup breadcrumbs

Drain the oysters and set aside. Melt 4 tablespoons of the butter in a heavy casserole. Add the onion and pepper and sauté until the onion is soft. Add the mushrooms and oysters and sauté for 5 minutes. In a separate pan, melt the remaining 4 tablespoons of butter. Stir in the flour. When smooth, add the cream and stir until boiling and thick. Add the cheese. Combine with the oyster mixture, and season with nutmeg, paprika, salt, and pepper. May be made ahead to this point and refrigerated overnight.

When ready to serve, grease a 9-by-13-inch casserole and fill with the prepared mixture. Top with the breadcrumbs and place under the broiler until browned and bubbling. If the mixture is cold, bring it to the simmer on top of the stove, then turn it into the casserole dish and broil as above.

Sausage and Apple Overnight Casserole

Serves 12

This is a fabulous-tasting easy casserole that can be made ahead and heated in the morning. It's ideal for putting in the oven before church on Easter morning, for instance.

2 pounds bulk sausage
9 slices bread
2 sliced apples
3/4 teaspoon dry mustard

9 eggs, beaten
1 1/2 cups (6 ounces) grated sharp
    Cheddar cheese
3 cups milk

Fry the sausage in a skillet, breaking it up as you cook it, and drain on paper towels. Reserve the fat. Place the sausage in a lightly greased 13-by-9-by-2-inch baking dish or divide between two 1 1/2-quart casseroles. Remove the crusts from the bread and cut it into cubes. Sauté the apples in the sausage fat. Combine the bread, apples, mustard, eggs, cheese, and milk, and mix well. Pour this mixture over the sausage, cover, and refrigerate overnight.

Sausage and Apple Casserole, continued

Preheat the oven to 350 degrees. Bake the casserole, covered, for 30 minutes. Uncover and bake another 30 minutes.

Cheese Puff and
Leftover Poultry Casserole

Serves 6

This is wonderful made with turkey, but if you are fortunate enough to have leftover quail or duck, stand back and listen for the applause. It is easy to make ahead and reheat.

1/2 recipe cream puff dough (p. 264)
1/2 cup Cheddar cheese

✿   ✿   ✿

Filling:

1/2 cup butter	Salt
4 onions, chopped	Freshly ground black pepper
1/2 pound mushrooms, sliced	1 tablespoon fresh thyme or
1/4 cup flour	1 teaspoon fresh sage
2 cups chicken or turkey stock	1/2 cup grated
3 cups cooked chicken, turkey, duck,	Cheddar cheese
or quail, roughly chopped	1/2 cup breadcrumbs, toasted
4 tomatoes, peeled, seeded,	(see p. 321)
and sliced	1/3 cup chopped parsley

Preheat the oven to 400 degrees. Mix the cream puff dough with the cheese in a food processor or mixer. Grease a shallow baking dish thoroughly. Take heaping teaspoonfuls of the dough and place around the sides of the dish. (Be sure there is a large space in the center of the dish for the filling once the dough has baked and expanded.) Place in the oven and turn down the heat to 350 degrees. Bake 20 minutes or until the dough is lightly browned, puffed, and firm. Do not remove from the oven until it is very firm.

For the filling: Melt the butter in a saucepan, add the onions, and cook until soft. Add the mushrooms and cook until tender, stirring when necessary. Remove the pan from the heat and add the flour, stirring. Return to the heat, pour in the stock, and bring to the boil. Simmer 2 minutes, stirring constantly. Remove from the heat, add the cooked meat and tomatoes, and season to taste with salt, pepper, and thyme or sage. Both filling and shell may be made ahead to this point and reheated separately before being put together.

Fifteen minutes before serving, preheat the oven to 400 degrees, fill the cream puff hollow with the filling, and sprinkle with the cheese and breadcrumbs. Place in the oven until the filling is heated through and the cheese is melted, about 25 minutes. Sprinkle with parsley and serve.

Crab Pie

Serves 4–6

This crab pie contains Madeira, a wine that was so important to the colonists it was used to toast George Washington's inauguration at Fraunces Tavern. Madeira parties became very popular in the late 1800s, but Savannah was a great Madeira city going back as far as April 7, 1763, the date Madeira prices were listed in the first issue of the *Georgia Gazette*. The city still has a Madeira Club, an élite group of intellectuals who meet monthly for lively conversation and an incredibly sumptuous meal. You may substitute dry sherry if you like.

Pie crust:

1 1/2 cups all-purpose soft-wheat flour (see p. 314)
Dash salt

1/2 cup butter
4–6 tablespoons water

✿ ✿ ✿

Filling:

2 cups white lump crabmeat, shells and membrane removed
2 tablespoons butter, melted
1 cup milk
1 cup heavy cream
4 eggs, slightly beaten

1/8 teaspoon mace
Dash salt
1/2 teaspoon freshly ground white pepper
1/2 teaspoon Worcestershire sauce
1/4 cup dry Madeira

To make the pie crust, sift together the flour and salt. Cut in the butter with a pastry blender or your fingers until the butter is the size of peas or butter beans. Add water as necessary to make a rollable dough. Flatten into a round and wrap. Chill the dough for 30 minutes. Roll out on a floured board to fit a 9-inch pie pan, preferably glass. Line the pie pan with the dough and crimp or flute the edges (see p. 233).

Crab Pie, continued

Preheat the oven to 375 degrees. To partially bake the crust, crumple a piece of wax paper or aluminum foil and place it over the dough, extending to the edges of the pan. Crumpling the paper prevents it from sticking to the crust. Pour metal pie weights, raw rice, or dried beans into the wax paper or foil, filling the shell. Place in the oven and prebake 15–20 minutes. Remove. Scoop out the weights and save to use the next time you make a pie crust. Carefully pull off the paper or foil and discard. Reduce the oven temperature to 350 degrees.

To make the filling, pick through the crabmeat, removing any shells and membranes. In a bowl, mix the melted butter, milk, cream, and eggs together. Add the seasonings, crabmeat, and Madeira. Pour into the partially baked crust. Place in the oven and bake 30–40 minutes. May be frozen and reheated.

Delicate Cheese Soufflés with Crabmeat Sauce

Serves 8

Soufflés have been my delight ever since I realized that they are not difficult to make. Making them ahead—even by a couple of days—and reheating them in the different way described below provides a new special treat. You may substitute cooked crawfish tails, peeled but unchopped, for the crabmeat.

Soufflés:
4 tablespoons butter
4 tablespoons flour
3 1/2 cups milk
1 1/2 cups grated Swiss, Parmesan, or Monterey jack cheese

5 egg yolks
Salt
Freshly ground black pepper
6 egg whites

✿   ✿   ✿

Sauce:
3 cups heavy cream
3/4 pound lump crabmeat, shells and membrane removed

2 tablespoons butter
Additional grated Swiss, Parmesan, or Monterey jack cheese

Butter well 16 three-inch tart pans, or 8 small soufflé dishes or ramekins, or 2 eight-inch nonstick frying pans.

Melt the butter in a saucepan and add the flour, stirring until smooth. Add the milk and bring to a boil, stirring constantly. Turn down the heat and let simmer a few minutes. Remove from the heat, add the cheese, and stir well. Add the egg yolks, one at a time, to the warm, but not hot, sauce, stirring constantly. Season to taste with salt and pepper. The soufflés may be made ahead to this point and refrigerated, covered with plastic wrap to prevent a skin from forming, or kept for a short time at room temperature.

In a large bowl beat the egg whites until they form stiff peaks and fold a small portion into the sauce base. This softens the mixture. Pour the rest of the sauce mixture on top of the egg whites and fold in. Pour into the tart pans, soufflé dishes, ramekins, or frying pans. (If the frying-pan handles are not ovenproof, you may want to cover them with foil to protect them.) The soufflés may be made ahead to this point and refrigerated or frozen.

When ready to cook, bring to room temperature. Preheat the oven to 400 degrees. Place the pans or dishes in the oven and bake 5 minutes for the tart pans, 15 minutes for the soufflé dishes or frying pans. Remove from the oven. If serving right away, remove from the dishes or pans. If not, let cool, then remove.

Boil the 3 cups of cream until reduced by 1 cup. When ready to eat, mix the cream with the crab and butter in a heavy saucepan until heated through. Pour the hot sauce into 8 heatproof dishes and add equal portions of the cooked and unmolded soufflés. Top with additional grated cheese. Place in the 400-degree oven for 5 minutes until glazed. Serve hot. This reheats well in a microwave, cream and all.

Fresh Corn Spoon Bread

Serves 6-8

Spoon bread is not a bread—it is the South's answer to the French soufflé. Its wonderful flavor comes from the corn milk, and it is light as air.

3 tablespoons butter
3 tablespoons fresh breadcrumbs
3 ears fresh corn, scraped (1½ cups)
⅓ cup corn meal
2 cups hot milk
1 green onion, finely chopped
    (2 tablespoons)

2 egg yolks
2 egg whites
2 teaspoons sugar
Salt
Freshly ground black pepper

Fresh Corn Spoon Bread, continued

Butter the bottom and sides of a 1 1/2-quart ovenproof soufflé dish with 1 tablespoon of the butter, and dust lightly with the breadcrumbs. Mix the corn with the corn meal and add the hot milk. Stir constantly over medium heat until the mixture comes to a boil and thickens. Melt the remaining butter in another pan, add the onion, and cook briefly until soft. Combine with the corn meal mixture.

In a separate bowl, beat the egg yolks until light. Add a little of the hot corn meal mixture to the egg yolks, then return to the hot mixture. The spoon bread may be made ahead to this point, covered, and refrigerated, and carefully reheated to lukewarm when you are ready to add the egg whites. One hour and 15 minutes before serving, preheat the oven to 325 degrees.

Beat the egg whites until stiff, then add the sugar. Add 1 spoonful of the egg whites to the corn meal–egg yolk mixture to soften, then pour the entire mixture on top of the egg whites and fold in. Pour into the prepared dish, place the dish inside a larger pan, and add hot water to a depth of 1 inch up the sides of the dishes. Bake 3/4–1 hour, until a knife inserted in the center comes out clean. Serve immediately.

Turnip Green and Tomato Sauce Soufflé Roll

Serves 6 as a starter

This is a flat soufflé, baked in a jelly roll pan. It is turned out, spread with a filling, and rolled up like a jelly roll. It's a good brunch dish, as well as a good starter. The roll may be made several days ahead, as indicated.

3/4 pound turnip greens, stemmed
1 tablespoon butter
Salt
Freshly ground black pepper

4 egg yolks, beaten
5 egg whites
4 tablespoons grated Parmesan cheese

✿   ✿   ✿

Filling:
1 recipe Tomato Sauce (p. 299)

Preheat the oven to 400 degrees. Oil a 10 1/2-by-15 1/2-inch jelly roll pan, then line with wax paper or foil. Oil the paper or foil.

Rinse the greens thoroughly several times. Place in boiling water and cook 5 minutes. Drain well. To remove excess water, press the greens between 2 plates facing the same way or squeeze very dry. Chop fine and place in a bowl. Stir in butter, salt, pepper, and egg yolks. You may do this up to several hours ahead and keep refrigerated, covered. If refrigerated, rewarm gently in a heavy saucepan over medium heat before proceeding.

Beat the egg whites to stiff peaks, fold a couple of tablespoons into the greens mixture to soften, then gently fold in the rest. Spread quickly and evenly on the prepared jelly roll pan and sprinkle with cheese. Place in the oven and bake until the soufflé has risen and is firm to the touch, about 10 minutes. This can be made several days ahead, left in the pan, covered with plastic wrap or foil, and reheated in a 350-degree oven.

To finish, cut off a piece of aluminum foil as long as the soufflé and place it on the counter. Turn the soufflé out onto the aluminum foil with the pan. Remove the pan and peel off the wax paper or foil that has adhered to the soufflé. Spread the hot Tomato Sauce on the soufflé and roll it up by lifting the foil underneath and pushing the soufflé into a roll. Place a platter at the end of the foil and make the final roll onto the platter. Decorate with any leftover sauce. May be made to this point an hour or so ahead. Reheat if necessary in a 350-degree oven.

Pimento Soufflé Roll with Goat Cheese

Serves 4–6

This is a deceptively simple dish to make and reheats easily, both filled and unfilled. It has all the qualities of a soufflé—light, enticing puffs of egg and air, wrapped around a creamy cheese filling, with the taste of pimentos and herbs. Today the South has many producers of goat cheese—in Virginia, Tennessee, and North Carolina in particular. Southern goat cheeses resemble some French goat

Pimento Soufflé Roll, continued

cheeses but are a bit different from the best-known California varieties. If you can't find goat cheese at your market, don't worry; any soft cheese will do.

Roll:

2 tablespoons butter
1 medium onion, chopped
2 jars pimentos, drained
1/3 cup goat cheese or a creamy
  cheese, such as Boursin

2 tablespoons fresh herbs (optional)
6 egg yolks
6 egg whites
Salt
Freshly ground black pepper

✿ ✿ ✿

Filling:

1 cup heavy cream
1 1/2 cups mild, creamy cheese
2 tablespoons fresh herbs (optional)

Salt
Freshly ground black pepper

Preheat the oven to 350 degrees. Oil a 10 1/2-by-15 1/2-inch jelly roll pan, and line with wax paper or foil. Oil the paper or foil.

To make the soufflé roll, melt the butter in a frying pan. Add the onion and cook until soft, 5–8 minutes. Remove the onion and place in a food processor or blender along with the pimentos, cheese, herbs, and egg yolks. Process until smooth and place in a large bowl. In a separate bowl beat the egg whites with a whisk or beater until stiff. With a metal spoon or a rubber spatula add a small dollop of the egg whites to the processed mixture, and fold. Place the mixture onto the remaining egg whites and fold in completely. Add salt and pepper to taste. Spread in the lined jelly roll pan.

Place in the oven and bake for 20 minutes. Remove. The soufflé may be cooled and refrigerated or filled and served immediately. If preparing ahead, reheat in the oven for 10 minutes before filling. To make the filling, heat the heavy cream in a saucepan and add the cheese and herbs. Bring to a brief boil and season with salt and pepper.

To finish, place a piece of aluminum foil as long as the soufflé on the counter. Turn out the soufflé onto the foil. Remove the pan and peel off the paper or foil that has adhered to the soufflé. Spread the hot cheese filling on the still warm soufflé and roll up like a jelly roll, lengthwise, by lifting the foil underneath and pushing the soufflé into a roll. Place a platter at the end of the foil and make the final roll onto the platter. Serve hot, cut into slices. May be reheated in the oven or microwave.

Hopping John Vinaigrette

Serves 6–8

You can use leftover Hopping John; serve hot or cold.

1 recipe Hopping John (p. 79)
1 medium onion, chopped
⅓ cup red wine vinegar
1 tablespoon Dijon mustard
1 cup peanut oil

Salt
Freshly ground black pepper
2 tablespoons chopped fresh basil
4 slices bacon, crisply fried
   and crumbled

Prepare the Hopping John. Drain the rice and peas and remove the fatback and hot pepper. Add the chopped onion.

    To make the vinaigrette, mix together the vinegar and mustard in a bowl and slowly whisk in the peanut oil. Add salt and pepper as needed. Combine with Hopping John and chopped basil. Top with the crumbled bacon.

Old-Style Pimento Cheese Spread

Makes 3 cups

Here it is, the old-time pimento cheese spread. Keep it in the refrigerator and spread it on white marshmallow (my name for store-bought) bread. Or serve it on celery as an appetizer.

12 ounces grated rat or
   Cheddar cheese

2 four-ounce jars pimento, drained
1 cup mayonnaise (p. 306)

Put all the ingredients in a food processor or blender and process until smooth.

Eggplant Relish

Makes 6 cups

Margaret Anne Sparks, who was my assistant at Rich's Cooking School for years before she became a top catering expert, swears by this as a special appetizer. It's easily made ahead and is very tasty served with crackers or Sour Cream Brittlebread (p. 27).

1/2 cup peanut oil
1 large eggplant
1 large onion, chopped
1/2 cup diced celery
1 fifteen-ounce can whole tomatoes,
    coarsely chopped
1–2 tablespoons tomato paste
    (optional)

2 tablespoons red wine vinegar
1/3 cup pitted and sliced black olives
1/3 cup pitted and sliced green olives
1 1/2 tablespoons capers
Salt
Freshly ground black pepper
2 tablespoons toasted pine nuts
1/2 cup raisins

Heat 1/4 cup of the oil in a skillet. Cut the eggplant into 1/2-inch cubes and add to the oil. Brown, adding more oil as needed, then remove. Add the onion and celery to the oil and cook 5 minutes or until soft. In a heavy saucepan, combine all the ingredients except the pine nuts and raisins and cook for 30 minutes or so over a low flame, stirring occasionally. Cool. Remove to a serving dish and top with pine nuts and raisins.

Fried Watermelon Rinds

Makes 2 cups

When the family is sitting around at home and there's "nothing to eat," try frying watermelon rinds. You'll be amazed at what a good snack these make, and everyone will love them as much as they do fried okra! Peel the rinds with a knife, cutting off the dark outside skin and inner layer down to the white part. Cut the white part of the rind into 1/2-inch cubes.

1/3 cup corn meal
1/3 cup all-purpose flour
1 teaspoon salt

Freshly ground black pepper
1 cup shortening or vegetable oil
2 cups watermelon rind, cubed

Mix together the corn meal, flour, salt, and pepper. Heat the oil to 350 degrees in a heavy 10-inch iron skillet. Roll the cubed rind in the corn meal mixture and add to the hot oil. Fry about 8–10 minutes until lightly browned. Stir gently and cook about 4–5 minutes more until browned all over. Drain on paper towels and season with salt and pepper. Eat while hot.

Stuffed Mushrooms

Serves 16

Stuffed mushrooms are good as an appetizer or as a vegetable side dish. When serving as finger food at a party, make them bite size so that your guests can just pop them in their mouths. They may be frozen before or after baking, defrosted and reheated, or kept in the refrigerator a day or two.

2 ten-ounce packages frozen chopped
    turnip greens or spinach
2 pounds small mushrooms, cleaned
1 1/4 cups butter
3 medium onions, chopped
3 cloves garlic, crushed with salt
    (see p. 315)

1/2 cup fine breadcrumbs
Salt
1/8 teaspoon dry mustard
Freshly ground black pepper
Freshly grated nutmeg
1/3 cup grated Parmesan cheese

Preheat the oven to 350 degrees. Defrost the greens. Drain very thoroughly by pressing between 2 plates facing the same way, and set aside. Remove the stems of the mushrooms, chop, and set aside. Melt the butter in a skillet and dip the mushroom caps into it until well coated on all sides. Place them, top down, on a greased baking sheet. Reheat the butter remaining in the skillet and sauté the onions, garlic, and chopped mushroom stems until very soft, about 10 minutes. Combine with the greens, add the breadcrumbs, salt, mustard, pepper, and nutmeg, and mix well. Taste and reseason. Fill each mushroom cap with this mixture, mounding it high, and sprinkle with grated cheese. Place in the oven and bake 10–15 minutes.

Buttered and Salted Pecans

Makes 2 quarts

It's always nice to have nut snacks handy to pull out when friends drop by or when you're just sitting around with the family watching TV. These will keep, if you can keep them hidden.

2 quarts shelled pecan halves
1 cup butter
Salt

Preheat the oven to 250 degrees. Spread the pecans on 2 baking sheets and dot with butter. Bake for 1 hour, stirring occasionally, making sure they don't burn. When the pecans are a nice brown, remove from the oven and salt while still hot. Cool. Store in a tightly covered container.

Peanuts with Hot Peppers

Makes 1 pound

With the new craving for hot stuff and the abundance of peanuts and peppers in the South, this is a natural innovation. I got the idea when my friend U.S. Ambassador Julius Walker returned from Africa with a jar of peanuts and hot peppers a friend had given him. They're wonderful to snack on anytime at all.

1 pound roasted peanuts
4–6 dried hot peppers, seeded and
**   chopped fine**
1 teaspoon salt (optional)

Toss the ingredients together and place in jars. Cover tightly. Lasts forever.

Ginger's Peach Omelet

Serves 2

Ginger is a gorgeous, red-headed young student-turned-assistant of mine. She always has a bevy of men offering her their arms as well as their hands, and this is what she fixes for a special breakfast or dessert with a special beau.

2 or 3 peaches, peeled and pitted	5 eggs
4 tablespoons butter	Freshly grated nutmeg
Juice of ½ lemon	Salt

Cut the peaches into chunks. Melt 2 tablespoons of the butter in a heavy sauce-pan. Add the peaches and the lemon juice and sauté over high heat briefly, 1–2 minutes. Remove and keep warm.

Beat the eggs with 1 tablespoon of water until frothy. Heat the remaining butter until sizzling hot in an omelet pan or well-seasoned small frying pan. Pour in the beaten eggs and give a good stir. Let the eggs cook and set 1–2 minutes, then peel back the set eggs and tip the pan so the raw portion runs under the cooked portion. Do this several times. When the eggs are just set but not overcooked, add the peaches, placing them over one-half of the eggs. Sprinkle with grated nutmeg and salt to taste. Fold the other half of the eggs over the peaches and slide the omelet out of the pan onto a plate.

Scrambled Eggs

Serves 4

I don't like scrambled eggs just for breakfast. I like them for a Sunday-night supper, when it's cold and rainy outside, served with crisp hot buttered toast. The secret to

Scrambled Eggs, continued

cooking them is to use low heat, avoid covering too much of the surface area in the frying pan or skillet, and add an egg at the end to keep the mixture moist.

3 tablespoons butter
6 eggs, beaten
1/2 cup whipping cream
1 egg
Salt
Freshly ground black pepper

2 tablespoons chopped herbs
   (optional)
1/2 cup sautéed sliced mushrooms,
   morels, artichoke hearts, or 1/4
   cup sliced truffles (optional)

Melt the butter in a heavy saucepan or in the top of a double boiler or bain-marie. Add the 6 eggs. Stir occasionally over low heat until they start to cook. Add the cream and stir occasionally to get large curds. When the eggs are still soft but nearly done, remove from the heat. Beat the last egg and mix it in gently. It will cook in the heat from the pan, and keep the other eggs moist. Season to taste, and add herbs if you wish. To serve, heat the other optional ingredients and add to the eggs. Reheat until heated through, 2–3 minutes. Scrambled eggs reheat well in a microwave.

Toad in the Hole

Serves 1

Don't laugh. This is absolutely the best way to fix eggs for Saturday breakfast.

4 tablespoons butter
2 slices bread
2 large eggs

Melt the butter in a heavy skillet large enough to hold both slices of bread. With a biscuit cutter cut a hole in the center of each bread slice. Place the bread in the butter and fry until browned on one side and turn. Crack the eggs separately and drop into the holes. Cook slowly until the eggs are fried and the bread browned, 3–4 minutes. If the bread browns before the eggs cook, cover and let sit for about a minute until done.

SOUPS, STEWS, and SALADS

Butter Bean or Lima Bean and Champagne Soup

Serves 10-12

This recipe was developed by Jimmy and Gwen Bentley when a group of us had gathered at their home to cook together one winter's evening. It was cooked in a kettle hanging on a swag in an open fireplace.

1 pound dried butter beans or limas
Ham bone, ham, or salt pork
3 celery stalks with leaves
1 large carrot
1 large or 2 medium onions
4 medium potatoes

1 large bay leaf
8 peppercorns
8 whole cloves
Salt to taste
1 bottle champagne, or to taste

✿   ✿   ✿

Garnishes:
Chopped ham (optional)
Fresh parsley, finely chopped

Rinse the beans and place in a large bowl. Cover with cold water by 2 inches and soak overnight. If you are short of time use the quick method as directed on the package.

To prepare the broth, combine 3 quarts of water with the remaining ingredients (except champagne and parsley) and simmer, covered, about 1 hour. Strain

Butter or Lima Bean Soup, continued

the broth and skim off any grease that may have risen to the top. Set aside the potatoes and any lean meat, discarding the bones and other vegetables. Mash the potatoes coarse. Drain the beans and add to the broth. Simmer until the beans are very tender, about 1–2 hours. Add the potatoes and bruise the beans well with a potato masher until the soup is thick. Chop the meat and add some of it to the soup. Correct the seasoning.

Before serving, add 1/2–3/4 of the bottle of champagne to the hot soup and stir to blend over medium heat. Serve with a garnish of the remaining chopped ham, if desired, and parsley, adding a few tablespoons of champagne to each soup bowl at the table as it is served. It causes an immediate fizzle and brings exclamations of joy and praise.

Cream of Carrot Soup

Serves 8

This soup is good to make when other fresh vegetables are not available. I often had it on the winter menu when I had my restaurant in Social Circle. It's a delicious and unusual soup, which may be made several days ahead and reheated gently.

3 tablespoons butter
6 carrots, peeled and sliced
1 onion, thinly sliced
4 cups chicken stock (p. 320) or
    canned broth

1½ tablespoons sugar, or to taste
1 clove garlic, crushed with salt
Freshly ground black pepper
¾ cup heavy cream
¼ cup cooked rice

Melt 2 tablespoons of the butter in a large saucepan or pot. Add the carrots and onion. Cover and cook over low heat until the onion is soft but not browned. Stir in the stock, cover, and simmer until the carrots are very soft, about 30 minutes. Remove the solids, reserving the liquid, and purée in a food processor or blender in small batches. Return to the stock, stirring. Add sugar and season to taste with garlic and pepper. Pour in the cream, bring to the boil, and remove from the heat. Whisk in the remaining 1 tablespoon butter, and add the cooked rice.

Iced Cucumber and Mint Soup

Serves 6–8

This cold soup can be made in large batches and kept for several days in the refrigerator, the cucumbers and shrimp being added just before serving. Serve in a glass or silver bowl for a lovely contrast. This recipe can be multiplied easily for a crowd. From my *Cooking of the South*.

3 cucumbers, peeled and diced	**1/2 cup heavy cream**
Salt	**2 cloves garlic, finely crushed**
1/2 cup tomato juice	**1 hard-cooked egg, grated or**
1/2 cup chicken stock, fresh	** chopped**
** (p. 320) or canned**	**1/4 pound fresh shrimp, cooked,**
2 cups plain yogurt	** peeled, and chopped**
	Fresh mint, finely chopped (optional)

Put the cucumbers in a colander, sprinkle with salt, and allow to drain for 30 minutes to remove the bitter juices. Rinse well, and set aside or refrigerate until needed.

Meanwhile, stir together the tomato juice, chicken stock, yogurt, cream, garlic, and egg until well blended. Chill. Add the cucumbers and shrimp just before serving. Garnish with chopped mint.

Pimento Soup

Serves 6–8

My friend Kay Goldstein, owner of the Proof of the Pudding, a local carry-out gourmet and catering firm, made this with sour cream when she first served it to me. It's nice either way and a lovely soup for outdoor dining.

Pimento Soup, continued

2 tablespoons butter
1 small onion, chopped
2 tablespoons flour
5 cups chicken stock, fresh or
    canned (p. 320)

Juice of 1/2 lemon
1 seven-ounce jar pimentos, chopped
    and drained
1 cup heavy cream

Melt the butter in a large saucepan. Add the onion and cook until it is soft but not browned. Stir in the flour. Add the chicken stock and lemon juice and bring to the boil, stirring continuously. When the liquid has boiled briefly and thickened slightly, remove from the heat.

    Purée 2 cups of the liquid with the pimentos in a food processor or blender. Combine with the remainder of the soup and refrigerate. When cool, blend in the cream. Serve chilled.

Sweet Potato and Bourbon Soup

Serves 4-6

This is a rich golden soup, quite uniquely Southern with the sweetness of the potato enhanced by the addition of bourbon.

3 tablespoons butter
4 medium sweet potatoes, peeled
    and sliced roughly
6 cups chicken stock, fresh or
    canned (p. 320)

1/3 cup bourbon
Salt
Freshly ground black pepper

Heat the butter in a large flameproof casserole or enamel pan. Add a layer of potatoes and brown on both sides. Remove and repeat until all are browned. Add 5 cups of the chicken stock. Cook, covered, until the potatoes are tender enough for a fork to pierce them easily. When they are tender, remove 1 cup of the potatoes and purée in a food processor fitted with a grating blade. Return to the soup and with a spoon break up the rest of the potatoes into large chunks. Taste. Stir in as much of the remaining cup of chicken stock as is necessary for a medium-thick soup. Add the bourbon and bring to the boil. Season with salt and pepper.

Tomato, Pepper, Garlic, and Onion Soup

Serves 8

My husband, David, and I ran a restaurant on the island of Majorca before moving to Social Circle, Georgia. The vegetables we grew and picked in our restaurant garden in Social Circle were much like those we had in Majorca—onions, garlic, bell peppers, and tomatoes. Here is a wonderful soup that is much like a Spanish gazpacho, yet distinctly Southern. It keeps a week, refrigerated, and is good hot or cold.

1 medium onion
2 cloves garlic
1 green or red bell pepper
1 medium cucumber, peeled
7 cups tomato juice, fresh or canned
1 one-pound can good-quality
    canned tomatoes

5 tablespoons red wine vinegar
1/3 cup breadcrumbs
Salt
Freshly ground black pepper

✿   ✿   ✿

Garnishes:
1 medium onion, chopped
1 red or green bell pepper, chopped
1 cup bread cubes, fried in
   3 tablespoons butter

1/2 medium cucumber,
   chopped, unpeeled

Purée the onion, garlic cloves, bell pepper, and cucumber in a blender or food processor. Add the tomato juice, tomatoes, vinegar, and breadcrumbs and process again. Season to taste with salt and pepper. Serve hot or chilled, with the garnishes in separate bowls to be added at serving time.

Turnip and Ginger Soup

Serves 6

This is a refreshing soup, and don't let the use of several pots daunt you — it's well worth the effort.

4 tablespoons butter
4 green onions, sliced and divided
    into green and white parts
5 cups chicken stock, fresh or
    canned (p. 320)
1 cayenne or other hot pepper
    (optional)
Dash Hot Sauce (p. 297)
    or Tabasco

½ pound turnips, sliced
½ pound turnip greens, stemmed
    and sliced in 1-inch pieces
1–2 tablespoons fresh ginger, grated
    or chopped
1 tablespoon soy sauce
Salt
Freshly ground black pepper

Melt the butter and add the white part of the onion. Sauté over medium heat about 3 minutes. Add the chicken stock, hot pepper, and Hot Sauce or Tabasco, and bring to the boil.

Meanwhile, place the turnip slices in a small pot of cold water and bring to the boil. If the turnips were small before slicing, boil 2 or 3 minutes; if they were large, 5–10 minutes will do. Remove and set aside when cooked.

In a separate pot, bring enough water to the boil to cover the sliced turnip greens. Add the greens. Cook 1 minute and drain. Add the turnips and turnip greens to the boiling stock along with 1 tablespoon of the grated or chopped ginger. Simmer 8–10 minutes. Remove from the heat, taste for seasoning, and add soy sauce, salt and pepper to taste, and any more ginger you think it needs. Top with the green slices of the onion just before serving. Serve hot.

Turnip Green and Cream Soup

Serves 6–8

Bobbi Sturgis came up with this recipe while helping me with this book. We wanted a colorful, flavorful soup and we got it. Let me introduce you to "likker." It's the "liquor" made by cooking vegetables in water.

3 cups turnip greens, washed
 and stemmed
4 tablespoons butter
1 large onion, chopped
1 clove garlic, mashed
8 turnips, peeled and sliced,
 about 6 cups

2 cups chicken stock, fresh or
 canned (p. 320)
1 cup milk
1 small hot pepper, chopped, or dash
 Hot Sauce (p. 297) or Tabasco
Salt
Freshly ground black pepper

Place the turnip greens in enough boiling water to cover. Boil 5 minutes, remove the greens, and set aside. Return the water you have just boiled the greens in (the "likker") to a boil and reduce to 2–3 cups. Meanwhile, melt the butter in a saucepan. Sauté the onion until soft but not browned. Add garlic, turnips, stock, milk, and the 2 cups of "likker," and continue cooking, covered, until the turnips are tender. Remove the solids and purée in a food processor or blender, then return to the soup.

Season to taste with the hot pepper, Hot Sauce, or Tabasco, and salt and pepper, adding more pot "likker" if necessary. Garnish with Cooked turnip greens.

Cream of Turnip Soup

Serves 4

This soup is good hot or cold. It's a surprise treat with its full rich flavor and smooth texture. May be made in advance.

4 tablespoons butter
1 large onion, chopped
8 medium white turnips, peeled and
 chopped, about 6 cups
1 clove garlic, chopped or crushed
2 tablespoons flour
1 cup chicken stock, fresh or
 canned (p. 320)

1 cup milk
2/3 cup sour cream
1/4 teaspoon nutmeg
1 teaspoon sugar
Salt
Freshly ground black pepper

Melt 2 tablespoons of the butter in a large saucepan. Add the onion and cook until soft but not browned. Blanch the turnips by placing them in a large quantity of water and boiling 5 minutes. Drain. Add the turnips and garlic to the onion and cook until the turnips are tender. Purée in a food processor or blender.

Cream of Turnip Soup, continued

In a separate pan melt the remaining 2 tablespoons of butter and stir in the flour until smooth. Add the chicken stock and milk. Bring to the boil, stirring constantly. Combine the puréed mixture with the stock mixture and blend thoroughly. Whisk in the sour cream, nutmeg, and sugar. Correct the seasoning with salt and pepper. If serving hot, reheat just before serving.

Turnip and Onion Soup

Serves 6

This soup is nearly a whole meal in itself, perfect for a Sunday-night supper, when you've had a full, rich meal earlier in the day. It will remind you of classic onion soup, with a twist. It may be made several days ahead and freezes well.

4 medium white turnips, grated
    to make 4 cups
8 tablespoons butter
8 medium onions, sliced to make
    4 cups
8 tablespoons flour
6–8 cups beef stock, fresh (p. 320)
    or canned

2 cups water (optional)
Salt
Freshly ground black pepper
8 thick slices French bread, toasted
1 cup grated Parmesan cheese

Place the grated turnips in a pot with enough water to cover. Bring to the boil and boil 1–3 minutes. Drain. Dry the turnips with a paper towel.

Melt 4 tablespoons of the butter in a large, heavy pan and add the onions. Cook over medium heat until they are a rich brown. Add the turnips and continue cooking until they have turned a light brown and the onions have caramelized to a nutty color. Add the remaining 4 tablespoons of butter. Stir in the flour a tablespoon at a time. Taste the beef stock. If it is particularly strong or salty, add only 6 cups stock and 2 cups water. Stir until the soup boils, turn the heat down, and simmer, slightly covered, for 30 minutes. Taste for seasoning and add salt and pepper if needed.

Sprinkle the toasted bread with the cheese. Place under a broiler until the cheese melts and turns slightly brown. To serve, ladle soup into individual bowls and top with the bread.

Zucchini and Pecan Soup

Serves 6–8

This soup is easily made, good cold or hot, and lasts several days in the refrigerator.

2 pounds medium zucchini, sliced
    but not peeled
2 medium onions, sliced
1 clove garlic, crushed or chopped
3½ cups chicken stock, fresh or
    canned (p. 320)

1 cup sour cream, heavy cream,
    or plain yogurt
Salt
Freshly ground black pepper

✿   ✿   ✿

Garnish:
3 tablespoons butter
½ cup pecan halves
    or chopped pecans

Combine the zucchini, onions, garlic, and chicken stock in a large saucepan or flameproof casserole. Bring to the boil. Lower the heat and simmer, covered, for 10 minutes until the zucchini is tender. Remove the solids, saving the liquid, and purée the solids in a blender or food processor. Return the puréed mixture to the liquid and stir. Blend in the sour cream, heavy cream, or yogurt, add salt and pepper to taste, and cool until ready to serve. If serving hot, reheat without boiling.

    For the garnish, melt the butter, add the pecans, and sauté until browned. When ready to serve, top the soup with the pecans.

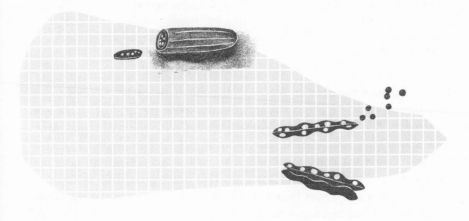

Vegetable and Sausage Soup

Serves 8

This garden soup is more than just a soup; it's dinner. Make it ahead, in the summer, freezing it for a long winter's night. It's also good in the late fall, when some of the vegetables are still fresh from the garden but there is a chill in the air. A word about the ham bone—it makes a tremendous difference in flavor.

2 quarts chicken stock,
    preferably homemade (p. 320)
1 ham bone (cured or smoked)
1 cup salt pork, diced
6 tablespoons butter
3 medium onions, chopped
2 cloves garlic, chopped
3 stalks celery, chopped
4 medium carrots, sliced on an angle
1 green bell pepper, seeded
    and chopped
1 tablespoon rosemary, crumbled
5 tablespoons fennel seed
1 bay leaf, crumbled
4 medium zucchini, sliced

1 cup mushrooms, sliced
3–4 cups cooked and drained crowder
    peas or black-eyed peas
2 pounds hot country bulk sausage,
    crumbled
Salt
Freshly ground black pepper
1/2 pound pasta, preferably pepper
    or turnip green, cut as vermicelli
6 fresh tomatoes, peeled, seeded, and
    coarsely chopped
2 cups coarsely shredded fresh
    turnip greens
1/2 cup chopped fresh parsley

✿   ✿   ✿

Garnish:
1/2 cup chopped fresh parsley
1/3 cup chopped fresh
    basil leaves
4 cloves garlic, chopped

2 cups freshly grated
    Parmesan cheese
French or Italian bread, sliced thick

In a large pot simmer the chicken stock with the ham bone for 10–15 minutes.

    Fry the salt pork in a large pot until crisp. Drain off the fat, leaving the salt pork in the pot. Add the butter, and heat until melted. Add the onions and garlic and cook until translucent. Add the celery, carrots, green pepper, rosemary, fennel, and bay leaf. Lower the heat, cover, and cook 5–8 minutes. Uncover, raise the heat, and add sliced zucchini and mushrooms. Toss over high heat for 3 minutes. Pour in the hot stock and ham bone and add the peas. Return to the boil, then reduce heat and simmer, uncovered, for 10 minutes. The vegetables should be fork tender. Remove the ham bone. Place the crumbled sausage in a skillet, and sauté 15 minutes or until done. Remove the sausage, drain, and add to the soup. Season to taste. The soup may be made ahead to this point and frozen.

When you are ready to serve, reheat to boiling, add pasta, tomatoes, and greens, and simmer until the pasta is done. Add 1/2 cup parsley to the soup. To make the garnish, combine 1/2 cup parsley, basil, garlic, and cheese. Top the soup with the garnish and serve with bread.

She-Crab Soup

Serves 6

This is a specialty soup of the Southern coast. The delicious eggs from the she-crab add a unique flavor and texture. When fresh she-crabs and their eggs are not available, substitute store-bought lump crabmeat and a couple of crumbled hard-cooked chicken egg yolks. Although sherry has been used in recent years, dry Madeira was the fortified wine of choice from the 1700s to Prohibition.

2 tablespoons butter	2 hard-cooked eggs (optional)
1 green onion, finely chopped	Salt
1 stalk celery, finely chopped	White pepper
2 tablespoons flour	Dash Hot Sauce (p. 297)
1 quart milk	or Tabasco
2 cups heavy cream	1/3 cup dry Madeira
She-crab, cooked and picked over to	1/2 cup heavy cream,
make 3 cups of lump crabmeat	whipped
and eggs (see p. 312)	Paprika

In a heavy saucepan, melt the butter, add the onion and celery, and cook until the onion is soft but not browned. Stir in the flour, then add the milk and cream and bring to the boil, stirring constantly. Remove from the heat and let cool a few minutes. Add the crabmeat with the eggs. Substitute crumbled yolks from hard-cooked chicken eggs if fresh she-crabs are not used. When ready to serve, warm the soup briefly to 180 degrees over very low heat, stirring. Do not allow to boil. Taste, season with salt, pepper, and Hot Sauce or Tabasco. To serve, place a small amount of Madeira in each soup bowl, add the soup, top with whipped cream, and sprinkle with paprika.

Crab Stew

Serves 4

This makes an ideal supper served with a dark green salad, crusty bread, and a light homemade fruit dessert. It's perfect for a chilly evening.

6 tablespoons butter
1 large onion, chopped
1 bunch green onions, chopped
2 stalks celery, chopped
1 cup water
3 peeled and diced potatoes, to make
    1½ cups

2½ cups lump crabmeat, shells
    and membrane removed
2 cups milk
Salt
Freshly ground black pepper
Tabasco

Melt the butter in a large pan, add the onion, green onions, and celery. Cook until soft. Add the water and bring to the boil, then add potatoes, and continue to cook until the potatoes are soft. Add crabmeat and milk and heat through without boiling. Season to taste with salt, pepper, and Tabasco, and serve immediately.

Oyster Stew

Serves 4

There is probably nothing simpler to make or more memorable than oyster stew. This is a wonderful main-course dish.

4 tablespoons butter
3 tablespoons finely chopped onion
1 stalk celery, finely chopped
½ cup milk
1 cup heavy cream
Salt

Freshly ground black pepper
1 teaspoon paprika
1 teaspoon Creole Seasoning (p. 297),
    optional
1 quart oysters and their liquid
Oyster crackers or saltines

Melt the butter in a heavy saucepan. Add the onion and celery and cook until soft but not browned, about 5 minutes. Add the remaining ingredients except the oysters and crackers, and bring to the boiling point. Remove from the heat and add the oysters and their liquid. Place back on the stove and heat through about 2 minutes, until the oysters are warmed throughout. Do not boil. Serve with the crackers.

Variation: Substitute chopped fennel for the celery, and top with a little shredded country ham or 3 cooked and quartered new potatoes.

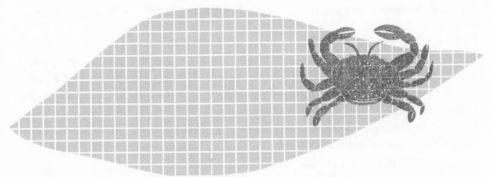

Abercrombie Brunswick Stew

Makes 3 gallons, serves about 30 people

Brunswick stew apparently received its name from Brunswick County, Virginia, although legend has it that the stew is named for the Earl of Brunswick, who visited the Deep South before the War Between the States. He observed that a succulent pork was being served to guests on the lawn while an equally succulent stew was being served to the laborers in the backyard. Like many an Englishman, he preferred the stew to the grill.

This is really an old-fashioned basic Brunswick stew—my friend Jimmy Bentley's version of the Abercrombie side of his family's stew. Some Southerners add okra, lima beans, garlic, and infinite other personal preferences, such as a few squirrels, a rabbit or two, and maybe a leg of venison. Some might even add boiled beef—Jimmy says it is absolutely atrocious in this stew; my friend Kate loves it.

Brunswick stew freezes well, and multiplies easily for a crowd of 100 when you are serving slaw and barbecue too. It is traditionally served with white loaf bread or crackling cornbread to sop it up. There are two kinds of stew, one to serve as a main dish, the other as a side dish with meats. If preparing as a side dish, add all the corn and potatoes. If using as a main dish, cut back on them.

Abercrombie Brunswick Stew, continued

8 medium onions, chopped
4 tablespoons pork drippings or
    4 tablespoons butter
2 cups seasoned chicken stock (add
    1 extra chicken bouillon cube)
2 three-pound chickens, cooked
    and boned
4–5 pounds pork (any cut), grilled,
    boned, and chopped
5 pounds tomatoes, chopped

1 quart ketchup
1 cup Mrs. Dull's (Abercrombie)
    Barbecue Sauce (p. 293)
2 cups chopped potatoes or instant
    potatoes (optional for
    quicker thickening)
1–2 pounds creamed corn
Salt
Freshly ground black pepper
Hot Sauce (p. 297) or Tabasco to taste

In a big black iron pot outdoors or in a large heavy pot indoors, cook the onions in the drippings or butter. Add the broth and bring to the boil. Add chicken, pork, tomatoes, ketchup, and barbecue sauce. Cook 6–8 hours outside or 1–2 hours inside to blend and thicken, stirring frequently so the stew does not stick to the bottom of the pot. Be cautious—it really will scorch the pot! Add the potatoes 1 hour before serving if the stew needs thickening. Add the corn 10 minutes before serving. Just before serving adjust the seasoning, particularly for black pepper (a good spice for pork) and the Hot Sauce or Tabasco.

Rabbit Stew

Serves 6

This is a lusty hunters' stew, although nowadays we don't use wild rabbits but buy them small and tender in the grocery store. Particularly good when made in advance, this stew also freezes and doubles well.

2 tablespoons butter
2 tablespoons oil
2 three-pound rabbits, cut in pieces
4 medium onions, sliced
3 cloves garlic, chopped or crushed
1 tablespoon brown sugar
1 twelve-ounce bottle beer or ale
1½–2 cups chicken stock, fresh
    (p. 320) or canned

1 bay leaf, crumbled
1 tablespoon chopped rosemary
2 tablespoons cornstarch
2 tablespoons white wine vinegar
Salt
Freshly ground black pepper

Melt the butter and oil in a heavy pot or casserole. Add the rabbit and brown on all sides in several batches. Remove the rabbit, add the onions to the fat, and cook for a few minutes until soft. Return the rabbit to the pot and add garlic, brown sugar, and beer. Add enough stock to cover, along with the bay leaf and rosemary. Cover and simmer for 1–1 1/2 hours, until the rabbit is tender, adding more stock if necessary. Fork-test for tenderness. When the rabbit is done, remove. In a small bowl mix the cornstarch and vinegar until smooth. Add a little of the hot liquid from the stew, then add the cornstarch mixture to the hot liquid and gently stir over heat until well blended. Taste for seasoning and add salt and pepper to taste. Return rabbit to the cooking pot or place on a platter and cover with sauce.

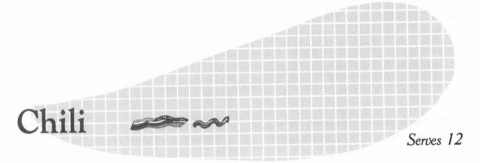

Chili

Serves 12

On a chilly night there's nothing more fun and filling than a big pot of steaming chili. Serve a gang! They will enjoy adding toppings of corn chips, lettuce, and cheese.

2 pounds ground round beef
1 pound ground pork
5 cups chopped onions
1 1/2 tablespoons chopped garlic
7 tablespoons chili powder
2 small cans chopped green
   chili peppers
3 sixteen-ounce cans tomatoes,
   crushed
3 tablespoons tomato paste
4 bay leaves, crumbled

1 tablespoon salt
1 tablespoon oregano
1 tablespoon red wine vinegar
1 tablespoon brown sugar
2 sixteen-ounce cans red kidney beans
   or pinto beans
1 bag corn chips
1 head lettuce, shredded (preferably
   red or leaf)
12 ounces sharp Cheddar cheese,
   shredded

In a large, heavy pot, brown the meat with the onions and garlic. Drain off the fat and stir in the chili powder. Add chilies, tomatoes, tomato paste, bay leaves, salt, oregano, vinegar, and brown sugar. Cover the pot and cook for 2 hours over low heat. Add beans and cook, uncovered, 30 minutes more. Serve with side dishes of corn chips, shredded lettuce, and shredded sharp Cheddar cheese.

Beef Stew with Fennel and Pecans

Serves 4-6

If you are as fond of fennel as I am, you'll enjoy the crunch of fresh fennel and the texture of pecans in this special stew. Fennel looks like celery and has a delicate licorice or anise flavor when cooked. If you absolutely must, substitute celery for the fennel, but whatever you do, cook the stew at least the day ahead of a dinner party. This recipe doubles easily, may be made up to three days ahead, frozen, and reheated, the fennel and pecans added just before serving. Cut the meat into large chunks for browning and cooking, then slice to bite-size pieces before heating.

3 pounds sirloin tip or chuck roast	Juice of 1 lemon
3 tablespoons bacon fat or drippings	1 tablespoon fennel seeds
2 medium onions, sliced	2½ cups beef stock (p. 320) or
4 tablespoons flour	canned beef bouillon
½ cup dry white wine	Salt
2 tablespoons chopped fresh rosemary	Freshly ground black pepper
1 teaspoon chopped fresh thyme	
1 clove garlic, finely chopped	
or crushed	

✿　✿　✿

Garnish:

4 tablespoons butter	1 cup toasted pecan halves
2 whole fennel bulbs, sliced,	1 orange rind, without the white,
with core removed, or	julienned
1-2 bunches celery, sliced	

Cut the beef into 2-inch squares. Heat the fat in a heavy flameproof casserole and add the beef. Do not crowd the pan; the cubes should not touch each other. Brown on one side to a deep mahogany color then turn with tongs and brown the other side. If the fat is good and hot this process shouldn't take more than 10 minutes. When the meat is browned, remove, and place the onions in the pan. Cook 3-4 minutes until they just start to brown. Remove from the heat and drain off all but 4 tablespoons of the fat. Add the flour, stir well, and return to the heat, then add wine, stirring until it comes to a boil. Remove from the heat again and add the browned meat, rosemary, thyme, garlic, lemon juice, and fennel seeds. Add only enough of the stock so that the liquid covers the meat. Stir all together, place back on the heat, and bring slowly to the boil. Cover, reduce to a simmer, and cook gently 1 1/2–2 hours until tender.

Remove from the heat, and if serving right away, degrease with paper towels or run ice cubes over the top. If serving the next day, cool uncovered, then refrigerate, covered, and remove excess fat the next day. It may also be frozen at this point. Check the size of the chunks of meat. If they are too large to serve attractively, slice them into bite-size pieces.

Reheat the stew over low heat and bring to the boil. Reduce heat and simmer 10 minutes or until heated through. When ready to serve, taste, add salt and pepper if needed, and place in an attractive serving bowl.

Up to 4 hours before serving, but ideally 10 minutes before, make the garnish. Melt the butter in a large frying pan. Add fennel or celery slices and sauté over medium-high heat for 5 minutes. Remove, add pecans, and sauté a few minutes. Blanch the orange rind in boiling water for 30 seconds. When ready to serve, reheat the fennel with the pecans, add to the stew, and top with the rind. Serve hot.

Beet and Sesame Oil Salad

Serves 6

Most everyone knows corn is best when cooked within minutes of being picked. But when my friend Laurie Garner of Atlanta served me a salad of fresh beets from her garden I discovered a pleasure equal to fresh corn. This is an adaptation of that salad. Its crimson slivers are particularly beautiful with broccoli flowerets.

3 medium beets (1½ pounds), cooked, peeled, and julienned, or canned beets
3–5 tablespoons dark sesame oil
1–2 tablespoons red wine vinegar

1–2 tablespoons chopped fresh herbs: lemon thyme, lemon balm, lemon grass, or ginger
Salt to taste
Freshly ground black pepper to taste

To cook the beets, clean and remove the green tops without cutting into the red skin. (Cutting the skin will make the beet bleed red when cooked.) Place whole, unskinned beets in a heavy saucepan of cold water. Bring to the boil and simmer, uncovered, about 30 minutes. Place in cold water and peel off the skins.

While the beets are still warm, toss them together with the remaining ingredients. Chill if desired or serve hot.

Beet and Sesame Oil Salad, continued

Variation: Sauté 2 cups broccoli flowerets in peanut oil for 2 minutes and add to the beets. Serve hot or cold as a vegetable side dish or a salad.

Grated Beet Salad

Serves 4–6

When the tomatoes are gone for the summer, we tend to use beets as color accent on our plates.

Dressing:

2 tablespoons wine vinegar	2 tablespoons Dijon mustard
1 tablespoon lemon juice	3 tablespoons vegetable oil
1 teaspoon sugar	1 tablespoon finely chopped parsley

✿ ✿ ✿

2 cups cooked or canned beets, grated	Freshly ground black pepper
Salt	2 tablespoons chopped chives or chopped green-onion ends

To make the dressing, combine the vinegar, lemon juice, and sugar, and stir. When the sugar has dissolved, add the mustard and oil and whisk until creamy. Sprinkle parsley over and mix lightly.

Place the beets in a bowl. Pour the dressing over them and season to taste with salt and pepper. Cover and refrigerate. When chilled, top with chives and serve.

Cabbage Slaw and Peanuts

Serves 6–8

When you want an unusual slaw, try this variation.

3 cups shredded cabbage	1/3 cup peeled and chopped cucumber
1/2 cup chopped celery	

3 tablespoons chopped onion
1 recipe Peanut Butter Mayonnaise
    (p. 306)
Dash Tabasco or Creole Seasoning
    (p. 297)

1 teaspoon Dijon mustard
Salt
Freshly ground black pepper
1/2 cup roasted, salted,
    and chopped peanuts

In a large bowl, toss together the cabbage, celery, cucumber, and onion. Add mayonnaise, Tabasco or Creole Seasoning, and Dijon mustard, and toss again. Taste and season with salt and pepper, top with peanuts, and serve.

Cole Slaw

Serves 10–15

This cole slaw feeds a crowd. It's especially good at pork barbecues since it's a light slaw with no eggs or mayonnaise. Some people like it very sweet, so I've allowed considerable latitude on the amount of sugar.

4–5 pounds cabbage, shredded
2–3 large Vidalia or salad onions,
    chopped
1 1/2 cups peanut oil

1 cup apple-cider vinegar
1 tablespoon Dijon mustard
Sugar to taste, 1 tablespoon to 2 cups
Salt and pepper to taste

Toss the cabbage and onions together in a large bowl. Place the oil, vinegar, mustard, and sugar in a saucepan and bring to the boil. While still hot, pour the dressing over the cabbage and mix. Chill, stirring from time to time.

Cucumber and Yogurt Salad

Serves 6

Cucumbers are so plentiful in the South that we have a myriad of ways to prepare them. With the advent of the lighter-eating era we are using cucumbers in new ways, such as this one with yogurt. The main thing to worry about with

Cucumber and Yogurt Salad, continued

cucumbers is that they may be bitter. This occurs most frequently when the weather is hot and dry. For that reason, degorging, which is salting, letting stand, then rinsing and draining, is always preferred. When my cucumbers are home grown I nibble a piece from every other one, just to double-check for bitterness. This refreshing salad is a good foil for a spicy dish.

4–6 cucumbers, peeled and sliced
Salt
2 cups plain yogurt, drained if watery
1 clove garlic, chopped or crushed

1 tablespoon fresh mint (optional)
3 tablespoons lemon juice
3 tablespoons vegetable oil
Freshly ground black pepper

Place the cucumbers in a colander or strainer and sprinkle with salt. Let stand 15 minutes or longer to release the bitter juices. Rinse well and dry. In a blender or food processor, mix together the remaining ingredients. Combine with the cucumbers in a bowl and refrigerate.

Eggplant Salad

Serves 6

This salad is good for fix-ahead occasions. A good accompaniment for cold meat and chicken, it's colorful and unexpectedly interesting with its range of textures and fullness of taste. It can be used as an appetizer when served with Sour Cream Brittlebread (p. 27). Boiling eggplant removes any possible bitterness.

2 eggplants, about 1½ pounds each
3 teaspoons peanut oil
2 onions, cut in ½-inch cubes

3 stalks celery, sliced
2 cloves garlic, chopped or crushed

✿   ✿   ✿

Dressing:
½ cup wine vinegar
Salt to taste
Freshly ground black pepper to taste

2 teaspoons chopped fresh thyme
1 tablespoon chopped fresh basil
¾ cup vegetable oil

✿   ✿   ✿

1/2 cup seedless raisins, plumped
    in warm water 10–15 minutes
    and drained
1/2 cup pine nuts

3 sweet red pimentos, roasted,
    peeled, seeded, and sliced thin,
    or 3 canned pimentos

Cut the eggplants into 1/2-inch cubes, leaving on the skin. Bring a large pot of water to the boil, add the eggplant, and cook, uncovered, over medium heat for 3–5 minutes, until tender but still firm. Drain well and set aside. Heat the oil, add the onions and celery, and sauté 5 minutes. Add garlic and cook a few minutes more.

    To make the dressing, in a large bowl combine the vinegar, salt, pepper, thyme, and basil; add the oil and mix well. Add the eggplant and toss. Cover with plastic wrap and marinate for several hours. One hour before serving, add the raisins, pine nuts, and red pimentos. Toss thoroughly to mix. Refrigerate until serving time.

Fennel and Apple Salad

Serves 10

This recipe cuts down quite easily, especially if you always keep a jar of the salad dressing ready in the refrigerator. Just slice up a bulb of fennel, add an apple or two, and there you have it.

3 bulbs fennel, sliced
5 apples, cored and sliced

1/2 recipe Sweet Southern Dressing
    (p. 298)

Combine and refrigerate.

Variation: May be made with 3 bunches of celery and 5 tablespoons ground fennel seeds, instead of the fennel.

Deen Terry's Ginger Salad

Serves 6–8

"Congealed" (jellied) salads are standard fare in the South. Usually I don't care for these sweet salads, but this is an exception. It's very nice served with roasted chicken or turkey.

Deen Terry's Ginger Salad, continued

1 envelope (3 ounces) lemon gelatin
1/2 cup boiling water
1 1/2 cups ginger ale
1 cup chopped dates

1 cup chopped apple, with peel on
3/4 cup chopped crystallized ginger
1/2 cup chopped pecans

✿   ✿   ✿

Sauce:
8 ounces cream cheese
About 1/4 cup sour cream

✿   ✿   ✿

Chopped crystallized ginger

Dissolve the gelatin in boiling water. Add the ginger ale, place in a 4- or 5-cup mold, and chill. When the liquid begins to get firm, stir in the dates, apple, ginger, and pecans. Chill until completely set.

To make the sauce, mix cream cheese with enough of the sour cream to make a well-blended sauce.

Unmold the salad and serve with the sauce. Top with chopped crystallized ginger.

Red Lettuce and Mushroom Salad

Serves 6

When we first moved to Social Circle, the only reliable lettuce we could find other than iceberg was red lettuce, so we became quite fond of it. We obtained our mushrooms from a local man who had converted an old rural schoolhouse in Madison, Georgia, into a sort of mushroom "greenhouse." The combination of mushrooms and lettuce became quite popular in our restaurant.

1 head red leaf lettuce

1/2 pound mushrooms, sliced

✿   ✿   ✿

Dressing:
1/3 cup red wine vinegar
1 cup vegetable oil
Salt to taste

Freshly ground black pepper to taste
1 tablespoon Dijon mustard

Wash the lettuce, dry thoroughly, and break into leaves. Arrange the leaves on plates. To make the dressing, in a bowl combine vinegar, oil, salt, pepper, and mustard. Place the mushrooms in the dressing, and toss well (this may be done several hours or a day in advance). To serve, use a slotted spoon to remove the mushrooms and place on the leaves.

Melon, Cucumber, and Tomato Salad

Serves 6

When my friends and assistants Carmen Sanders and Candy Thrasher returned from their first six weeks at the Cordon Bleu in London, they made this salad to show students how to adapt a recipe learned in one country to the ingredients of another country. Cherry tomatoes, for instance, are hardly used in Europe and England but are some of our most flavorful tomatoes. The look of this salad is spectacular, making it ideal for a buffet.

1 cucumber, washed but not peeled
1 cantaloupe or honeydew melon
1 pound fresh cherry tomatoes

✿   ✿   ✿

Dressing:

1/3 cup wine vinegar
1 cup peanut or vegetable oil
1/2 teaspoon Dijon mustard
Salt to taste

Freshly ground black pepper to taste
Sugar to taste
3 tablespoons chopped fresh parsley, mint, and chives, mixed

Cut the cucumber into cubes, sprinkle lightly with salt, and place in a colander. Slice the melon lengthwise from top to bottom in 6 equal wedges. Seed the melon and remove the flesh from the rinds, leaving the rinds intact. Set the rinds aside. Chop, cube, or ball the melon flesh. Rinse the cucumber of all salt and dry. Mix the cucumber, melon, and tomatoes together. Chill. Arrange the melon rinds in a glass bowl by placing them on their ends, forming a tulip petal design. Fill the bowl with the chilled salad. Combine the dressing ingredients and pour over the salad.

Mushroom, Pumpkin Seed, and Lettuce Salad

Serves 10

Pumpkins were a crucial staple of the South during the depression, and are still a popular vegetable. In this recipe dried pumpkin seeds add just the right touch to a simple salad.

Dressing:
2 tablespoons Dijon mustard
2/3 cup wine vinegar
2 cups peanut oil

Salt
Freshly ground black pepper

☆   ☆   ☆

Salad:
2 pounds mushrooms, sliced
1 head red leaf lettuce
1 bunch spinach, or Bibb or Boston
    lettuce

1/4 pound dried pumpkin seeds, pine
    nuts, or dried sunflower seeds

In a bowl, mix together the mustard and vinegar and slowly add the oil. Season with salt and pepper to taste. Marinate the mushrooms in the dressing until ready to serve. Wash the lettuce and spinach (if using), dry thoroughly, and break into leaves, discarding the spinach stems. Arrange the lettuce and spinach in a bowl and top with the mushrooms, seeds, and dressing.

Tuna Salad

Serves 2-4

This salad made from fresh grilled tuna is unforgettable.

6 ounces to 1/2 pound tuna fish, grilled
    (p. 134)

6 ounces to 1/2 pound cooked
    green beans or peas

Chopped mixed herbs (optional)
1 cucumber, sliced ⅛-inch thick
French dressing (1 tablespoon Dijon
　　mustard, 2 tablespoons vinegar,
　　5 tablespoons oil)

Anchovies, drained
Black olives
1 pound tomatoes, quartered

Place a layer of fish (you may break it up if you wish) on the bottom of a bowl and a layer of vegetables over it. Sprinkle with some of the optional herbs, then the cucumber. Drizzle with some of the salad dressing, then make a lattice of the anchovies and put the olives in the lattice diamonds. Surround with the tomatoes, rounded sides up. Brush the tomatoes with the dressing and spoon the remaining dressing over the entire salad. Garnish with more of the herbs, if desired.

Cooked Zucchini Salad

Serves 6

We have a custom when going to special outdoor events—like our Steeplechase, as well as football and baseball games—of opening up the back of the station wagon and laying out a feast fit for a king. We call this "tailgating." This recipe is perfect for such an occasion.

5 tablespoons butter
2 pounds zucchini, sliced
1 onion, chopped
Salt
Freshly ground black pepper

3-4 tablespoons peanut oil
2-3 tablespoons wine vinegar
2 tablespoons chopped fresh dill or
　　fresh chives (optional)
Zucchini blossoms (optional)

Melt the butter in a large saucepan. Add the zucchini, chopped onion, salt and pepper to taste, and cover. Cook about 15 minutes over low heat, until the zucchini is fork tender. In a bowl, mix together the oil and vinegar. Add the zucchini and onion and toss. Taste and add more oil, wine vinegar, salt, and pepper as needed. Refrigerate. Add the optional herbs and blossoms when ready to serve.

Vidalia Onion and Bell Pepper Salad

Serves 12–15

Beautiful, big red salad onions do as well as Vidalias in this salad, but since Vidalias are a Georgia product, I have to brag about them. They are the sweetest onions you'll ever eat, and this salad gets better the longer you keep it. It lasts up to a week in the refrigerator, and is great all week long.

3 large Vidalia or red salad onions,
    sliced
3 bell peppers, cored, seeded, and
    sliced, preferably 1 yellow, 1 red,
    and 1 purple, or a mixture of red
    and green

✿   ✿   ✿

Dressing:

1 cup peanut oil
1/2 cup red wine vinegar
1/2 teaspoon chopped fresh basil
1 teaspoon chopped fresh lemon balm
    (optional)
1 teaspoon chopped rosemary,
    preferably fresh

1 teaspoon chopped thyme, preferably
    fresh
1 tablespoon chopped fresh parsley
Salt
Freshly ground black pepper
1 1/4 teaspoons Dijon mustard

Place the onions and peppers in a large bowl.

To make the salad dressing, mix all the ingredients in a food processor or with a whisk in a medium-sized bowl. Pour over the onions and peppers and toss once or twice before refrigerating. May be eaten right away, but is best made at least a day ahead.

SIDE DISHES
and
VEGETABLES

Asparagus

I love asparagus so much I collect a variety of antique asparagus tongs, a wonderful utensil for eating individual asparagus spears. Asparagus is technically a finger food, held at the stalk with fingers or tongs. Do not overcook it — it should never be limp or droopy.

2 pounds asparagus
4 tablespoons butter (optional)

Cut off the thick ends of the asparagus. Peel the asparagus from the bottom up to the first of the little offshoots. Place in a frying pan and add enough boiling water to cover. Cook until done, usually 3–5 minutes for small spears, 5–8 minutes for large spears. Remove. Reheat in the butter or liquid or serve cold in a salad.

Black-eyed Pea Snaps

Serves 4

Black-eyed peas are best when they are young and tender, and still in their "snaps." A "snap" is a tiny pod full of immature peas.

2 cups black-eyed pea snaps   **Salt**
3 tablespoons butter   **Freshly ground black pepper**

Bring a large pot of water to the boil, add the snaps, and boil 8 minutes. Drain. When ready to eat, heat the butter in a frying pan until it turns slightly brown. Add the snaps, sprinkle with plenty of salt and pepper, and reheat, tossing in the butter, about 5 minutes.

Black-eyed Peas, Traditional Style

Serves 8

Some Southerners would not consider having a New Year's party without serving this dish. As the saying goes, turnip greens on New Year's bring you greenbacks all year long, and black-eyed peas bring you a lucky day for each one you eat. My Virginia friend Jane Bradley says this topping is traditional in her family. I offer it for variety but not because it's part of my recipe.

4 cups fresh or frozen black-eyed peas
4 three-inch pieces fatback or
**   streak-o'-lean (see p. 314)**
2 hot peppers (optional)

Place the peas, water to cover, fatback, and hot peppers in a heavy pan and bring to the boil. Cover, reduce heat, and simmer 1 hour or until the peas are soft. Serve the peas with their juice, the "pot likker." If you use dried peas, place in enough water to cover, bring to the boil, then turn off the heat and let sit 1 hour, drain, and proceed.

Jane Bradley's Topping

1 medium onion, chopped
Pinch sugar
Salt

Freshly ground black pepper
1/2 cup apple-cider vinegar

Combine the ingredients and let sit 1 hour. Serve on top of black-eyed peas.

Green Black-eyed Peas, New Style

Serves 4

Black-eyed peas are green when they are new on the vine. In this recipe they stay green, and don't turn the brown color mature beans assume when left on the vine or cooked a long time. They have a little crunch, and are quite different from the softer texture of fully ripened, traditionally cooked black-eyed peas. When shelling peas, save the "snaps," or tender pods in which the peas are so tiny they cannot be shelled. Break or snap these pods into pieces and cook them with the shelled peas.

2 cups black-eyed peas, and "snaps"
4 cups boiling water
3 tablespoons butter
2 tablespoons chopped fresh savory
    and/or thyme

Salt
Freshly ground black pepper

Place the peas in a pot with the water and bring to the boil. Add butter, and let boil for 20 minutes. Add the herbs, salt, and pepper. Serve the peas hot and slightly crunchy in their "pot likker."

Black-eyed Peas with Duck Giblets

Serves 6

When my friends the Bentleys and I grilled a duck one day, it occurred to us to use duck fat rather than the traditional streak-o'-lean (see p. 314) in cooking these peas and, my goodness, are they good this way! Serve them with Grilled Duck with Muscadine Sauce (p. 166), Brown Rice with Pecans (p. 103), and Celery and Carrots with Ginger Sauce (p. 82).

Duck fat
Duck gizzards, heart, and neck
2 pounds canned black-eyed peas, or
Black-eyed Peas, Traditional Style
(p. 76), with their liquid
1 cayenne pepper, split and seeded

Pull off any excess fat from a duck. Place in a saucepan over low heat, and let the fat cook until it melts. Remove any hard pieces, and leave 1/4 cup of fat in the pan. Cut up the gizzards and heart of the duck, saving the liver for another use. Break the neck in a few places, leaving whole but cutting into it enough to extract flavor. Place the gizzards, heart, and neck in the fat and cook over high heat a few minutes, browning nicely. When browned add the cooked peas and their liquid, and the split and seeded cayenne pepper. Simmer over low heat, covered, for 30 minutes, then remove and discard the bones. This shouldn't need salt and pepper, but taste for seasoning and add if necessary.

Hopping John

Serves 6–8

Hopping John is traditionally served on New Year's Day. The black-eyed peas are said to represent each Southern soldier who died for the South during the War Between the States.

2 cups dried black-eyed peas
    or cowpeas, soaked
    overnight and drained
1 piece fatback (salt pork;
    see p. 314), slashed
    in several places
1 hot red pepper

1 medium onion, chopped
Salt
Freshly ground black pepper
1 cup uncooked rice
4 tablespoons drippings, preferably
    bacon

Place the peas in a large pot, cover with water, and add 3 cups more water. Add the fatback, red pepper, onion, salt, and pepper, and bring to the boil. Cover, reduce the heat, and simmer until the peas are tender. Add more water as needed. Remove the peas, and reserve enough liquid in the pot (about 3 cups) to cook the rice. Add the rice and drippings to the pot. Bring back to the boil, cover, reduce the heat, and simmer until the rice is cooked, about 30 minutes. Return the peas to the pot, stir together, and cook for a few minutes more. Turn into a large dish and serve.

Butter Beans with Fresh Herbs

Serves 8

Some say butter beans are small baby limas but real butter-bean aficionados say butter beans are fatter than baby limas. So be it; this recipe works for fat butter beans or skinny baby limas. (Large limas, like Fordhooks, have to be cooked longer.) I like to start them in boiling water even though some people believe this causes the beans to split more easily. You can start them in cold water if you like.

This is a new way of cooking a very traditional Southern vegetable. Another

Butter Beans with Fresh Herbs, continued

optional addition is a tablespoon of caraway seeds and 1/2 chopped onion, with or without the herbs.

1 quart freshly picked and shelled Salt
    butter beans or 2 packages frozen Freshly ground black pepper
3–4 tablespoons butter
Chopped fresh lemon thyme, lemon
    balm, and/or basil (optional)

Place the butter beans in a large pot of boiling water. Add butter and optional herbs. Boil, uncovered, 20 minutes or until slightly crunchy but cooked. If you like the Old South–style softer bean, cook 30 minutes or longer. Some liquid should remain in the pot. Place this in the serving dish with the beans and season before serving.

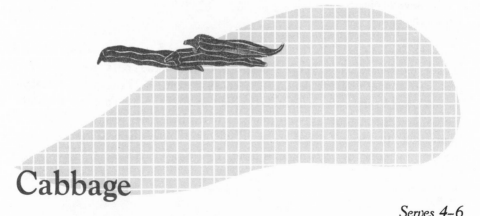

Cabbage

Serves 4–6

Here it is—the most delicious cooked-cabbage recipe you ever hope to eat.

1 head cabbage Salt
2 cups water Freshly ground black pepper
1/2 cup butter

Cut out the hard core of the cabbage. Slice the cabbage into 4–6 wedges. Bring the water to the boil and add the wedges along with the butter. Continue to boil for 20–30 minutes. Remove the cabbage when it is still crisp, yet tender. Boil down the water in the pan for a couple of minutes. Taste it for seasoning and add salt and pepper to taste. Dish up the cabbage, and pour the "pot likker" over it.

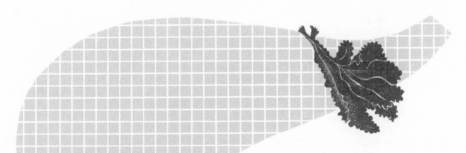

Limed Carrots and Parsnips over Red Slaw

Serves 20

My friend Lee Hopper makes this salad, a wonderful alternative when fresh greens are not available. The parsnip is the unexpected delight. Assemble ahead of time, pouring the dressing over just before serving.

6 medium carrots, peeled
   and julienned
3 large parsnips, peeled and julienned
Juice of 3 limes

1/3 cup olive oil
1 small head red cabbage, cored and
   shredded
1 bunch celery, sliced thin

✿ ✿ ✿

Dressing:
1 1/2 cups mayonnaise (p. 306)
1 small onion, quartered
1/4 cup balsamic or red wine vinegar

✿ ✿ ✿

Topping:
2 cups coarsely chopped pecans

In a steamer, steam the carrots and parsnips until just done. Drain and place in a bowl. Whisk together the lime juice and oil, then pour over the carrots and parsnips and place them in the refrigerator to cool.

    Combine the cabbage and celery in a large bowl. To make the dressing, place the mayonnaise, onion, and vinegar in a food processor or blender and process until smooth. Pour over the cabbage and stir in. Drain off any excess juice.

    To serve, place a nest of slaw on a plate and top with carrots and parsnips. Garnish with pecans.

Baby Carrots Glazed with Butter and Herbs

Serves 6–8

Baby carrots from the garden are a special treat in the spring after months of the large woody ones.

2 pounds baby carrots, scraped
3 tablespoons butter
2 tablespoons chopped herb,
    preferably lemon balm, lemon
    thyme, or mint

Salt
Freshly ground black pepper

Place the carrots in a heavy saucepan and barely cover with water. Add the butter and cover. Bring to the boil, reduce the heat, and cook 15 minutes or until still firm but easy to pierce with a fork. Remove the cover and boil down until the liquid has evaporated and the carrots are coated with butter. Watch them carefully or they will burn. Add the chopped herb and season with salt and pepper.

Celery and Carrots with Ginger Sauce

Serves 4

Sweet and wonderful tasting—this dish proves that there are creative ways to last out the winter when there are no decent vegetables to be found. If you can keep some mint growing somewhere, somehow, you will certainly make it through the winter.

6 tablespoons butter
8 stalks celery, stringed and sliced on
    the diagonal
8 large carrots, or more small ones,
    sliced on the diagonal

1/2 cup sugar
1 1/2 teaspoons to 1 tablespoon
    chopped fresh ginger
1 handful small fresh mint leaves,
    about 1/3 cup

Melt the butter in a heavy pan. Add the celery and carrots. Cover and cook over low heat until crisp but tender. Mix together the sugar and ginger and add to the pan. Stir the celery and carrots in the sugar-ginger mixture slowly and gently until they are well glazed and slightly browned. If the mint leaves aren't small and pretty, chop coarse; otherwise leave them whole. Dish up, stirring in the mint.

Celery and Pepper Bundles

Serves 4

This is a little fancy but looks so pretty on a plate it's worth the effort. If you can't find green or red bell peppers, particularly in the winter, try using a strip of canned pimento.

1 green or red bell pepper, seeded   **Salt**
1 bunch celery   **Freshly ground black pepper**
1/4 cup butter

Cut the pepper into 1/4-inch rings and blanch in boiling water 2–3 minutes. Remove and set aside. Cut each stalk of celery into 3–3 1/2-inch lengths, 1/4-inch thick. Melt the butter. Add the celery and cook over low heat 5 minutes. Divide into 4 bundles of 4 or 5 pieces of celery and put a ring of blanched pepper around each bundle. When ready to eat, reheat the bundles in a microwave or place in a pan with a little butter added to it and cover. Season with salt and pepper.

Fried Collards and Turnip Greens

Serves 4

This is a versatile dish. You can serve it as a vegetable or as a bed for fried quail or other fowl. It stays crisp a very long time and may even be refrigerated and reheated in the oven or microwave.

Fried Collards and Turnip Greens, continued

1 pound turnip or collard greens, stemmed	**Salt (optional)**
	Freshly ground black pepper (optional)
Peanut oil	**Cayenne pepper (optional)**

Rinse the greens thoroughly several times. Dry very well with paper towels and shred into 1/2–3/4-inch-wide pieces. Pour in enough oil to reach the halfway mark of a heavy skillet or deep-fat fryer and heat. When hot, add the dry greens by the handful, until the pan is full.

Fry until crisp, about 5 minutes. Remove with a slotted strainer (I prefer the Chinese kind) and place on a paper towel to drain. Continue to fry until all the greens are cooked. Taste. I add little or no seasoning, but you may want to add salt, pepper, or cayenne pepper.

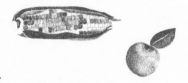

Fried Corn

Serves 6–8

In this old country recipe the corn is really not fried but is called fried since it's stewed in an iron skillet. The best kind of corn to use is field or country corn—which has colorful names like Silver Queen or Truckers' Favorite. Field corn isn't as sweet as what we call "sweet" corn, but its kernels are bigger. You can, of course, use sweet corn. The starch from the corn milk makes this a rich, thick corn dish.

10 ears corn on the cob	**8 tablespoons butter**
1 ounce fatback (salt pork), cut into thin slices	**Salt**
	Freshly ground black pepper
1 cup water	

Place an ear of corn on its end in a shallow bowl or pan. Slice the tips of the corn kernels from the cob with a sharp knife. Then scrape the kernels to remove the remaining corn and "milk" left next to the cob. Repeat with each ear of corn. Place the fatback in a 10-inch iron skillet or heavy frying pan. Cook until crisp and remove, leaving the drippings in the pan. Add the corn with its milk to the pan of fatback drippings along with the cup of water. Bring to the boil, stirring. Add the butter and salt and turn down to low heat. Cook, stirring frequently, about 30 minutes. Add more water if necessary. Perfect fried corn should be thick and sticky. Taste and season.

New-Style Fried Corn

Serves 10

This combination of sweet fresh corn and fresh herbs cooked quickly over high heat will surely become one of your favorite ways to cook corn. Any sweet corn, yellow or white, will do.

10 ears corn on the cob
6 tablespoons butter
2 tablespoons chopped fresh
    thyme or basil

Salt
Freshly ground black pepper

Slice tips off the corn kernels and scrape the corn as described for Fried Corn (preceding recipe), saving all the milk. Melt the butter in a frying pan or iron skillet. Place the corn and its milk in the frying pan and cook 3–4 minutes, stirring constantly. Season with the herb, salt, and pepper.

Green Beans

Serves 6–8

There are a number of varieties of green beans grown in the South. Our most common are pole beans, large beans whose vines need the support of a pole, and half-runners, which are smaller and "half-run" on the ground. If you use pole beans, cut them into small diamonds by slicing on the diagonal. This is a relatively new

Green Beans, continued

method of cooking beans in the South—traditionally they are cooked a long time with fatback.

2 pounds green beans, ends and strings removed	**Salt** **Freshly ground black pepper**

Bring a large quantity of water to the boil in a large pot. Add the beans and cook about 7 minutes. Drain. Rinse with cold water to stop the cooking. Season with salt and pepper and set aside or refrigerate. When ready to eat, reheat in one of the following ways.

Green Beans Tossed in Butter

4 tablespoons butter
1 recipe Green Beans
Salt
Freshly ground black pepper

Melt the butter in a large frying pan. Toss the beans in the butter 2–3 minutes, until heated through. When they start to brown, remove from the heat and toss with salt and pepper to taste.

Green Beans Tossed in Butter and Pecans

Add 1 cup chopped pecans sautéed in 2 tablespoons butter to the beans and toss together with salt and pepper.

Green Beans in White Butter Sauce

I had a dinner party one night, and decided to toss the green beans in some leftover White Butter Sauce I had in the refrigerator. What was the one recipe everyone asked me for? The Green Beans in White Butter Sauce, of course.

1 recipe White Butter Sauce (p. 301) **1 recipe Green Beans**	**Salt** **Freshly ground black pepper**

Melt the sauce completely in a large frying pan. Add the beans and toss over high heat until the beans are completely coated. Serve hot. Season with salt and pepper if desired.

Green Beans and Tomato Conserve

You will want to serve this over and over again for dinner parties and family gatherings.

1 recipe Green Beans
2 tablespoons butter

1 recipe Tomato Conserve (p. 304),
at room temperature

Bring the beans to the table hot, tossed in butter. Top with the conserve.

Green Beans and New Potatoes

Serves 6–8

These beans are cooked in the time-honored Southern way—with fatback. They are cooked a long time, probably because in the old days they were put on in the morning before people went out to the fields to work, so the beans would be ready by lunchtime. The fatback was considered crucial for nutrition and an important source of seasoning. Some Northerners think our beans are greasy but we country folk love them.

3 pounds green beans, broken in
**   1-inch pieces**
1/4 pound fatback (salt pork)

1 teaspoon salt
14 small new potatoes, scrubbed

Combine the beans, fatback, salt, and water to cover in a heavy Dutch oven. Bring to the boil and cover. Reduce the heat to low and cook 30 minutes. Add the potatoes, cover again, and cook for an additional 30 minutes. Remove the lid and cook down until no liquid remains and the beans are slightly browned, just a few minutes.

Greens and "Pot Likker," Old Style

Serves 4–6

Both collard and turnip greens were traditionally cooked in this manner. They have always been an important staple and source of calcium in our diets. And, since they like poor soil, they're often found growing alongside a road or in a hilly, rocky place where nothing else will grow. We just stop the car, get out, and fill up two large brown paper bags with greens and cook them up old style. There are stories about how hard they are to wash—some people claim they wash them wrapped in a pillowcase in the clothes washer.

4 pounds turnip or collard greens, stemmed	Salt
¼ pound fatback (salt pork) or streak-o'-lean (see p. 314)	Freshly ground black pepper

Rinse the greens thoroughly several times, then put them in a large pot of boiling water and boil for 2 minutes. Drain, discarding the water to remove the bitter taste. Fill the pot again with water and bring to the boil. Place the greens back in the pot. Cut into the fatback in several places without slicing it into pieces, and add to the pot. Bring to the boil, cover, turn down to a simmer, and cook 2–3 hours. Taste and add salt and pepper as desired. Serve greens with their juices or serve "pot likker" separately as a soup with cornbread.

Greens with Coriander Seed and Browned Butter

Serves 4

I particularly like this recipe with turnip greens, but spinach and collards may be used as well. Some of my New York City friends who have always said "I don't eat turnip greens" like these. But longtime Southerners who like their greens long cooked and with fatback will feel these may "take a little getting used to."

2 pounds greens, washed, veined, and stemmed
6 tablespoons butter
2 teaspoons ground coriander seed

2 tablespoons chopped fresh basil (optional)
Salt
Freshly ground black pepper

Place the greens in a large pot of boiling water. Bring back to the boil and cook 5 minutes. Drain. Pour cold water over the greens to stop the cooking. Drain again. Melt the butter in a large frying pan, and cook until it turns a nutty brown color. Add the coriander seed and basil. Toss the greens in the butter until well coated and heated through. Taste for seasoning and serve hot.

Grits with Cream and Cheese

Serves 4

Many people have had grits only for breakfast with butter, unless they live here where grits are eaten at all times and for all meals. This recipe is for dinner and is a very special dish you'll always remember.

1/2 cup quick grits
2 cups heavy cream
2–3 tablespoons butter
Salt

Freshly ground white pepper
1/2 cup freshly grated Parmesan, Swiss, or Monterey jack cheese

Place the grits and cream in a heavy saucepan, stirring. Cook the grits according to package directions, substituting cream for water. Stir occasionally, being careful they don't burn. If grits begin to separate and turn lumpy, add water to keep them creamy. Remove from the heat, taste, add the butter and salt and pepper to taste, then stir in the cheese. May be made ahead and reheated over low heat or in a microwave.

Fried Spicy Cheese Grits Pieces

Serves 8

This is a good use for leftover grits, and can be eaten like bread, as a snack, first course, or side dish. It's easy to make the base ahead and reheat later the same day.

2 cups grits, cooked
3 cloves garlic, chopped
2/3 cup grated extra-sharp Cheddar
    or Monterey jack cheese
Freshly ground black pepper to taste
1 hot pepper, finely chopped
Salt to taste

1 tablespoon Hot Sauce (p. 297) or
    Tabasco
4 tablespoons bacon drippings or
    peanut oil
1 egg, lightly beaten
1 cup breadcrumbs

Butter an 8-inch square pan and refrigerate or freeze until cold. Reheat the grits and add garlic and cheese. Taste and add the pepper, hot pepper, salt, and Hot Sauce or Tabasco. Spread the grits in the buttered pan and place in the freezer for 30 minutes, or refrigerate overnight until solid. When ready to eat, heat the drippings or oil in a large, heavy frying pan. Cut the cold grits into squares. Dip the squares into the egg, then coat with breadcrumbs, and fry until crisp on each side, 3–4 minutes.

Grits with Rosemary and Grapes

Serves 4

A perfect complement to Turkey Breast with Pecan Butter and Grapes (p. 164), this dish will win the hearts of those who never eat grits. It is particularly good with a strong Southern grape, like muscadines or scuppernongs. If these are not available, green grapes are better than red ones.

5 cups turkey or chicken stock, boiling
1 cup grits
1–2 tablespoons chopped or
    whole rosemary

1 cup grapes, preferably scuppernongs
    or muscadines, halved
    and seeded
1 tablespoon butter

Salt
Freshly ground black pepper
1 cup pecan halves, toasted

Bring the stock to the boil and add the grits, rosemary, and grapes. Cook 30 minutes, until thick and cooked. Add butter and taste for salt and pepper. Add pecans and serve.

Grits with Yogurt and Herbs

Serves 8

Grits are good cooked in most any liquid. For years they were cooked only in water, probably because it was available and not costly. Now they are cooked in a variety of liquids. I love them cooked with yogurt, but you might like to try them with sour cream or whipping cream.

3 cups plain yogurt
2 cups milk
1¼ cups quick grits
2 tablespoons butter

5 tablespoons chopped fresh lemon
balm, thyme, or mint
½ cup whipping cream

Bring the yogurt and milk to the boil in a medium-sized saucepan. Stir in the grits. Cover and bring back to the boil. Cook as directed on the grits package, substituting yogurt for water. Stir frequently. If needed, add more liquid: yogurt, water, or cream. When grits are cooked, add butter, herbs, and whipping cream. This dish may be made a couple of hours ahead and reheated in the same pan or in a microwave. Keep covered well with plastic wrap until reheating and serving time.

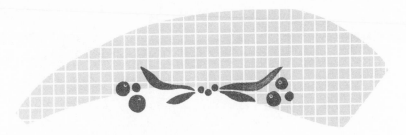

Fried Okra

Serves 6

Okra was brought to the Southeastern United States by slaves who came from the Congo regions of Africa via the West Indies. It can be cooked in a variety of ways and is used in many gumbos since it has the wonderful quality of thickening any liquid it's cooked in. Fried okra must be served immediately; prepare it at the last minute when the rest of the meal is all ready to be served. It may seem that this recipe calls for a great deal of okra, but frankly, the family will snitch the first batch while you're cooking the second in the kitchen.

2 pounds okra
1/2 cup corn meal
1/2 cup flour
2 teaspoons salt

2 cups peanut oil
Salt
Freshly ground black pepper

Wash and drain the okra. Cut off the caps on the stem ends and cut okra into 1/4-inch slices or pieces. In a bowl combine the corn meal, flour, and salt, add half the okra, and toss. Spread out on a flat surface to dry for a few minutes, then toss in corn meal and flour again.

Meanwhile, pour in enough oil to reach halfway up the side of an iron skillet or frying pan and heat. Test to be sure the oil is hot enough by adding one piece of okra. If it sizzles, add the floured okra in batches. Leave enough room in the pan to turn the okra without layering it. Brown lightly on both sides. Resist the temptation to turn the okra too soon. If you stir too much, the corn meal will fall to the bottom of the pan and burn. Remove when browned and crisp on both sides, and place on paper towels. If necessary, drain out the oil and wipe the bottom of the pan clean. Pour the drained oil back into the pan and repeat with the second batch. Season with salt and pepper.

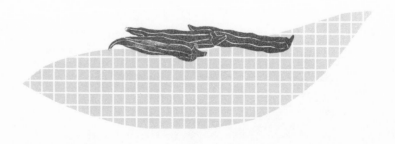

Onion Flowers with Pecans

Serves 6

When I crave something to eat but don't know what it is I want, I bake an onion and eat it all by myself. But, when the family comes for a Sunday or holiday dinner, I think baked onions are a must. This is a beautiful variation, and there's never any left. From my *Cooking of the South.*

6 large sweet onions
6–8 tablespoons melted butter
Salt

3–4 tablespoons chopped pecans
Freshly ground black pepper

Preheat the oven to 350 degrees. Make an onion flower out of each onion by first peeling the onion, leaving the root end intact. Place the onion on a cutting board, root end down. Cut the onion in parallel slices 1/4 inch apart, cutting from the top almost to the root end. Do not cut through the root end. Rotate the onion and slice again at right angles to the first cut, making a grid or chrysanthemum design. Don't worry about any loose onion sections in the middle.

Lightly oil a baking dish. Place the onions on their root ends in the baking dish. Pour butter over until the onions are well coated and there is extra butter in the pan for basting. Salt to taste. Bake for 1–1 1/2 hours, basting several times. Add a few chopped pecans to the center of each onion and continue baking 30 minutes longer. Remove from the oven and season with pepper.

Pepper Pasta

Makes 1–1 1/2 pounds

The idea for this pasta was conceived one day when Paul Prudhomme was in the cooking school at Rich's. He eyed me making traditional pasta and said, "You know, I could make Cajun pasta." Struck with the idea, I promptly added peppers to what I was making, and lo and behold, pepper pasta was born.

Pepper Pasta, continued

3 tablespoons finely chopped hot peppers	1 tablespoon peanut oil
3 cups all-purpose or bread flour	1 teaspoon salt
3 eggs	1–3 tablespoons water

In a large bowl mix together all the ingredients but the water. Knead on a floured surface or in a food processor, adding water as necessary to keep the dough smooth, moist, and pliable, but not sticky. When kneading by hand knead the dough about 10 minutes. In a food processor, the total time will be a little more than 1 minute. Cover with plastic wrap and let rest 30 minutes or so.

Feed the dough through a pasta machine or roll out by hand on a floured surface until very thin. Cut into strips or shapes, as desired. To prevent sticking, let the dough dry on a rack or a floured surface for 15–30 minutes before cooking. The pasta may also be wrapped in plastic wrap and refrigerated up to 24 hours or frozen to be cooked later.

To cook, drop the fresh pasta into rapidly boiling water for a very brief time, 2–3 minutes, if very thin. The thinner and fresher the pasta, the shorter the cooking time. Dried pasta can take up to 10 minutes in boiling water. To test, do as one of my Italian teachers did: extract a piece and throw it against the wall or ceiling to see if it sticks. It's supposed to hit and then drop off. Better yet, eat a piece. When cooked it will be slightly resistant to the bite. Drain and serve with any of your favorite pasta sauces, or with butter and grated Parmesan.

Pepper Pasta and Cheese

Serves 6

Macaroni and cheese has long been a popular Southern side dish. The first mention I found of it was in Mrs. Randolph's *The Virginia Housewife* (1836). She gave a recipe for a macaroni pudding. Now we use fresh pasta. Any pasta will do, and this will stand out in your memory.

1 pound Pepper Pasta (preceding recipe), cut into fettuccine	1/2 cup flour
1 cup butter	4 cups milk
	Salt

Freshly ground black pepper
1 1/2 pounds sharp
    Cheddar cheese, grated
1 1/2 cups breadcrumbs

Preheat the oven to 350 degrees. Butter a large baking dish and bring a large pot of water to the boil to cook the pasta.

    Meanwhile, make the cheese sauce: Melt 1/2 cup of the butter in a large, heavy saucepan. Add the flour and stir until smooth. Add the milk and bring to the boil, stirring constantly. Season with salt and pepper and add 1 cup of the cheese. Cover with waxed paper or aluminum foil to prevent a skin from forming, and set aside while cooking the pasta.

    Add the pasta to the boiling water and cook until nearly tender (see Pepper Pasta directions, preceding recipe). Drain well. Put a layer of the drained pasta in the buttered baking dish and sprinkle with some of the cheese. Repeat until all the pasta is layered, finishing with cheese. Pour the sauce over it all. Melt the remaining butter in a large frying pan. Add the breadcrumbs, and toss in the butter. Sprinkle on top of the casserole, which may be made ahead to this point. When ready to serve, bring the casserole to room temperature and place in the oven until heated through, about 20 minutes.

Turnip Green Pasta

Makes 3/4 pound

This is a Southerner's answer to spinach pasta. Try it in my Crazy Lasagna (p. 200)—or any time you would use spinach pasta.

1/3 cup turnip greens, cooked   2 large eggs
    and drained   3/4 teaspoon salt
2 cups bread flour   2 tablespoons water

Place the greens, 1 cup of the flour, the eggs, and salt in a food processor. Process until the mixture forms a ball, adding more flour or water as necessary to make a smooth but not sticky dough.

    Hand method: Knead 1 cup of the flour, the eggs, and salt together on a floured board. Finely chop the cooked and drained turnip greens. Combine with

Turnip Green Pasta, continued

the flour mixture and blend completely, adding water or flour as necessary to make a smooth but not sticky dough.

Cover with plastic wrap and let rest about 30 minutes. On a floured surface roll the dough out by hand or feed through a pasta machine until very thin. Cut as desired and let dry on a rack or floured surface.

Cook the pasta by dropping into rapidly boiling water for 2–3 minutes until it is tender but you feel a slight resistance to the bite. Drain, sauce, and serve.

Fettuccine with Tomato-Mint Sauce

Serves 4

This quick supper dish is ideal with our indigenous foods.

3 or 4 slices bacon or streak-o'-lean
   (see p. 314)
2 tablespoons butter
1 pound tomatoes, canned or fresh,
   drained and seeded,
   juice reserved
Handful coarsely chopped fresh mint
   leaves and stems

Salt
Freshly ground black pepper
Sugar
½ pound cooked fettuccine, preferably
   Pepper Pasta (p. 93) or Turnip
   Green Pasta (preceding recipe)

Fry the bacon or streak-o'-lean in a heavy skillet until browned. Remove, drain on a paper towel, then crumble slightly and set aside. Add butter to the fat in the skillet. Tear the tomatoes apart into large chunks and add to the skillet with the tomato juice. Simmer until the sauce is slightly thickened. Add the mint and heat through. Season to taste with salt, pepper, and a pinch of sugar. Serve over cooked pasta and top with the crumbled bacon or streak-o'-lean.

English Peas with Green Onions and Thyme or Mint

Serves 6–8

Thomas Jefferson is credited with bringing many new vegetables to this country, among them green peas. The colloquial designation for these peas is "English peas." In the early days, green peas were cooked much longer than they are today. They have a natural affinity for herbs.

3 cups shelled fresh English peas
1 tablespoon chopped fresh mint
    or thyme
1–2 leaves iceberg or romaine lettuce
1 small bunch green onions, trimmed
    of roots and outside layers

5 tablespoons butter
1/2 cup chicken stock (p. 320)
Salt
Freshly ground black pepper

Place the peas, herb, lettuce, onions, and butter in a pan. In another pan bring the stock to the boil and add to the rest of the ingredients. Bring back to the boil and continue cooking, covered, until the peas are done, yet slightly crunchy, about 6–8 minutes. Taste for seasoning and add salt and pepper as desired.

Poke Sallet

Serves 2

Poke is short for pokeweed, which grows abundantly in the South but is not commercially marketed—or even planted. It used to be an important vegetable to country cooks because it grows abundantly in yards and fields in the spring. Some people find its wild and tender taste the most flavorful of the Southern greens. The word *poke* originated from the Algonquin Indian term "puccoon." A poke was also a sack country people used to gather greens, cotton, and other field necessities. *Sallet* is an old English term and to us it means a "mess of greens." This is the traditional way to serve this spring weed. The recipe makes only 1 cup, but it may

Poke Sallet, continued

be doubled or tripled easily. You'll get only 1 pound of leaves out of 1 1/2 pounds picked poke sallet. Be sure to remove all stems and berries; these should not be eaten. Leaves up to 6 inches long may be used but most people prefer the smaller, younger leaves. Wash as you would any green. Make the base recipe, then vary it in one of these ways.

1 pound poke sallet leaves

Place the poke sallet in a gallon of cold water, bring to the boil, uncovered. Drain, rinse in cold water, and squeeze well.

Poke Sallet with Green Onions and Bacon   *Serves 2*

4 strips bacon
2 green onions, chopped
1 cup cooked poke sallet

Place the bacon in a frying pan and cook until crisp. Add the chopped green onions and cooked poke sallet and heat through.

Poke Sallet with Scrambled Eggs   *Serves 2*

1 cup cooked poke sallet
2 eggs, beaten
2 tablespoons bacon drippings

Combine the poke sallet, eggs, and bacon grease in a frying pan over medium heat. Stir around with a wooden spoon until the sallet is well heated, with pieces of scrambled egg throughout.

Potatoes and Green Beans Vinaigrette

Serves 6–8

This may be served hot or cold, but be sure your vegetables are hot when tossed in the vinaigrette. Hot vegetables absorb flavor quickly, so when they have cooled the flavor is even more enhanced. This is the trick for a perfect potato salad, too.

1 pound green beans
2 pounds new potatoes

✿   ✿   ✿

Vinaigrette dressing:
3/4 cup vegetable oil
1/4 cup white or red wine vinegar
1 teaspoon Dijon mustard
1 small clove garlic, crushed

Salt
Freshly ground black pepper
1/4 teaspoon sugar

✿   ✿   ✿

2 tablespoons chopped fresh herbs
    such as basil or tarragon (optional)

Remove tips and strings from the beans, but leave the beans whole. Boil in salted water to cover until still crunchy, 7–10 minutes. Remove from the heat, drain, and immediately rinse with cold water to stop the cooking and set the color.

Meanwhile, boil whole, unpeeled new potatoes in salted water to cover until done, 20–30 minutes. Drain. Make the vinaigrette (see below). While still hot, peel quickly and toss them in half the vinaigrette, adding the herbs if you wish.

If serving warm, stir the green beans with 2 tablespoons of the vinaigrette in a saucepan and warm them gently before adding to the potatoes. If serving cold, simply toss the cooked beans with 2 tablespoons of the dressing and gently mix with the potatoes. Drizzle the remaining dressing over all, and serve either lukewarm or cold.

To make the vinaigrette, whisk the oil into the vinegar, mustard, and garlic; add salt, pepper, and sugar to taste.

New Potatoes with Mustard Seed

Serves 10

My friend Alma is a great dinner-party giver. Occasionally she asks me to develop a recipe to go with a particular dish she has in mind to serve. Here's one that is a fine accompaniment for roast beef.

40–50 new potatoes,
  about 3–4 pounds
½ cup bacon or meat drippings
  or butter
5–6 tablespoons mustard seed

5–6 tablespoons Dijon mustard,
  to taste
Salt
Freshly ground black pepper

Preheat the oven to 350 degrees. Scrape the potatoes. Heat the drippings or butter in a roasting pan and add the potatoes. Place in the oven and roast, turning every 15 minutes, until browned all over, about 1 hour. Remove from the oven, toss in the mustard seed, and return to the oven for another 5 minutes. Remove and add the mustard, tossing with a spoon to coat the potatoes lightly. Add salt and pepper to taste.

New Potatoes with English Peas

Serves 4–6

The cream makes this a special-occasion vegetable dish for Thanksgiving, Christmas, or a company meal. The slightly runny sauce is like a gravy, with the vegetable juices flavoring the cream. The middle strip of the red new potatoes contrasts nicely with the green of the English peas.

12 small new red potatoes, washed
8 tablespoons butter
1 medium onion, sliced
2 cups shelled English peas

2 tablespoons flour
½ cup heavy cream
Salt
Freshly ground black pepper

Peel a waistband around the potatoes with a swivel peeler or knife. Rinse and place in a heavy pot, with just enough water to cover. Bring to the boil and cook, uncovered, until the potatoes are done, about 30 minutes. Meanwhile, heat 3 tablespoons of the butter in a frying pan. Add the onion and sauté until tender, about 5 minutes. Add the peas and cooked onion to the potatoes about 10 minutes before the potatoes are cooked.

In the frying pan, melt the remaining 5 tablespoons of the butter and stir in the flour, making a soft roux. Add heavy cream to the roux, stirring continuously, to make a white sauce. Bring to the boil. Pour the sauce into the undrained vegetables and bring to the boil, adding salt and pepper to taste. May be made ahead and reheated.

Dripping-Cooked Potatoes, Onions, and Turnips

Serves 6-8

Cooking root vegetables together with meat drippings is a wonderful way to add flavor.

3 turnips, peeled	4–8 tablespoons drippings, butter,
3 medium potatoes, peeled	or oil
3 medium onions, peeled	1 tablespoon rosemary
3 medium carrots, peeled	

Cut the vegetables into quarters. Cover the turnips with water in a saucepan, bring to the boil, and boil 5 minutes. Drain. Heat the drippings in a large, heavy flameproof pan. Add all the vegetables and brown on one side.

Preheat the oven to 350 degrees. Place the pan with vegetables in it in the oven and cook 1 hour, turning every 15 minutes until browned and crisp all over. Crumble rosemary on top and serve hot.

Oven-Crisp Potatoes

Serves 4–6

If you hunger for a crisp potato, but don't want to deep-fat fry, try these. I think they're especially delicious with Grilled Lemon and Herb Chicken (p. 148). For a little variety sprinkle with 3 tablespoons fresh chopped herbs before baking.

4 potatoes, peeled and sliced 1/8 inch thick 2 tablespoons peanut oil	Salt Freshly ground black pepper

Preheat the oven to 400 degrees. Place the sliced potatoes on 2 well-oiled or nonstick cookie sheets, in a single layer or slightly overlapping. Brush with oil and sprinkle with salt and pepper. Place in the oven and bake 20 minutes, turning once, until lightly browned and crisp on both sides.

Rice with Parmesan and Champagne or Scuppernong Wine

Serves 6–8

Rice is not the staple it was when we had large rice plantations, but it remains an integral part of our cuisine. We have expanded and adapted our cooking methods to include some from Europe. This risotto-like dish was developed in one of my classes held in Sea Island, Georgia. I was teaching risotto and John Wright, president of Domaine Chandon Vineyards, got up and simultaneously made his version of this dish, using sparkling wine. I've tried it with local scuppernong wine and, with its sweetness, it's equally pleasing to the Southern palate.

4 tablespoons butter
1 or 2 cloves garlic, finely chopped
2 cups white rice
3 cups champagne or
    scuppernong wine

Salt
Freshly ground white pepper
4 tablespoons freshly grated
    Parmesan cheese

Melt 2 tablespoons of the butter in a large frying pan. Add garlic and fry gently for a few minutes. Add the rice. Stir and fry for 4–5 minutes until the grains are opaque. Add 1 cup of the wine. Season and stir occasionally until the liquid is absorbed. Add more wine in small amounts, stirring, until the rice thickens and the grains are creamy, with just a little bite. Be careful; this burns easily. Taste for seasoning. Add salt and pepper if desired.

Remove from the heat and dot with the remaining 2 tablespoons of butter and sprinkle with Parmesan cheese. Cover and let sit 5 minutes, for the cheese to melt. Stir with a fork, not a spoon, and turn into a hot serving dish.

Brown Rice with Pecans
Serves 4

Gwen Bentley developed this side dish to go with our black-eyed peas, duck giblets, and Grilled Duck with Muscadine Sauce (p. 166).

1/2 cup coarsely chopped pecans
2 tablespoons butter
1/4 cup chopped green onions, green
    part reserved for garnish

1/4–1/2 cup dried currants
1 cup brown rice
2 1/2 cups chicken stock

Brown the pecans in the butter, being careful not to burn them. Remove the pecans and set aside. Add the white part of the chopped green onions to the butter and cook briefly until soft. Bring the stock to a boil in a separate pot and add the cooked onions and butter, currants, and rice. Cook, covered, until the liquid is absorbed, about 45–60 minutes. To serve, toss the hot rice with the browned pecans and garnish with the chopped green onion tops.

Basil and Garlic Rice or Grits

Serves 4

We started serving this in our restaurant in 1971, and people still ask me for the recipe. Using grits is every bit as good as using rice.

4 cups hot cooked rice or grits
3–4 tablespoons Basil and
    Garlic Butter (p. 302)
1/2–3/4 cup freshly grated Parmesan or
    Swiss cheese

Salt to taste
Freshly ground black pepper

Preheat the oven to 350 degrees. Mix all the ingredients together and place in a buttered baking dish. Place in the oven and heat through for 10 minutes.

Lemon Rice

Serves 6

This is great for dinner parties and goes particularly well with lamb and chicken. Cook the rice ahead, then reheat in the pan as directed.

1/2 cup butter
1 teaspoon salt
1 teaspoon black mustard seed

1 teaspoon turmeric
3 cups cooked white rice
Strained juice of 1 lemon

Melt the butter in a saucepan. Add the salt, mustard seed, and turmeric, and stir until they are well blended and the mustard seeds dance in the pan. Add the rice and lemon juice and heat through, stirring constantly.

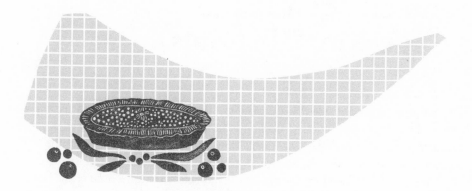

Squash Casserole

Serves 6–8

What would summer be without a squash casserole? This one has a wonderful melt-in-your-mouth consistency and a crunchy nut topping. Serve it slightly hotter than lukewarm with your favorite chicken or ham recipe.

2 medium onions, chopped
1 green bell pepper, seeded
   and chopped
1 red bell pepper, seeded
   and chopped
1 1/4 cups butter
2 cloves garlic, chopped

2 pounds yellow crookneck or
   zucchini squash, sliced
2 cups grated sharp Cheddar cheese
4 eggs
1 1/2 cups chopped pecans
Dash Hot Sauce (p. 297) or Tabasco
1 cup breadcrumbs

Preheat the oven to 350 degrees.

In a frying pan, sauté the onions and peppers in 1/4 cup of the butter until soft. Add the garlic and cook briefly. In a pot filled with boiling salted water cook the squash until tender, 5–10 minutes. Drain, put in the food processor, and process until fine, or mash with a potato masher. Return the squash to the pot, add 1/2 cup of the butter, 1 cup of the cheese, the eggs, the sautéed onions, peppers, and garlic, 1 cup of the pecans, and Hot Sauce or Tabasco. Mix well.

Pour into a casserole buttered with 2 tablespoons of the butter. Mix together the breadcrumbs and the remaining cheese and pecans and spread on top of the casserole. Dot with the remaining butter and bake 3/4–1 hr.

Sautéed Squash and Zucchini Blossoms

Serves 4

The flowers from vegetables are surprisingly flavorful. They are both male and female. The male flowers do not bear any "fruit," so they are best stuffed or used as a pretty, flavorful garnish. The female flowers can be distinguished by the tiny vegetable protruding from the flower. The flower disappears as the fruit grows. Quite frequently you see tiny zucchini in the garden with just a little of the flower left. They are also quite charming, and could be used in this recipe.

2 tablespoons butter
1 pint flower blossoms, partially
    opened, washed and
    carefully dried

Salt
Freshly ground black pepper
1 tablespoon chopped fresh thyme
    or basil

Heat the butter in a large skillet. Add the flowers and cook, turning until they burst into full blossoms, just a few minutes. Do not brown. Season with salt, pepper, and herbs.

Candied Sweet Potatoes

Serves 4

Gooey sweet potatoes are still one of the South's staple items on the Thanksgiving and Christmas tables.

4 medium or 3 large sweet potatoes

1/2 cup melted butter

1 cup granulated sugar

1/4 cup water

Salt to taste

Freshly ground black pepper to taste

Peel the potatoes and cut into 1/2-inch slices. Combine butter, sugar, and water in a frying pan and add the sweet potatoes. Cover and simmer 30 minutes. Remove cover and cook 30 minutes more, or until cooked through.

Sautéed Sweet Potatoes with Pecans

Serves 4-6

Many people have sweet potatoes only at Christmas and Thanksgiving, cooked with marshmallows, brown sugar, and other sweets. But the potato is correctly named. It is a sweet potato and is particularly satisfying simply sliced and sautéed. This is a delicious way to round out a meal. Leftovers are lovely, too, a naturally sweet treat in the middle of the night, when you can't sleep.

3 sweet potatoes

6–8 tablespoons butter

1/2 cup chopped or halved pecans

Peel the sweet potatoes and slice as thin as possible. Melt 3 tablespoons of butter to cover the bottom of a large, heavy skillet. Add enough potatoes to cover the bottom of the pan. Cook until lightly browned, with perhaps a speck of black in them, then turn gently and brown the other side. Remove to a serving dish. Add 3 more tablespoons of butter and the remaining potatoes and cook until lightly browned. Remove potatoes to a serving dish. Add the remaining 2 tablespoons of butter to the skillet, toss in the pecans, and brown ever so lightly. Pour over the potatoes.

Fried Green Tomatoes

Serves 2

Make these for a special breakfast on a Saturday. I like them with fried eggs. My friend Sue always has them with grits.

2 green tomatoes
1/2 cup flour or corn meal, seasoned
     with salt and pepper
1/3–1/2 cup butter

Cut the tomatoes into thick slices; thin slices tend to disintegrate. Coat on both sides with the seasoned flour or corn meal. In an iron skillet, heat the butter until sizzling hot, but do not brown. Reflour the tomatoes and place in the skillet in one layer. When golden brown, turn and brown the other side. Drain on paper towels. Repeat with any slices that remain. Serve immediately.

Ginger Tomatoes

Serves 6–8

We like to think Southern tomatoes are the best in the world. When coupled with home-grown ginger and green onions, they are something new and wonderful-tasting. Ginger grows very easily—we just stick it in the ground or a flowerpot.

4 tomatoes, about 1 pound, unpeeled   **Salt**
2 tablespoons vegetable oil   **Sugar**
1 slice fresh ginger about the size of   **4 green onions, green part only,**
     a quarter, slivered or chopped   **sliced thin**

Wash the tomatoes and cut each into 6 wedges. Heat the oil in a large frying pan over high heat. Add the ginger to the oil and let it sizzle for a few seconds, stirring it with a wooden spoon. Add the tomatoes and toss them quickly in the ginger until just heated through and coated with the oil. Don't let the tomatoes get mushy. Add a dash of salt and sugar. Sprinkle the green onion tops over the tomatoes and dish them up hot.

Sliced Tomatoes and Gravy

Serves 2

I can't think of anything better than a lush, sun-and-vine-ripened tomato fresh from the garden. When the crop comes in, the first thing you do is make a sandwich with white bread, homemade mayonnaise, and tomato. For dinner that night, you could slice up a tomato and sprinkle it with fresh basil. But, for a real treat, have it the way we do in the South for a light lunch or supper, topped with gravy. If you want to be really Southern, slice up a cantaloupe and top the cantaloupe as well as the tomato with the gravy. I realize this sounds very odd, but it's the way we country folk like to eat. "Sweet" milk is the country term for non-buttermilk.

2 fresh garden tomatoes, sliced

✿   ✿   ✿

Gravy:
2 tablespoons drippings or chicken fat   **1 cup sweet milk**
2 tablespoons flour   **Chicken bouillon granules (optional)**

Arrange the tomatoes on 2 plates. To make the gravy, melt the fat in a heavy saucepan and add flour, stirring briefly over medium heat. Add sweet milk and stir until it comes to a full boil, adding the bouillon granules for extra flavor. Serve the gravy over the sliced tomatoes.

Turnips and Cream

Serves 10

Turnips are a much-misunderstood vegetable. They are so frequently treated diffidently, as a second-class potato or as the ugly duckling of root vegetables. Southern turnips are sometimes called white turnips in other parts of the country — they are purple on the outside and white, not yellow, on the inside. They go handsomely with game, pork, and especially with Thanksgiving and Christmas turkey and ham. May be made a day ahead and reheated; leftovers freeze well.

3 pounds white turnips, peeled and
    sliced 1/8 inch thick
Salt
Freshly ground black pepper
2 tablespoons chopped fresh parsley,
    tarragon, thyme, and/or oregano,
    or 1 1/2 tablespoons dry
    mixed herbs

3 cloves garlic, finely chopped or
    crushed with salt
1 cup grated Swiss cheese
1 cup grated Parmesan cheese
1/2 cup butter
1 1/2–2 cups heavy cream
1/2 cup fresh breadcrumbs

Butter a long casserole dish. To blanch, place the turnips in a large pot of cold water and bring to the boil. If the turnips are young and small, boil 3 minutes. If they are large, boil 8–10 minutes, until they are tender and have lost their sharp taste. Drain. Spread a layer of turnips to cover the dish (they may overlap slightly), and sprinkle with salt and pepper. Mix the herbs with the garlic and sprinkle one-third over the turnips. Now combine the 2 cheeses and sprinkle the turnips with one-third of the mixture. Dot with one-third of the butter. Continue to layer until you've added all the turnips to the dish, finishing with cheese on top of the third layer. Pour cream over the entire dish and sprinkle with breadcrumbs and the remaining butter. May be made ahead to this point. When ready to serve, preheat the oven to 400 degrees. Bake 45 minutes or until the cheese is melted and the breadcrumbs are nice and browned. Serve hot.

Turnips and Red Peppers

Serves 4

Turnips are one of the South's favorite foods, as are red peppers. This is a tasty combination and quite good with roast chicken, pork, or quail.

1 pound small white turnips, peeled
  and sliced
6 tablespoons butter
1 pound red bell peppers, seeded
  and sliced

2 large cloves garlic, finely chopped
1 teaspoon salt
Freshly ground black pepper to taste

Place the turnips in a pan of boiling water for 2–3 minutes if they are small and 8–10 minutes if they are large. Drain. Melt 3 tablespoons of the butter in a large, heavy skillet. Add the red peppers, turnips, and garlic, and stir-fry over moderate heat, adding more butter if necessary. Cook until the turnips are tender when pierced with a knife but peppers are still crunchy. Season with salt and pepper.

Grated and Sautéed Turnips

Serves 6

1 pound turnips, peeled and grated
4 tablespoons butter
Salt

Freshly ground black pepper
1/2 cup pecan halves, sautéed in
  3 tablespoons butter

If the turnips are small, they do not need blanching. If they are larger than an egg, bring a large pot of water to the boil and blanch them by cooking 1–2 minutes, to remove the strong taste. Drain well and dry with paper towels. Heat the butter in a large skillet or frying pan. Add the turnips and toss in the butter for 5 minutes. Taste and add salt and pepper as desired. May be made ahead to this point. When ready to eat, add the pecans and toss over high heat 2–3 minutes.

Grated and Sautéed Turnips, continued

Grated Turnips with Carrots

Proceed as above, using 1/2 pound of turnips and 1/2 pound of carrots.

Grated Turnips with Carrots and Herbs

Add 3 tablespoons fresh herbs, preferably mint or basil, when reheating.

Grated Turnips and Onions

Serves 3 or 4

2 turnips, grated
3 tablespoons butter
1 onion, sliced
1 clove garlic, finely chopped
1 slice ginger, finely chopped

2 tablespoons chopped fresh herbs
   (optional)
2 tablespoons Hot Sauce (p. 297),
   optional
2 tablespoons soy sauce (optional)

Place the grated turnips in a pot of water and bring to the boil. Boil 5 minutes. Drain and dry thoroughly. Heat the butter in a pan, add the onion, and cook for 5 minutes. Add the garlic, turnips, and flavorings and toss together, cooking for a few minutes over medium heat.

Grated Turnips and Zucchini

Serves 4–6

This colorful vegetable dish may be made ahead and reheated in a microwave oven or a frying pan. It should have a crispy crunch, and is very tasty and good with every kind of meat and fish I can think of.

3 turnips, grated
3 zucchini, grated
4–6 tablespoons butter
Salt to taste

Freshly ground black pepper to taste
2 tablespoons fresh herbs: basil,
    thyme, or oregano (optional)

Place the grated turnips in a pan of cold water and bring to the boil. Boil for 5 minutes. Drain. Place the grated zucchini in a colander, salt well, set aside for 5 minutes to drain. Rinse well. Drain again. Pat the turnips and zucchini well with paper towels to dry. Heat the butter in a large frying pan, add the turnips and zucchini, and toss for 5 minutes. Season with salt, pepper, and optional fresh herbs.

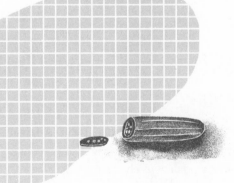

Grated Zucchini

Serves 6

When you want a vegetable that can be prepared either quickly at the last minute or ahead and reheated briefly, try this. It's low in calories, delicious, and easy to prepare. For a little variety add garlic, sour cream, or tomato sauce if you wish.

Grated Zucchini, continued

Salt

2–2½ pounds zucchini, grated

6 tablespoons butter

2–3 tablespoons minced shallots, scallions, or onions

Freshly ground black pepper

Salt the zucchini in a colander and let drain to remove excess juice. Rinse, squeeze, and dry the zucchini. In a large skillet, melt 3 tablespoons of the butter. Add the shallots, scallions, or onions, then the zucchini. Toss for 4–5 minutes over high heat until tender but crunchy. Taste for salt and pepper. The zucchini may be prepared to this point several hours ahead of serving. Set aside uncovered. Cover when cool. Shortly before serving, place over high heat and toss it in the pan with the remaining 3 tablespoons of butter. Turn into a hot dish and serve immediately.

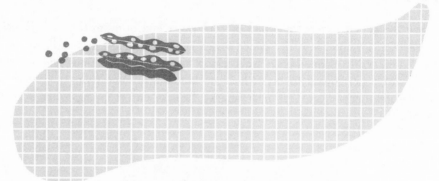

Charcoal-Broiled Vegetables

Serves 6–8

These vegetables are wonderful with any simple grilled meat or fish. They are best right off the grill, but may also be cooked under the broiler—they just won't pick up that delicious charcoal flavor. The vegetables are cooked sequentially, according to their individual cooking times, so add to the grill as you prepare each one and remove when cooked, working as fast as possible. Leftovers can be kept a few days in the refrigerator for snacking. Serve hot, lukewarm, or cold.

2 large onions

Vegetable or olive oil

3 green or red bell peppers

Salt

Freshly ground black pepper

2 medium eggplants, halved lengthwise

3 large, firm ripe tomatoes, halved

4 zucchini, cut into ½-inch-thick slices

2 or 3 cloves garlic, chopped

2–3 tablespoons fresh herbs

Make an onion flower out of each onion by first peeling the onion, leaving the root end intact. Place the onion on a cutting board, root end down. Cut the onion in parallel slices 1/4 inch apart, cutting from the top almost to the root end. Do not cut through the root end. Rotate the onion and slice again at right angles to the first cut, making a grid or chrysanthemum design. Brush with oil and place on a hot grill, turning until the onion has browned and opened up or "flowered."

Add the whole peppers to the hot grill next to the onions. Turn the peppers until all the skin is charred. Remove the peppers from the grill and place in a paper or plastic bag and seal to create steam; this will make it easier to peel off the skin. After 10–15 minutes, peel, seed, and cut the peppers into 2-inch strips. Place in a bowl, drizzle with oil, and sprinkle with salt and pepper. Toss and set aside.

Make shallow cross-hatched cuts in the meat of the eggplant, spaced about 1 inch apart. Sprinkle with salt and place in a colander for at least 15 minutes for the bitter juices to drain away.

Meanwhile, place the tomatoes, cut sides down, on the grill and turn when slightly charred. Remove from the grill, cut in strips, and add to the peppers.

Rinse and dry the eggplant. Brush with oil on the cut side of each half and place on the grill, with the cut sides down. Don't let the eggplant char. Cook until tender, brushing occasionally with oil. Remove from the grill, slice, add to the other vegetables, and season to taste.

Now place the zucchini slices on the grill and cook until browned on both sides. Remove to the bowl with the other vegetables and add garlic and herbs. Taste for seasoning. Top with the onion flowers for decoration. When serving, pull apart the onions.

Marinated Vegetables

Serves 12

These vegetables are wonderful hot, cold, or at room temperature. I like to cut them uniformly—they look prettier and have a crunchier texture. They reheat easily.

Marinated Vegetables, continued

3 medium zucchini, cut in finger-size
    pieces (2½ inches long,
    ½ inch wide)
3 or 4 carrots, cut in finger-size pieces
⅔ cup white wine (see Note below)
⅓ cup wine vinegar
⅔ cup water
1 tablespoon coriander seeds, crushed
1 teaspoon thyme, preferably fresh
1 teaspoon fennel seeds

3 bay leaves, crumbled
5 or 6 large onions, cut into
    4–6 wedges, then separated
    into layers
3 or 4 green or red bell peppers, cored,
    seeded, and cut in finger-length
    pieces
⅓–½ cup peanut oil or olive oil
Salt
Freshly ground black pepper

Place all the ingredients except the onions, peppers, oil, and salt and pepper, in a large non-aluminum saucepan or flameproof casserole. Bring to the boil, reduce the heat, and simmer for 5 minutes. Add the onions and peppers, bring back to the boil, and boil 5 minutes more. The vegetables should be soft enough to put a fork into, but still crunchy. Add the oil and season with salt and pepper.

Note: You may omit the white wine. If you do, increase the wine vinegar to ⅔ cup.

SEAFOOD
and
GAME

Low Country Seafood Boil

Serves 16

If you should make friends with people from Hilton Head Island, South Carolina, or towns along the coast of Georgia, you are likely to be invited to a low country seafood boil. It's called "low" country because that marshy countryside is as low as it can be—sea level. Eat this outdoors with people you love. A cookout on the beach is enchanting. This recipe cannot be cut down and still be as good!

8 medium potatoes
8 large onions, preferably Vidalia
2 pounds hot country sausage,
    preferably links, cooked, with
    their drippings
6 heads of garlic, broken into cloves
3 hot red peppers, chopped
6 lemons, halved

1 cup apple-cider vinegar
Salt
16 ears fresh corn, husked
Hot Sauce (p. 297) or Tabasco
Freshly ground black pepper
6 pounds raw shrimp in shells
    (30–35 per pound)
16 live blue crabs

☆　☆　☆

Cocktail sauce:
4 cups ketchup
6 tablespoons horseradish
2 tablespoons lemon juice

Low Country Seafood Boil, continued

To serve:
4 pounds butter, melted
2 pounds sour cream

Fill a copper water-bath canner or large pot a little more than half full with water. Place over fire and bring to the boil. Quarter the potatoes and onions and add to the boiling water. Bring back to the boil and cook for 20 minutes. Add the sausage and drippings, garlic, hot peppers, lemons, and vinegar. Simmer 15 minutes. Add the salt and corn and bring back to a rapid boil. The vegetables should be just done. Taste for seasoning and add more salt if necessary, Hot Sauce or Tabasco, and pepper to taste.

   Add the shrimp and crabs; this will bring down the heat. Simmer until the crabs and shrimp are done, about 5 minutes. Remove the potatoes, sausage, corn, crab, and shrimp, and heap onto a large serving platter. Discard the onions, garlic, peppers, and lemons. To make the cocktail sauce, mix all the ingredients together. To serve, have butter melted and ready for the corn, sour cream for the potatoes, and cocktail sauce for the seafood.

Shrimp Pilau

Serves 4

This recipe from my cousin Weida's collection is one she serves to company as well as family. It's similar to Chinese fried rice, yet very different. We pronounce it "pur-loo."

4 tablespoons butter
1/2 cup finely chopped celery
2 tablespoons chopped bell pepper
2 cups medium whole shrimp, peeled
1 tablespoon Worcestershire sauce
1 teaspoon cayenne pepper

1 tablespoon flour
Salt
Freshly ground black pepper
3 cups cooked white rice, hot
4 slices fried crisp bacon and
its drippings

Melt the butter and add celery and bell pepper. Cook until soft. Meanwhile, sprinkle the shrimp with Worcestershire sauce and mix cayenne and flour together. Stir shrimp in the flour and add to the butter mixture. Stir and simmer until the shrimp are cooked, about 5 minutes. Season with salt and pepper. Combine with the hot cooked rice and bacon, crumbled, with its drippings. Serve hot.

Spicy Hard-Shell Crabs

Serves 4

This is the time-honored hard-shell crab recipe. You usually invite a crowd, spread layers of newspapers on the table or the floor, and crack, pick, and eat for hours. Be sure to have plenty of napkins and beer on hand.

12 live blue crabs
1/2–3/4 cup favorite seasoning — Paul
    Prudhomme's Louisiana Cajun
    Magic, Old Bay, or Creole
    Seasoning (p. 297)
Butter, melted

Place a steaming rack in the bottom of a large pot. Add 1 inch of water and bring to the boil. Add live crabs in layers, sprinkling each layer with the seasoning mixture. Bring to the boil and cover. Reduce the heat to low and steam 15–20 minutes, until the crabs turn from blue to red. Combine the melted butter and additional seasoning to taste, and serve the crabs with plenty of this butter sauce.

Sautéed Soft-Shell Crab

Serves 1

This is a wonderful main course. It's distinctly Southern when prepared with pecans.

2 or 3 soft-shell crabs   **1 tablespoon oil**
4–5 tablespoons butter   **1–2 tablespoons pecans or almonds**

Prepare the crabs by removing the eyes, dead-men, and sand sack (see p. 312). Heat 3 tablespoons of the butter and the oil in a heavy skillet until hot and

Sautéed Soft-Shell Crab, continued

sizzling. Add the crabs. Sauté a few minutes on each side. Remove to warm plates. Meanwhile, brown the pecans or almonds in 1–2 tablespoons butter. Pour over the crabs and serve.

Broiled Soft-Shell Crabs

Serves 1

Broiling soft-shell crabs is one of the most traditional methods of cooking these delicacies. We like our spicy variation. Use the seasoning according to your taste.

2 or 3 soft-shell crabs
Juice of 1 lemon
2–3 tablespoons peanut oil
2–3 tablespoons favorite seasoning —
    Paul Prudhomme's Louisiana
    Cajun Magic, Old Bay, or
    Creole Seasoning (p. 297)

Salt
Freshly ground black pepper

Prepare the crabs by removing the eyes, dead-men, and sand sack (see p. 312). Cut each crab in quarters and drizzle lemon juice and oil over. Sprinkle with seasoning, salt, and pepper to taste. Broil, first with the shell up until crisp, then turn. Broil a total of 3–5 minutes, depending on size.

Mussels in Lemon and Wine with Herbs

Serves 4

Mussels will stay alive on ice or in the refrigerator for several days. Unfortunately, unless you feed them, they shrink in size and lose their plumpness. When I was chef of a restaurant in Majorca we got our mussels straight from the ocean, brought them back to the restaurant, threw them in the sink with ocean water, and fed them a flake-like oatmeal for several days. One word of caution, don't use mussels taken during or just after a storm—they will be gritty. To clean, scrape off any debris and pull off the beard from the shiny black shell. Rinse. The sand settles to the bottom of the sink or bowl, so be sure you don't pour the gritty water back over the mussels. Always serve in a soup bowl with the broth and thick, crusty bread.

8 dozen mussels, cleaned
   and scrubbed
Juice of 2 lemons
1½ cups white wine
1 onion, chopped

4 tablespoons chopped fresh basil
Salt
Freshly ground black pepper
1 lemon, decorated

Place the mussels in a large, heavy pot with lemon juice, wine, and onion. Cover and heat just until the shells open. Add the basil, taste for seasoning, and add salt and pepper if needed. Serve hot with the broth and add a lemon that you have cut with a zigzag design.

Oysters Dario

Serves 2

This recipe doubles quite easily. It's an ideal Sunday supper for two, and is named after my friend Peggy's dog, who loves oysters.

6 tablespoons butter
2 tablespoons Chili Sauce (p. 300)
½ cup heavy cream
½ pint oysters, with liquor
Salt
Freshly ground black pepper

Worcestershire sauce
Lemon juice
2 pieces of white loaf bread, toasted,
   buttered, and halved
3 tablespoons chopped fresh parsley

Melt the butter in a small non-aluminum saucepan. Add Chili Sauce and cream, and heat to a simmer. Add the oysters with their liquor and continue to simmer to heat through, being careful not to allow the mixture to boil. Season to taste with salt, pepper, Worcestershire, and lemon juice. Pour over buttered toast points. Garnish with parsley.

Cicero's Oyster Roast

Serves 10–12

When the oysters are fresh, my friend Cicero has an oyster roast for 500 people or so. The fresh taste of a plump oyster roasted in its shell, then dipped in butter, is one of life's great pleasures. Croaker sacks are the large burlap bags that were once used to put croaker fish in to sell.

1 croaker sack oysters (1 bushel)
Butter, melted
Saltine crackers

Heat 2 turpentine burners (or any heavy-duty propane or outdoor burner), or make a pit wood fire. Place a sheet of heavy steel, 3 feet by 4 feet by 1/8 inch thick, over the fire and heat until very hot. Wash the oysters if they are muddy and place on the hot steel. Put a croaker sack or burlap bag on top of the oysters. Take a water hose or spray bottle and spray the sack with enough water to create steam. Continue steaming until the oysters open just slightly. If they open all the way, they will be too dry. Shovel the oysters onto plywood serving tables and serve with butter and saltine crackers. Use oyster knives to finish opening.

An alternative method is to use a thin lard can. Pound a hole in the top with an ice pick. Fill an 8-ounce Coke bottle with water, then pour it into the bottom of the can. Fill the can half full with oysters. Replace the top. Set on the burner. When steam starts escaping through the ice-pick hole, they're ready!

Fried Catfish

Serves 6

"Just-fried" catfish—crispy on the outside with a juicy inside—is a true rural Southern gastronomic experience.

6 catfish, cleaned, or 12 fillets
2 cups buttermilk
2 cups white corn meal

Salt to taste
Freshly ground black pepper to taste
Oil for frying

Soak the catfish in buttermilk 30 minutes to overnight.

Mix corn meal, salt, and pepper in a paper bag. Drain the catfish and drop into the bag, one at a time, and shake until coated. Heat 1 1/2 inches oil to 360 degrees. Measure the thickness of the catfish and for each inch of thickness fry 5 minutes on each side until golden brown. Drain on a paper towel. Serve hot.

Boiled Crawfish

Serves 8

Although frozen crawfish tails are available, there is no comparison between frozen and fresh crawfish. Like shrimp, crawfish should be cooked in the shell. Usually they are cooked in batches, since a generous serving is 3 pounds per person. This will yield only 1/2 pound of tails per person! The best way to keep all the crawfish hot without overcooking is to place each batch, when barely cooked, in a Styrofoam ice chest. They will continue cooking while in the insulated container and be perfect for eating. Overcooked crawfish are hard to peel.

24 pounds crawfish in their shells
1 pound commercial crab boil
    (see p. 319) or Creole Seasoning
    (p. 297)

Juice of 4 lemons
5 onions, sliced
48 new potatoes, unpeeled
24 ears corn

Wash the crawfish. Bring a large pot of water to the boil with the crab boil or Creole Seasoning, lemon juice, and onions. If possible, use a pot that has its own drainer. Add some of the live crawfish to the pot and return to the boil, covered. When the water boils, or steam is visible, remove the crawfish immediately from the boiling liquid. Place them in a large Styrofoam container and cover. Repeat this procedure with the remaining crawfish, leaving the liquid in the pot.

When all the crawfish are done, put the cleaned potatoes in a string onion sack and drop into the boiling crawfish liquid. Boil 15–20 minutes, until done. Remove the sack, empty out the potatoes, and keep warm. Put the corn in the

Boiled Crawfish, continued

onion sack and place in the still boiling liquid. Cook about 5 minutes after it has returned to the boil or until the corn is done. Drain. Serve the crawfish with the potatoes and corn on an oilcloth tablecloth with lots of napkins.

Billy's Baked Shad with Corn Butter and Sautéed Roe

Serves 4–6

Every year we make a "big do" about the shad running. Friends get together and order up a quantity of fresh shad and roe to be shipped from Russo's in Savannah. We all pitch in and do the cooking. Here's the way Billy McKinnon cooked it this year. Cook the roe and shad simultaneously.

The roe:

2 single roe, 6–8 ounces	8 tablespoons butter
Salt	2 tablespoons olive oil
Freshly ground black pepper	

✿　✿　✿

The shad:

2 shad fillets, boned, 2½ pounds each	Freshly ground black pepper
2 cups flour	5 tablespoons butter
Salt	Juice of 1 lemon

✿　✿　✿

Corn butter sauce:

1 or 2 hot red peppers, seeded and chopped	2 cups heavy cream
5 tablespoons fresh corn off the cob	4 tablespoons butter
Juice of 2 limes	Salt
	Freshly ground black pepper

Preheat the oven to 400 degrees.

To prepare the roe, first season it with salt and pepper. Heat the butter and oil to sizzling in a heavy pan and add the roe. Slash the roe with a knife a few times to prevent blistering. Turn down the heat to very low and let cook 5 minutes before turning. Remove to a warm plate when just pink inside.

To prepare the shad, first remove the skin, then coat the shad in flour seasoned with salt and pepper. Melt 2 tablespoons of the butter, and pour onto a long baking sheet. Place the shad on the sheet, dot with the remaining 3 table-spoons of butter, and sprinkle with the lemon juice. Bake 10 minutes per inch of thickness, about 7 minutes.

For the corn butter sauce, place the peppers and corn in the lime juice in a heavy pan and boil briefly until the juice is reduced by half. Add the cream and butter and boil until the cream is reduced and thick. Taste and add salt and pepper if necessary.

Place the shad on a serving platter, surround with the sautéed roe, and top with corn butter sauce.

Cicero's Sautéed Shad Strips with Roe and Turnip Green Sauce

Serves 6–8

Here is an exciting way to cook shad. You may serve the poaching butter as a second sauce if you like. Laurie and Cicero Garner courted during shad season and their candlelight dinners consisted of just-netted shad cooked at the side of the Savannah River. They celebrate each year with a shad roast.

The roe:
3 single roe, 6–8 ounces each
2 tablespoons salt

1 1/2 cups butter, melted
Juice of 1 lemon

☆ ☆ ☆

The sauce:
2 shallots, chopped
Juice of 1 lemon
2 cups heavy cream

4 tablespoons butter
1/2 pound blanched and chopped
    turnip greens

☆ ☆ ☆

The shad:
3 shad fillets, boned, 1 1/4 pounds each
10 strips bacon, fried, with drippings
    reserved
8 tablespoons butter

1–2 cups flour
Salt
Freshly ground black pepper

To prepare the roe: Place it in a bowl of ice water with 2 tablespoons of salt. Let stand 30 minutes to firm up, then drain. Cut approximately 2 inches off one end of

Cicero's Sautéed Shad Strips, continued

a roe for the sauce. Place all of the remaining roe in a heavy saucepan. Cover with the melted butter and the lemon juice. Slash the roe a couple of times to prevent bursting. Cover and poach in the butter until the roe is light pink inside, usually 10–15 minutes. Be careful not to boil. Drain, reserving the poaching liquid.

To make the sauce: Boil the shallots with the lemon juice until the liquid is nearly gone. Add the cream and butter and boil until thick, about 5 minutes. Add the well-drained greens and the reserved uncooked roe. Set aside. When ready to serve, reheat the sauce, adding a little of the roe poaching liquid if desired. The roe poaching liquid may also be served in a separate bowl as a second sauce.

To prepare the shad: Remove the skin and cut each of the 2 wide center portions into 2 vertical strips to equal the thinner side strips. Cut all 6 strips in half horizontally. Ten minutes before serving time, heat enough of the bacon drippings and butter to cover the bottom of a heavy frying pan. Season the flour with salt and pepper, and toss the shad in the flour to coat. Add the shad in batches to the sizzling fat. Sauté a few minutes on each side and remove. Add more fat and heat until sizzling. Cook the remaining fish.

Place the shad on a hot serving platter, surround with the roe and top with the bacon strips. Serve the sauces separately.

Flounder Stuffed with Shrimp

Serves 2

Sometimes incorrectly called sole, after its flatfish cousin, flounder is found in shallow water, or near the bottom of the sea. The head is a tasty part of the fish, but you may remove it if delicacy dictates. Its two eyes are disconcerting to some. With the head on, the fish, boned and stuffed from underneath, appears whole. When you cut in and discover the secret pocket of shrimp and sauce, it's a wonderful surprise! I have done this recipe with two very small flounder for individual servings.

1 large flounder, cleaned and gills removed	8 tablespoons butter 1 tablespoon flour

1/2 cup milk
1/4 cup mushrooms, sliced
2 ounces peeled shrimp
3 tablespoons heavy cream
Salt

Freshly ground black pepper
Dash cayenne pepper
2 tablespoons chopped fresh thyme
 (optional)
2 tablespoons breadcrumbs

Place the fish, dark skin side down, on a plastic board. With a very sharp knife, cut down to the backbone from the head to the tail of the fish, leaving both the head and tail intact. Make a cut perpendicular to the center cut to form a T at the head end of the fish. This cut will facilitate opening the pocket.

To remove the backbone, keeping fillets whole, slide the knife against the backbone on either side of the incision. Leave the skin attached. With scissors, snip down the outer edges of the exposed small bones and through the top and bottom of the backbone. Sliding the knife under the backbone, wedge the bone out. The backbone should be clean of flesh. This leaves a pocket for the stuffing, with the fillets still in place and the fish whole but boneless. Refrigerate the flounder until ready to cook.

To make a white sauce: Melt 2 tablespoons of the butter in a saucepan, add the flour, and blend in the milk. Bring to the boil, stirring. Boil rapidly about 2 minutes. Melt 2 tablespoons of the butter in a frying pan. Toss the mushrooms in the butter over high heat, remove the mushrooms, and add to the white sauce. If the shrimp are large, chop; add with the cream to the sauce. Bring back to the boil. The shrimp will be only partially cooked. Remove the sauce from the heat and season to taste. Place the shrimp sauce as filling inside the pocket of the fish. Turn the fish over, with the uncut side up, and place in a well-buttered baking and serving dish.

Preheat the oven to 400 degrees. In a saucepan melt the remaining 4 tablespoons of butter. Brush the fish with half of the melted butter and sprinkle with the breadcrumbs. Pour on the remainder of the butter. Measure the thickness of the fish, with the stuffing. Bake, basting occasionally, 10 minutes for every inch of thickness. Serve flounder hot in its baking dish.

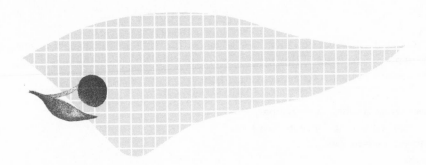

Grilled Grouper

Serves 4

Grouper, a really Southern fish, makes a wonderful light meal. This variation is particularly nice.

2 grouper steaks, 1½–2 inches thick
2 tablespoons soy sauce
1 slice fresh ginger, chopped

1 cup pecan shells, whole pecans in
   the shell, crushed, or hickory
   chips (optional)

Place the fish steaks in a shallow bowl. Mix together the soy sauce and fresh ginger and pour over the steaks. Soak the pecan shells, pecans, or hickory chips in water for 30 minutes. Heat the grill, drain the pecan shells, pecans, or hickory chips, and add to the coals. When the coals are very hot, remove the fish from the marinade and place on the hot grill rack. Grill approximately 5 minutes per side for each inch of thickness, depending on the heat of the coals. The grouper may break up a bit, into large flaky chunks, so be prepared to remove it with a slotted spatula or fish spatula. Serve hot.

Baked Stuffed Snapper

Serves 2

Susan Puett makes this on their boat when her husband has just caught a great big red snapper. The meat of this fish, common from the Carolinas through Florida, is mild, moist, and lean—a perfect eating fish.

1 three-pound whole red snapper,
   cleaned and scaled with head on
2 tablespoons peanut oil

✿　✿　✿

Stuffing:

3 tablespoons butter
4 or 5 green onions, chopped
1 green pepper, chopped
1 tomato, peeled, seeded,
    and chopped
3 tablespoons chopped fresh parsley
1 teaspoon chopped fresh thyme
    (optional)

1 teaspoon chopped fresh basil
    (optional)
4 black olives, pitted and sliced
Salt
Freshly ground black pepper
Juice of 1 lemon
1 lemon, sliced

Preheat the oven to 350 degrees. Oil a baking dish. Rinse the fish and its cavity well. Brush the fish with oil, including the cavity.

To make the stuffing: Melt the butter in a skillet and add onions and green pepper. Cook until the onions are nearly soft and the pepper still crunchy. Add the tomato, herbs, olives, and salt and pepper to taste. Place the stuffing in the cavity of the fish.

Make 2 or 3 diagonal slashes in the skin of the fish and place in the baking dish. Measure the thickness of the fish and bake 10 minutes for every inch of thickness, about 30–40 minutes. Remove to a warm platter or serve from the baking dish. Pour lemon juice over the fish and decorate with lemon slices.

Sea Trout with Roasted Pecans in Creole Sauce

Serves 6

Paul Prudhomme is one of the most talented chefs I know. He is very dear to me, and I cook nothing Creole or Cajun that doesn't have, somewhere in the recipe, something he taught me. He taught a variation of this recipe at Rich's Cooking School. It is different from the one in his book, however.

Sea Trout in Creole Sauce, continued

6 six-ounce fresh sea-trout fillets, bones
    saved to make stock for sauce
Creole Seasoning (p. 297) or Paul
    Prudhomme's Cajun Magic
2 eggs

1 cup milk
2 cups flour
1/2 cup butter, melted
3 tablespoons vegetable oil

✿   ✿   ✿

Pecan butter:
1 cup roasted and chopped pecans
1/4 cup butter
Juice of 1/2 lemon

1 teaspoon Worcestershire sauce
1 teaspoon Tabasco

✿   ✿   ✿

1 recipe Creole Brown Fish Sauce
    (p. 300)

Preheat the oven to 350 degrees. Generously sprinkle the trout with the seasoning. Beat the eggs and milk together. In a separate bowl combine the flour and more seasoning, and dredge the trout fillets with it. Dip in the egg wash and dredge with the flour again.

Preheat a 9-inch ovenproof skillet and add 1/2 cup melted butter. Heat the butter to foaming and add the fillets. Brown one side, then turn over and place the trout in the oven to finish cooking, about 5 minutes. Remove the trout from the skillet and set aside on a warm platter.

To make the pecan butter, place 1/2 cup of the chopped roasted pecans in a blender or food processor and purée. Add the butter, lemon juice, Worcestershire sauce, and Tabasco, and blend well. Brush the pecan butter over the trout, top with the remaining chopped pecans and the Creole Brown Fish Sauce.

Brilliant Blue Trout

Serves 8

There is a natural slick coating on freshly caught trout that turns a brilliant blue when the fish are poached quickly in a pan of boiling acidulated water. This coating is formed by the tiny microbes in lake water that adhere to the skin of the trout. For this recipe to work, that natural coating should not be disturbed when handling and cleaning the fresh trout. When cleaned and cooked properly, the trout will automatically right itself in the pan so that it appears to be swimming with its tail curved. Originally a European dish, blue trout has now become a specialty in fine American restaurants like the Frog and Owl in Highlands, North Carolina, and the Marketplace in Asheville, North Carolina. At the Frog and Owl the fish is caught from its own trout stream. At the Marketplace, a fish tank is always kept full of fresh fish. It is possible to clean your trout, replace it in lake water carefully, and freeze it, with the slick coating intact. It will not assume the swimming position, however, once frozen.

8 freshly caught rainbow trout
Wine vinegar, warmed
Juice of 2 lemons

1 recipe White Butter Sauce (p. 301)
4 lemons, halved and cut
   decoratively

Follow these cleaning directions very carefully: Hold the live trout in the air with one hand, securely placing your fingers in the gills from the bottom. Hold tight. Do not let the fish touch any surface and disturb the natural coating. With your other hand, club the fish on the back of the head to kill it. Still holding the fish in the air, insert a small, sharp knife in the vent on the belly. Make a cut from the vent all the way up to the head. Pull out the gills and the innards in one tug. Rinse the insides gently, making sure water does not splash onto the coated skin of the fish. Return the fish, carefully, without rubbing it, into a vat of lake water or cold water.

Select one or two pots large enough to cook 8 trout without touching each other. Add enough water to fill the pot three-quarters full and bring to the boil. Add 2 tablespoons of lemon juice per fish. Remove the fish from the holding vat, sprinkle with warm vinegar, and plunge individually into the boiling water, belly down. Let the water return to the boil. The fish are done when the eyes bulge out, about 3 to 5 minutes for a 10-inch trout. Remove the trout carefully with a slotted spoon or Chinese strainer, without rubbing the sides. Drain. Place on plates or a platter and serve with White Butter Sauce and lemon halves.

Quick Rainbow Trout with Pecans

Serves 2

This is a great last-minute dish.

2 rainbow trout, cleaned with heads on
1/4–1/2 cup all-purpose flour
Salt
Freshly ground black pepper
5 tablespoons butter
3 tablespoons chopped pecans

Juice of 1/2 lemon
1 tablespoon finely chopped fresh
herbs: parsley, thyme, chives,
basil, lemon balm, and/or
oregano

Measure the thickness of each trout. Season the flour with salt and pepper, then roll each trout in it. Heat a heavy iron skillet with 3 tablespoons of the butter. When the butter is sizzling hot, add the fish and brown. Turn. Allow 10 minutes for each inch of thickness, about 5 minutes on each side. Remove the fish to a warm platter.

To make the sauce, wipe the skillet clean with paper towels and place it over high heat with the 2 remaining tablespoons of butter. When hot, add the pecans and cook until browned. Add lemon juice, herbs, and salt and pepper to taste, and heat through quickly. The sauce will foam and sizzle rapidly for a few seconds. Remove from the heat and immediately pour the foaming sauce over the fish. Eat at once.

Grilled Tuna Steak

Serves 4

This is probably the best tuna you will ever eat in your life. Like other fish steaks, tuna can be marinated in fancy things, but when all is said and done, it's best done simply. To those who don't like fish—it tastes like steak! Try this with shark steaks too.

2 tuna steaks, 1½–2 inches thick
Juice of 2 lemons
Salt
Freshly ground black pepper

2 cups pecan shells, whole pecans,
  cracked, or apple wood, soaked
  in water for 30 minutes

Marinate the steaks in lemon juice for 30 minutes. Prepare the grill and add the shells or wood to the coals. Place the tuna on the grill over very hot coals, season liberally with lemon juice, salt, and pepper, and cook 10 minutes per inch of thickness, turning once. The steaks should be brown on both sides.

Marinated Fresh Tuna

Serves 2

This recipe was developed by Annabelle Stubbs of Albany, Georgia, after her husband caught a 100-pound yellow-fin tuna off the Florida Gulf Coast. They allowed 2/3 pound per person and made one recipe of marinade per pound of fish. When marinated and grilled this way, fresh tuna looks and tastes like a yummy cross between grilled chicken and pork. The mint adds a refreshing and unique flavor.

Marinade:
1/2 cup peanut oil
1/2 cup white wine or 1/4 cup
  lemon juice
2 tablespoons chopped fresh parsley

2 tablespoons chopped fresh mint
2 cloves garlic, chopped

1 pound tuna steaks, 1 inch thick   ✿   ✿   ✿

To make the marinade, mix together the oil, wine, parsley, mint, and garlic. Pour over the tuna steaks and marinate 3–4 hours, turning at least once.

Prepare the grill. To cook, let excess marinade drip off the steaks. Place the steaks on the grill over very hot coals and cook about 5 minutes per side for each inch of thickness. Turn once.

"All Day While You're Hunting" Food

Serves 6

A hunting friend once described to me what he likes to eat when he goes out hunting for the day. It sounded so good I decided to try cooking it at home.

2 rabbits, cut in 5–7 pieces
Salt
Freshly ground black pepper
2 tablespoons chicken fat
    or drippings

8 stalks celery, without leaves, cut
    in half
6 carrots, peeled
6 potatoes, peeled and halved
Chicken stock or bouillon to cover

Season the rabbits with salt and pepper. Heat the chicken fat in a Dutch oven. Place the rabbits fleshy side down in the hot fat and brown on both sides. Add the celery, carrots, potatoes, and chicken stock. Cover, turn heat to low, and simmer for several hours. Presto—a hot lunch when you return from the hunt or the shopping mall!

Rabbit and Dumplings

Serves 6

This rabbit dish is so delicious it will make you think of home and country, ideal for a cold rainy night. Rabbit is usually sold already cut up and packaged in the grocery store.

1 cup flour
1 teaspoon salt
1 teaspoon freshly ground
    black pepper
1 rabbit, cut in 7 pieces

¼ cup oil
4 cups chicken stock
1 hot pepper
1 cup milk

✿   ✿   ✿

For the dumplings:

1 cup self-rising flour	¼ cup shortening
2 teaspoons freshly ground black pepper	⅓ cup milk

Combine the flour, salt, and pepper. Then evenly flour the rabbit. Heat the oil in a heavy flameproof casserole and brown the rabbit in the oil. Add the chicken stock and hot pepper and simmer 30 minutes or until done. Remove the rabbit, cover, and keep warm.

Add milk to the stock in the casserole and bring it to the boil. To make the dumplings, mix flour, pepper, and shortening together in a bowl. Add milk and mix with a fork to make a dough. Drop, a teaspoonful at a time, into the boiling rabbit broth. Cover, reduce heat, and simmer 10 minutes. To serve, place the rabbit back in the casserole under the dumplings and warm through. You may instead reheat the rabbit in the oven, remove to a platter, and pour the dumplings and steamy broth over.

Barbecued Quail

Serves 2

These wonderful quail can be split or left whole. The hot vinegar sauce adds the final touch.

5 tablespoons Hot Sauce (p. 297)	4 quail, whole or split
1 cup buttermilk	4 tablespoons apple-cider vinegar

Mix 3 tablespoons of the Hot Sauce with the buttermilk. Add the quail and marinate for 30 minutes or overnight in the buttermilk mixture. Remove the quail from the buttermilk bath and pat dry. Prepare the grill. Place the quail over hot coals, or under the broiler, skin side down if split, and cook until browned. Turn and brown the other side, cooking until done to your liking.

To make the sauce, mix the remaining 2 tablespoons of the Hot Sauce with vinegar. Serve the sauce with the barbecued quail.

Variation: After grilling the quail, brush with ½ cup melted Hot Pepper Jelly (p. 303), then pass the rest at the table.

Hot Fried Quail

Serves 2

This is pleasantly hot and spicy and quite lovely served on fried turnip greens or collard greens. We eat two kinds of quail in the South, the Pharaoh and the Bob-White. The Bob-White is an all-white-meat bird and is found in local stores quite frequently. The Pharaoh is a mixture of dark and white meat, mostly dark, and is a European variety, now cultivated in the South.

5 tablespoons Tabasco	Salt
1 cup buttermilk	Freshly ground black pepper
4 quail	2 tablespoons cayenne or red pepper
1 cup flour	Peanut oil

✿   ✿   ✿

Sauce:
2 tablespoons Hot Sauce (p. 297)
    or Tabasco
1/4 cup apple-cider vinegar

Mix the Tabasco with the buttermilk. Split each quail in half, cutting down the backbone and breastbone. Marinate 30 minutes or overnight in the buttermilk mixture. Sift the flour with the salt, pepper, and cayenne. Remove the quail from the buttermilk and dredge in flour. Fill a frying pan half full with peanut oil and heat to 350 degrees. Add the floured quail, skin side down, and fry, turning once, until crispy and browned and fork tender. Serve immediately with the sauce.

    To make the sauce, mix Hot Sauce or Tabasco and vinegar.

Bobbi's Quail Stroganoff

Serves 4

Bobbi Sturgis, one of my assistants, and I developed this recipe while working on recipes for my classes at The Cloister, the famous Georgia resort at Sea Island. It may be made ahead and frozen, using Bob-White or Pharaoh quail.

5 tablespoons butter	1/4 cup dry white wine
1 tablespoon oil	1/4 teaspoon oregano
8 quail	1/4 teaspoon paprika
1 medium onion, chopped	1/2 teaspoon rosemary
1/4 cup finely chopped celery	1/4 teaspoon sage
1/4 cup sliced fresh mushrooms	Salt to taste
1 tablespoon flour	Freshly ground black pepper to taste
3/4 cup milk	1/2 cup sour cream

Preheat the oven to 350 degrees. Melt 2 tablespoons of the butter and the oil until sizzling hot in a frying pan. Add the quail and brown, breast sides down. Then turn and brown all over. Place the quail in a buttered baking dish, breast sides up.

To make the sauce, melt the remaining 3 tablespoons of butter in the frying pan. Add the onion and celery and mushrooms and cook until soft. Stir in the flour, then add the milk, stirring constantly until the sauce boils and thickens. Stir in the wine and seasonings. Pour over the birds.

Cover the baking dish tightly with aluminum foil and bake 25 minutes. Remove from the oven and add sour cream to the sauce surrounding the quail, whisking it in with a fork. Bake, uncovered, an additional 10–15 minutes until the sauce is thickened.

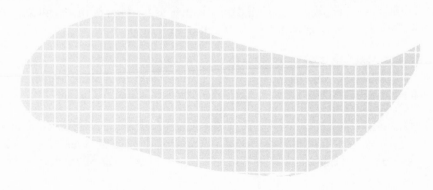

Grilled Doves with Oysters

Serves 4

I especially savor this combination of doves and oysters. Doves tend to be dry if cooked whole, so I wrap them in bacon—this keeps them moist and enhances their flavor.

8 doves
8 oysters
8 slices bacon

Stuff each dove with an oyster, then wrap in bacon. Prepare a grill or preheat the oven to 400 degrees. Place the doves on a rack on the grill or smoker; cover and cook until done. Or cook, uncovered, in the oven for 20–30 minutes until done.

Blind Duck Breast Sandwich

Serves 4

This is Charlestonian Conrad Zimmerman's recipe for cooking duck when he goes duck hunting. I've never been duck hunting so I don't make this in a duck blind, but it may be cooked in the blind on a burner, as he does, or in a civilized kitchen, as I do. Eat, chasing with brandy if you need warming up.

4 ducks or duck breasts (mallard, pintail, or Long Island)
8 tablespoons butter

Salt
Freshly ground black pepper
8 thick slices rye bread

If the ducks are not skinned, pull up the skin of each at the neck, insert a knife, and cut the skin the length of the breast as you would unzip the front of a jacket. Pull the skin back, exposing the raw meat. Cut the breast meat off the bone, about the size of a hamburger. Melt the butter in a large frying pan over high heat. Add the duck breasts. Cook a few minutes on each side, until browned outside, barely pink inside. Season. Make a sandwich, each breast between 2 pieces of bread.

Sam Goolsby's Marinated Venison with Oyster Sauce

Serves 6–8

Sam Goolsby has written two fabulous Southern game cookbooks. He's a wonderful person, a very good hunter, and a great cook. His recipes range from the conservative to the eclectic, and they all work. This is a take-off of his recipe for venison steak stuffed with oysters. For a variation, leave the roast whole and smoke until done after marinating overnight.

1 boneless venison loin or tenderloin
6–8 strips bacon

✿ ✿ ✿

Marinade:
5–6 cloves garlic, chopped fine
4 tablespoons soy sauce
1 cup vegetable oil

4 tablespoons good red wine
4 tablespoons Oyster Sauce (p. 298)

✿ ✿ ✿

5 tablespoons butter
Hickory or pecan shells or whole
**   pecans, crushed and soaked in**
**   water 30 minutes (optional)**

Cut the venison into 3/4-inch to 1-inch steaks. Wrap with bacon and secure with string, as you would a filet mignon. Mix together the marinade ingredients. Place the meat in the marinade and marinate 2–3 hours. Remove, shaking off any excess.

Heat the butter in a large, heavy frying pan or iron skillet, add the steaks, and cook briefly, turning once, until rare. To grill the steaks, place over hot coals to which hickory or pecan shells or pecans have been added.

Grilled Venison Steaks

Serves 4

Grilling is one of the tastiest ways to cook venison steaks. As always, the grill should be hot.

4 venison steaks, 1 1/2 inches thick
1 cup red wine
1 medium onion, chopped

Creole Seasoning (p. 297) or
Paul Prudhomme's Louisiana
Cajun Magic, to taste

Marinate the steaks overnight in the red wine and onion. When ready to cook, prepare the grill. Remove the steaks from the marinade and pat dry. Sprinkle with Creole Seasoning or Cajun Magic on one or both sides, as desired. Place the steaks on a hot grill and cook about 5 minutes on each side.

CHICKEN
and
OTHER
POULTRY

Roast Chicken

Serves 4

My favorite dinner is roast chicken and crisp potatoes. I like my chicken moist, so I favor an unstuffed chicken. When I have dressing, say for a Sunday family dinner, I cook and serve it in a separate dish. Also, I prefer just the pan juices rather than a thick gravy. Some people would call this Baked Chicken, and that's okay.

3 1/2-pound roasting chicken	2 cups chicken stock,
4 tablespoons butter	preferably fresh (p. 320)
3 or 4 sprigs tarragon or rosemary	

Preheat the oven to 400 degrees. If possible, remove the chicken from the refrigerator 30 minutes before cooking. Rub the chicken all over with 3 tablespoons of the butter, placing the remaining tablespoon of butter inside the chicken with the sprigs of tarragon or rosemary. Tie the legs together so the chicken keeps its shape while it cooks. Place it, breast side up, in a roasting pan with enough stock to reach a depth of 1 inch up the sides of the chicken. Save the remaining stock. Roast about 1 1/4 hours, turning a few times. The chicken should be well browned on all sides when done. If the chicken is cold when placed in the oven, it will take longer to cook. To test for doneness, insert a knife or skewer in the flesh of the thigh. If juices run clear, the chicken is done. Let rest for 10 minutes before carving.

Roast Chicken, continued

Meanwhile, place the roasting pan on the stove over low heat, add the remaining stock, and boil until reduced to a saucelike consistency, stirring and scraping the pan well. Strain into a small sauceboat and taste for seasoning. Arrange the chicken on a warm serving dish and spoon some of the sauce over it. Serve the remaining sauce from the sauceboat. This dish is best served right away, but it may be reheated for 10–15 minutes in a 350-degree oven.

To carve: Hold the chicken firmly with one hand. With a sharp knife, cut the skin between the leg and the breast. Pressing the flat of the knife against the carcass, take the leg in your other hand and bend it out until the bone breaks away from the carcass.

Slide the knife around the leg joint, cutting down toward the the tail of the chicken, keeping the knife between the oyster (that succulent little piece of meat sitting in the middle of the lower back) and the backbone. The leg is now separated from the carcass with the oyster attached. Remove the other leg in the same manner.

For full servings with some of the breast attached to each wing, make a 45-degree cut with a knife or scissors diagonally across the breast, through the bone, to below the wing. Pull the wing and its breast piece away from the backbone. Repeat with the other wing. Pull off the remaining breast meat in 1 or 2 pieces, leaving the ribs and backbone. Divide the legs by cutting through the joint, leaving a portion of the thigh attached to the drumstick. Reassemble on a serving platter to look like an uncarved whole chicken.

Roast Chicken Stuffed with Peanuts

Serves 4

The flavor peanuts give a traditional roast chicken is incredible. This is the only way I like a stuffed chicken. It's a version of an old Virginia recipe.

2 cups chopped roasted
    unsalted peanuts
1 hot red pepper, chopped
1 large red onion, chopped
1 three-pound roasting chicken

3 tablespoons butter
About 3 cups chicken stock,
    preferably homemade (p. 320)
Salt
Freshly ground black pepper

Preheat the oven to 400 degrees. Mix together the peanuts, hot pepper, and onion. Stuff inside the chicken. Tie the legs of the chicken together and rub the chicken with butter. Place in a roasting pan with chicken stock to a depth of 1 inch up the sides of the chicken. Place in the oven and roast 1–1 1/2 hours, until brown and the juices run clear when a leg is pierced, turning occasionally to brown all over. Remove from the oven, place on a plastic board, carve, and remove stuffing. Meanwhile, add the remaining stock to the pan juices. Place on the stove over low heat and boil until well reduced and slightly thickened. Taste for salt and pepper and season if necessary. Place the carved chicken on a platter and surround with the peanut stuffing. Strain the sauce and serve separately.

Hot Barbecued Chicken

Serves 4

Mary Nell Reck, a famous Tex-Mex cook, made a variation of this dish when she was a guest on my television show. It doesn't need turning or basting, and is cooked skin side up. The butter may be omitted, making this quite a nice diet dish.

1 chicken, about 2 1/2–3 pounds	2 teaspoons ground cayenne or
Juice of 1 1/2 lemons	hot ground pepper
2 cloves garlic, crushed with	1 tablespoon paprika
1 tablespoon salt	2 tablespoons butter, melted
1 tablespoon freshly ground	
black pepper	

Split and butterfly the chickens by cutting down the backbone and opening the chicken, leaving the breast attached. Squeeze lemon juice over the chicken. Mix together the garlic, peppers, and paprika, and add to the melted butter. Pour over the chicken. If possible, let the chicken sit overnight, uncovered, in the refrigerator.

    Prepare the grill. Place the chicken, breast side up, on the grill. Cover the grill and cook chicken for 50 minutes, until crisp. Or preheat the oven to 350 degrees and bake the chicken for 50 minutes or until done. Don't turn. If the skin is not crispy, place the chicken under the broiler to crisp the skin and brown, watching carefully so that it doesn't burn.

Grilled Lemon and Herb Chicken

Serves 4

This chicken is weighted to make it flat for even cooking, since it is to be broiled or grilled. Otherwise, the legs tend to be uncooked when the breast is ready.

1 chicken
Juice of 3 lemons
2½ tablespoons crushed fresh
    rosemary or chopped ginger
¼ cup olive or peanut oil
Salt

Freshly ground black pepper
2 cups pecan shells or whole pecans,
    cracked and soaked in water
    1 hour (see p. 316), optional
½ cup soft goat cheese or Boursin
    (optional)

Place the chicken on a cutting board, breast side down. Split and butterfly the chicken by cutting down the backbone, then crack the chicken on either side of the backbone at the ribs by pressing down with the heel of your hand so that it will lie flat. Place the chicken in a roasting pan and pour the juice of 2 lemons over it. Place a heavy weight like a marble slab or a heavy pan weighted with a brick on top of the chicken. Refrigerate several hours or overnight. The goal is to have the chicken completely flat and level. When ready to cook, combine the rosemary or ginger and oil with the juice of 1 lemon. Brush on the chicken.

If roasting, preheat the oven to 350 degrees. Place the chicken, skin side up, in the oven, and roast for 30–45 minutes. Remove when it starts to brown and place under the broiler for 10–15 minutes until crisp. If grilling, prepare the grill to very hot and add drained pecans or shells, if desired. Place the chicken, skin side down, on a grill rack about 6 inches from the heat, and grill for 45 minutes, turning the chicken when browned. Check for doneness by wiggling a leg and checking the juices, which should run pink for a moment and then clear. If you wish, place the goat cheese or Boursin on top of the cooked chicken and run under the broiler or leave on the grill until the cheese is soft and warm, about 5–10 minutes.

Jean Sparks's Fried Chicken

Serves 4

This Alabama recipe for pan-fried, medium-crust chicken can be altered by reflouring for a thicker crust or knocking off excess for a lighter one. Jean is adamant that Crisco makes the best fat for frying.

1 three-pound chicken, cut up	Salt
1½–2 cups Crisco or	Freshly ground black pepper
other shortening	1 cup flour

Rinse the chicken pieces and drain in a colander. Melt Crisco or other shortening in a 12-inch skillet so that the skillet is no more than half full. While the shortening is heating, liberally salt and pepper the chicken. Spread flour on wax paper or on a baking sheet and roll the still damp seasoned chicken in the flour. Knock off any excess flour.

When the shortening registers 360 degrees on a frying thermometer, or sizzling hot when tested with a small piece of chicken, flour the chicken again, and knock off any excess. Add the chicken, skin side down, dark meat first, in the center of the skillet, then the white meat. The pieces can touch, but try not to crowd the chicken in the skillet. Cover loosely. Reduce the heat to medium-high and cook 9–10 minutes, or until dark golden. Remove the cover, turn the chicken with tongs, and cook 8–10 minutes more, uncovered. Drain on paper towels. Chicken should be dry and crisp, not greasy.

Chicken Gravy

Serves 4

Chicken gravy isn't just for chicken—it's for all the things that go with chicken. Serve it over biscuits, mashed potatoes, rice, even fresh sliced cantaloupe!

Chicken Gravy, continued

2 tablespoons chicken fat	1/4 teaspoon freshly ground
2 tablespoons all-purpose flour	black pepper
1/2 teaspoon salt	1 1/2 cups milk

Remove the chicken drippings from the skillet except for the 2 tablespoons of fat. Be sure to leave the browned particles in the skillet. Reserve and store the removed fat for another time. Add the flour to the skillet and stir over medium heat until browned. Add salt and pepper, stir in milk, and bring to the boil. Continue stirring while gravy boils for 2 minutes. If it gets too thick, add a little more milk. Serve hot, unstrained.

Butter-Fried Chicken

Serves 4

New York Times food writer Craig Claiborne visited Rich's Cooking School as we were testing fried-chicken recipes. He gave us one of his recipes for fried chicken. A Mississippi native, he said he liked his chicken well seasoned and pan-fried in butter and lard. We followed his suggestion and made this chicken, which has incredible flavor.

1 three-pound chicken, cut up	1 cup flour
3 cups milk	1 1/2 cups lard
Salt	1/2 cup butter
Freshly ground black pepper	

Cover the chicken with milk and soak, preferably overnight. Remove from the milk and season with salt and pepper. Mix more pepper with the flour, using 2 teaspoons pepper per cup of flour, and salt to taste. Melt enough lard and butter to come no more than halfway up the sides of a 12-inch iron skillet. Heat to 360 degrees, or until the fat sizzles when tested with a small piece of chicken. While the fat is heating, shake the chicken dry and flour evenly with the seasoned flour. Add the chicken skin side down to the skillet, dark meat in first, placed in the center, then the white meat on the outside, and brown. Turn, reduce the heat to low, and fry, uncovered, until the chicken is browned on both sides and thoroughly cooked, 20–30 minutes in all. Drain on paper towels.

Herb-Fried Chicken or Rabbit

Serves 4

Chickens and rabbits are excellent fried this way. They taste nearly the same, but the rabbit has a slightly different aftertaste. If your rabbits are small, adjust the portions.

1 three-pound chicken or rabbit, cut up	1 egg, mixed with 1 teaspoon water 1 cup flour
Salt	1 teaspoon rosemary, crumbled, dried
Freshly ground black pepper	or fresh

2 tablespoons chopped fresh herbs:
    oregano, thyme, basil, rosemary,
    parsley, or a combination
	1 teaspoon paprika
	Freshly ground black pepper
	1 1/2–2 cups oil for frying

Sprinkle the cut-up meat with salt, pepper, and the herbs. Dip into the egg mixture. Mix the flour with the rosemary, paprika, and pepper and dredge the chicken or rabbit pieces with the flour mixture. Pour oil into a 12-inch iron skillet to a depth of 1/2–3/4 inch and heat. When the oil registers 360 degrees on a frying thermometer, add the floured chicken or rabbit, skin side down. Put the dark pieces in first, in the center of the pan, adding the white meat last. The pieces can touch but not overlap. Turn when browned. Continue cooking until done: juices will run clear when the meat is pierced, after about 30 minutes.

Chicken with Cucumbers

Serves 4

Cucumbers grow so easily down South, they nearly rival kudzu for vine space. They are usually served raw in salads. But try cooking them with chicken and you open up another set of possibilities. The combination is fragrant; the color is lovely. This dish can be made ahead, several days in advance, and can be frozen. It reheats easily in the oven or microwave.

Chicken with Cucumbers, continued

1 three-pound chicken, cut up
2 tablespoons butter
2 tablespoons oil
¾ cup dry white wine or white
    grape juice

¾ cup chicken stock, fresh or
    canned (p. 320)
3 medium cucumbers
Salt
Freshly ground black pepper

Dry the chicken so that it will brown nicely. Heat the butter and oil in a large, heavy casserole until sizzling hot. Add the chicken and brown the skin side first, then turn and brown the other side. Add the wine and stock, and bring to the boil. Turn down to a simmer, cover, and cook over medium heat without boiling for about 30 minutes.

    Peel, halve, and slice the cucumbers. Remove the cover from the casserole, add the cucumbers, and cook 15 minutes more, until the chicken is tender. Remove the cucumbers and chicken and keep warm, leaving the juices in the pan. Boil until they are reduced by half. Season to taste with salt and pepper. Place the chicken on a platter, surrounded by or topped with the cucumbers. Moisten the chicken with some of the juices, and pass the rest at the table. If serving from the casserole dish, return cucumbers and chicken to pan, leaving the cucumbers on top of the chicken for an attractive presentation.

Chicken with Pecans

Serves 4

This is a fabulous dish to make when you're having company over for dinner. It looks so elegant for such a simple dish, and everyone will think you slaved over the stove for hours cooking it. It is even better made the day ahead and reheated in the oven or microwave. It also freezes well.

1 three-pound chicken, cut up
4 tablespoons butter
2 tablespoons oil
1 cup chicken stock, fresh or
    canned (p. 320)
½ cup white port or ¼ cup
    lemon juice

Salt
Fresh ground black pepper
⅓ cup heavy cream
1 cup chopped pecans or walnuts
2 tablespoons chopped fresh parsley
    or other fresh herb (optional)

Dry the chicken so it will brown nicely. Heat 2 tablespoons of the butter and the oil together in a large, heavy frying pan or casserole until sizzling hot. Brown the chicken, skin side first, then turn and brown the other side. Add the chicken stock and port, season with salt and pepper, and bring to the boil. Turn down to a simmer, cover, and cook over medium heat without boiling until the chicken is tender, about 30 minutes.

Remove the chicken to a platter. Skim fat off the liquid left in the pan and boil until reduced by half. Stir in the cream. Sauté the chopped nuts in the remaining 2 tablespoons of butter in another small pan. Add to the sauce. Taste for seasoning, add parsley, and spoon over the chicken.

Chicken with Rice and Garlic

Serves 6-8

This is a new twist on the old theme of chicken and rice, combining the two with whole baked garlic cloves. Whole garlic is a pleasure to eat by itself, baked until soft as directed below. You just pop each clove out of its skin and spread on crisp toast. It has a sweet, fruity taste—a far cry from the strong taste of raw garlic.

2 whole heads garlic
2 tablespoons butter or oil
1/3 cup oil
2 chickens, cut up
2 medium onions, chopped
1 1/4 cups uncooked rice
1 sixteen-ounce can Italian plum
    tomatoes, with their juice
2 1/2-3 cups chicken stock,
    preferably fresh (p. 320)

1/3 cup black olives,
    preferably Niçoise
3 tablespoons chopped mixed
    rosemary and thyme,
    preferably fresh
4 ounces Boursin, Montrachet,
    or other soft cheese, cut up
Salt to taste
Freshly ground black pepper to taste

Preheat the oven to 300 degrees. Place the unpeeled heads of garlic on a sheet of aluminum foil. Drizzle with 2 tablespoons butter or oil, wrap tightly, and bake for an hour. Remove and squeeze out one of the cloves. It should pop out of the skin easily and be of a spreadable consistency. Try eating it to be sure it is soft enough. If not, return the heads of garlic, wrapped, to the oven for another 15 minutes. When done, remove from the oven, cool slightly, pop all the cloves out of their skins, and set aside.

Chicken with Rice and Garlic, continued

Meanwhile, heat the 1/3 cup oil in a large heavy skillet or casserole. Dry the chicken. Add, skin side down, and brown, in batches if necessary. Turn and brown other side. Remove. Add the onions and cook until soft. Then add the rice and cook about 5 minutes. Add the tomatoes with their liquid and break up slightly. Add stock to the rice mixture a little at a time, and cook until the liquid is absorbed each time before adding more, stirring if necessary. When all the stock has been absorbed, remove the rice from the heat and add all of the remaining ingredients except the garlic. Cook, covered, 20 minutes. Add garlic. May be made ahead to this point and refrigerated. To serve, simmer long enough to heat through.

Country Captain

Serves 6–8

This was originally an English dish, which came in through the back door via Savannah, we think. But don't tell that to anyone in Columbus, Georgia! They think Mrs. Bullock, an important socialite in Columbus, invented it for General Patton or Franklin Delano Roosevelt, who both loved it! FDR's "Little White House" was near Columbus in Warm Springs, Georgia. The President went there for rest and to bathe in the therapeutic waters. My stepfather worked in the White House for ten years and told me many stories of FDR's enjoying Country Captain at his summer retreat.

2 whole chickens, cut into pieces
1/2 cup flour
Salt to taste
Freshly ground black pepper to taste
1/2 teaspoon Hungarian paprika
1/4 teaspoon cayenne pepper
4 tablespoons butter
2 tablespoons oil
3 onions, chopped

4 green bell peppers, chopped
2 cloves garlic, finely chopped
3 teaspoons curry powder
1 teaspoon ground mace
2 one-pound cans tomatoes,
   liquid reserved
1/2 cup currants or raisins
6 cups cooked rice
1/2 cup toasted blanched almonds

Rinse the chicken and place in a colander to dry. Mix together the flour, salt, pepper, paprika, and cayenne. Place the slightly damp chicken in the flour and coat on both sides. Meanwhile heat the butter and oil in a large 12-inch chicken fryer or frying pan. Place the chicken in the hot fat, skin side down. Fry until the chicken is a nice golden brown and turn. When the other side is browned, remove from the pan. Add the onions, peppers, garlic, curry powder, and mace to the pan. Cook until the onions are soft but not browned. Add tomatoes and their liquid. Return the chicken to the pan, skin side up, cover, and simmer until tender, about 30 minutes. Remove the chicken. Stir the currants into the sauce, and serve the chicken and sauce on hot rice. Garnish with toasted almonds.

Chicken Pot Pie

Serves 4

There is nothing more heart-warming and comforting than chicken pot pie—its wonderful flaky crust and the marvelous aroma of cooked chicken and mushrooms. Well, get ready to be *fed* and feel loved! Try to find a pretty pie dish or at least a glass one rather than the metal kind. The chicken and the stock may be cooked 2 days ahead, or cooked and frozen until ready to use, and the pastry may be shaped and refrigerated or frozen. There is no bottom crust to this pie.

1/3 recipe Rapid Puff Pastry (p. 231)
1 three-pound chicken
1 carrot, sliced
1 onion, sliced
1 teaspoon thyme
Small bunch parsley stalks
6 peppercorns
2 bell peppers (preferably 1 green,
    1 red), seeded, cored, and
    sliced thin

5 tablespoons butter
1 cup sliced mushrooms
4 tablespoons flour
4 tablespoons heavy cream
Salt
Freshly ground black pepper

✿   ✿   ✿

Glaze:
1 egg
1 tablespoon water

Roll the pastry out on a floured board into a round piece 1/8 inch thick and 2 inches wider than the pie dish. Cut off a 1-inch strip from the circumference of the round and save. Make decorations from any excess pastry: leaves, flowers, and so forth. Wrap and chill the round until ready to use.

Chicken Pot Pie, continued

To make the stock and cook the chicken, place the chicken in a large pot and cover with water. Add the carrot, onion, herbs, and peppercorns. Bring to the boil, then turn down to a simmer. Partially cover and simmer until the chicken is done, about 1–1 1/2 hours. Remove the chicken to cool, straining the stock and returning it to the pot. Bring the stock back to the boil, and cook until reduced to 1 1/2 cups. Skim fat from the stock either by chilling in the refrigerator and spooning off, removing with ice cubes, or running a paper towel across the top. Set aside. After the chicken has cooled, take the meat off the bones, then shred into bite-size pieces.

Bring a small pot of water to the boil and add the peppers. Blanch in the boiling water for just a few minutes. Drain. Meanwhile, melt 1 tablespoon of the butter, add the mushrooms, and cook for several minutes, until tender.

In a separate pan, melt the remaining 4 tablespoons of butter, then add the flour. Stir together until smooth, then cook slowly until golden. Add stock and bring to the boil. Add cream and cook rapidly to a thick, syrupy consistency. Remove from the heat and add the shredded chicken, peppers, and mushrooms. Season with salt and pepper and cool so that the crust doesn't melt when you place it over the pie. Pour into the pie dish.

Dip a finger into water and run it along the edge of the pie dish to dampen. Place the 1-inch strip of pastry around the rim of the dish. Dampen again with water, then place the large round of pastry on top and flute all around the rim. Remove excess dough with a sharp knife. Make a 1-inch hole in the center for the steam to escape.

Preheat the oven to 425 degrees. Prepare the glaze by mixing the egg with water. Brush the dough with the glaze. Add the decorations, setting one aside to use as a cover for the hole. Brush again. Place the pie on a baking sheet to collect any drippings that may bubble over while it cooks. Add the reserved decoration to the pan. If the dough is too soft to hold a shape, chill the pie for half an hour before proceeding. Place in the oven and bake 15 minutes. Turn heat down to 350 degrees, and bake 25–30 minutes more, until the dough is puffed and brown. Check the decoration that is being cooked separately after 15 minutes and remove from the oven pan if it is getting too brown. When the pie is done, remove from oven, place the decoration over the hole, and serve hot.

Chicken and Oysters

Serves 2-4

This dish is more a stew than anything else, easy to make and good for a cold night. Bobbi Sturgis, who helped with the testing and typing for this book, developed it one blustery day when we needed a quick hot meal. It is delicious served over rice.

2 tablespoons butter
1 medium onion, chopped
1 stalk celery, chopped
1 clove garlic, minced
4 chicken breast halves, boned,
    skinned, and cut into strips

1½ cups shelled oysters,
    with their juice
Salt
Freshly ground black pepper

Heat the butter and sauté the onion and celery about 5 minutes. Add the garlic and cook a few minutes longer. Add the chicken and brown on both sides. Add the oysters with their liquid, and cook just until the edges of the oysters begin to curl. Taste and correct seasoning with salt and pepper, if necessary.

Chicken and Pepper Dumplings

Serves 8

Chicken and dumplings is the ultimate belly warmer for hungry souls. Everything may be cooked ahead except the dumplings, which should be prepared when the chicken is ready to be reheated and served. You're in for quite a surprise when you bite into the dumplings—the pepper will dance in your mouth.

Chicken and Pepper Dumplings, continued

1 three-pound chicken
4 cups chicken stock, fresh
   (p. 320) or canned
1 hot pepper, whole
1 carrot, chopped

1 onion, cut in quarters
1 cup milk
Salt
Freshly ground black pepper

✿   ✿   ✿

Dumplings:
1 cup all-purpose soft-wheat flour
   (see p. 314)
1 teaspoon baking powder
1 teaspoon salt

1 tablespoon freshly ground
   black pepper
1/4 cup shortening
1/3 cup milk

Place the chicken in a heavy flameproof casserole. Add the chicken stock and vegetables, cover, and bring to the boil. Reduce the heat and simmer until the chicken is tender, 1 1/2 hours. Remove the chicken, hot pepper, carrot, and onion from the pot, and discard the vegetables. Skim the fat off the broth and boil down until tasty. Cool the chicken until you are able to handle it, then remove the meat, discarding the skin and bones, and tear into bite-size slivers. Return the chicken to the broth and set aside while you are making the dumplings. The dish may be done ahead to this point, refrigerated or frozen, and reheated later with the milk and dumplings added. Fifteen minutes before serving, add the milk and bring to the boil. Taste for seasoning, add salt and pepper as desired, then add the dumplings.

    To make the dumplings, combine the flour, baking powder, salt, and pepper. Cut in the shortening with a knife or pastry blender until it resembles coarse meal. Add the milk until you have a very soft dough. Drop the dumplings, a teaspoonful at a time, into the boiling chicken broth. Cover, reduce heat, and simmer 10 minutes. The dumplings will swell and break up a bit.

    Serve hot from the casserole.

Chicken Breasts in Madeira Cream

Serves 4

Julia Child made a version of this very easy, fast recipe famous. Madeira was the wine served predominantly in the South in colonial days. It is said that George

Washington drank a pint a day. Thomas Jefferson used it extensively for entertaining and cooking.

1/4 cup butter
6 chicken breast halves, skinned and
    boned

✿   ✿   ✿

Madeira cream sauce:
1/4 cup beef stock (p. 320) or
    canned beef bouillon
1/4 cup dry Madeira
1 cup heavy cream
Salt to taste

Freshly ground black pepper to taste
1/4 cup sliced mushrooms sautéed
    in butter (optional)
2 tablespoons finely chopped parsley

Preheat the oven to 400 degrees. Heat the butter in a heavy flameproof casserole until slightly browned. Add the chicken and brown lightly for 30 seconds on each side. Put the lid on the casserole and place it in the oven. Cook 6–8 minutes, until the chicken springs back when touched. Do not overcook. Remove to a hot serving dish, cover, and keep warm while making the sauce. Or the chicken may be frozen at this point, thawed in the refrigerator, and reheated.

    To make the Madeira cream sauce, add stock and Madeira to the casserole with the pan juices. Boil until reduced by half. Add cream and boil until slightly thickened. Add salt, pepper, and mushrooms, and heat thoroughly. Spoon enough sauce over the chicken to cover completely. Sprinkle with parsley. If made ahead, reheat the chicken in the sauce until warmed through.

Grilled Chicken Breasts with Hot Pepper Jelly

Serves 2–4

Try these chicken breasts brushed with Hot Pepper Jelly, then grilled with the ever-so-subtle flavor of pecans. They are wonderful!

1 cup pecan shells or whole unshelled
    pecans, cracked, soaked in water
    1/2 hour (optional)

4 chicken breasts
1/3 cup Hot Pepper Jelly (p. 303)
1/3 cup dry white wine or apple juice

Grilled Chicken Breasts, continued

Prepare the grill and let the coals burn until white and hot. Add the drained pecans. Place the chicken breasts, skin side down, on a rack over the hot coals. Cover the grill. Meanwhile, mix together the Hot Pepper Jelly and wine or apple juice. Check the chicken after 15 minutes. The skin should be browned. Turn. Brush with the pepper-jelly-and-wine or juice mixture. Cover the grill again. Baste the chicken with the pepper-jelly mixture occasionally. Remove the chicken when it's dark brown and crisp—total time about 30 minutes. Boil any of the pepper-jelly mixture that has remained and pass at the table.

Spicy Fried Chicken Breasts

Serves 4-6

We Southerners like our chicken spicy hot these days. Try changing this recipe a bit, using a cut-up rabbit.

4 whole boned chicken breasts
Salt to taste
Freshly ground black pepper to taste

2 tablespoons cayenne pepper
1 cup flour
Oil for frying

Season the chicken breasts with salt, pepper, and 1 tablespoon of the cayenne pepper. Add the other tablespoon of cayenne pepper to the flour and mix with salt and pepper. Dredge the chicken breasts with the seasoned flour. Heat enough oil in a large skillet so that the chicken will be covered when added to it. When 360 degrees, add the chicken in one layer; do not crowd. Turn when browned. Remove when golden on both sides and place on paper towels to drain.

Stir-Fried Collards, Chicken Breasts, and Peanuts

Serves 4

You may decide to change the mood and flavor of this completely by adding a slice of ginger the size of a quarter, chopped, and 2 tablespoons of soy sauce rather than the Hot Sauce. It's an easy and healthful supper!

1 pound collards or turnip greens, washed, stemmed, and sliced
1 or 2 chicken or vegetable bouillon cubes
4 chicken breast halves, boned

3 tablespoons peanut oil
2 tablespoons Hot Sauce (p. 297) or Tabasco
1/3 cup chopped roasted peanuts
1 tablespoon butter

Place the greens in a large pot of boiling water with the bouillon cubes. Boil for 5 minutes, then drain. Meanwhile, cut the chicken breasts into 1-inch pieces. Heat the peanut oil in a large frying pan and add the chicken breasts. Toss over medium heat for 3–5 minutes, until nearly done. Add the greens and Hot Sauce or Tabasco and toss until the greens are heated through and coated with the juices of the chicken and the Hot Sauce or Tabasco. In a separate pan, melt the butter and stir in the peanuts. Sprinkle over the chicken and greens before serving.

Fast Unstuffed Turkey with Peanut Dressing

Serves 12–15

This is a desperation turkey. It's for those times when you can't cook ahead, when you somehow ruined your first turkey, or when you have only two hours to cook everything in, which often happens to me on Thanksgiving because I like to go to church in the morning. The turkey cannot be stuffed; it must be completely

Unstuffed Turkey, continued

defrosted (still in its sack, of course, to prevent the growth of bacteria), and it must not be more than 14 pounds, although it can weigh as little as 12 pounds.

    In case you think I don't know better, I must tell you the difference between stuffing and dressing. Stuffing is Northern. Dressing is Southern. Dressing gets baked beside the turkey, in a pan, basted with the turkey juices. Stuffing goes inside the bird. Some Southerners do call dressing stuffing. But most of them are transplanted Northerners.

1 turkey, 12–14 pounds	4–6 cups chicken or turkey
½ cup butter	stock (p. 320)
1 medium onion, chopped	Salt
1 medium carrot, chopped	Freshly ground black pepper
4 or 5 sprigs fresh rosemary or	
2 tablespoons dried rosemary	Peanut Dressing (following recipe)

Preheat the oven to 500 degrees. Butter a piece of aluminum foil and place in the bottom of a roasting pan. Place the turkey, breast up, on the foil and rub all over with butter. Place some of the onion and some of the carrot and all of the rosemary inside the turkey. This isn't stuffing; it's added for flavor. Pour in stock to a depth of 1–2 inches up the sides of the turkey. Now turn the turkey breast side down, so the juices from the turkey and the stock will keep the breast moist. Sometimes a turkey doesn't want to stay put, in which case just leave it breast side up.

    Roast for 1 hour. There will be a lot of steam in the oven. Carefully remove the turkey from the oven, closing the door rapidly so that very little steam is released. If the stock has boiled down to less than 1 inch, add enough to bring it up to 2 inches. Turn the turkey breast side up, and return it to the oven. When the oven has returned to a temperature of 500 degrees, reduce the heat to 450 degrees, and roast for 1 hour more.

    Remove the turkey; check for doneness with a meat thermometer or by piercing to see if the juices run clear. Let sit 30 minutes before carving. You should have some wonderful pan juices. If the juices seem fatty, skim off fat with a paper towel. Add any remaining stock to the pan. Place the pan over high heat, and bring the juices to the boil, stirring constantly. Taste. Reduce until rich and flavorful. Season with salt and pepper. Serve with Peanut Dressing.

Peanut Dressing

Makes 2 quarts

4 cups shelled, roasted, and ground
    unsalted peanuts
3 cups toasted breadcrumbs
5 tablespoons melted butter
2 egg yolks
3 tablespoons finely chopped
    fresh sage

Salt
Freshly ground black pepper
2 tablespoons chopped hot red
    pepper or cayenne (optional)
About 3 cups chicken stock, fresh or
    canned (p. 320)

Preheat the oven to 350 degrees. Mix the peanuts, breadcrumbs, butter, egg yolks, and sage together. Season as desired with salt and pepper and optional red pepper. Add enough of the stock to make a moist mixture. Place in a greased baking dish and bake 30 minutes. If too dry, heat and add chicken stock to moisten as desired. Halve this recipe if serving with chicken.

Cornbread Dressing

Serves 8–10

Dressing is best made from fresh breadcrumbs, but old crumbs or crumbs from the freezer will do. This is a very moist dressing. Double if serving with a large turkey.

4 tablespoons butter
2 large onions, chopped
1 stalk celery, chopped, to make
    1/2 cup
1/2 teaspoon fresh thyme
3 cups cornbread crumbs
3 cups biscuit crumbs

4 eggs, beaten to mix
2 1/2–3 cups chicken stock,
    preferably fresh (p. 320)
1 tablespoon chopped fresh sage
Salt
Freshly ground black pepper
2 teaspoons poultry seasoning

Preheat the oven to 500 degrees. Melt 2 tablespoons of the butter in a heavy saucepan. Add the onions and celery and cook until tender. Melt the remaining 2 tablespoons of butter in the oven in a 9-by-13-inch ovenproof baking dish.

Cornbread Dressing, continued

Remove the onions and celery to a large bowl and mix in all remaining ingredients. Pour into the buttered baking dish. Bake until browned, 30 minutes.

Turnip Green Stuffing

Stuffs 1 boned chicken

Use as a stuffing for boned chicken. Double the recipe for turkey. This is also good as a dressing.

2 pounds turnip greens, cleaned
    and stemmed
2 tablespoons butter
2 medium onions, chopped
1 clove garlic, finely chopped
1 cup fresh Boursin or other
    soft cheese, crumbled or grated
3 eggs, beaten
1 cup cornbread crumbs or
    cooked grits

1 tablespoon chopped fresh
    lemon balm
1 tablespoon fresh thyme
1/2 teaspoon chopped fresh sage
1 tablespoon Tabasco
Salt
Freshly ground black pepper

Blanch the turnip greens in boiling water about 3 minutes to remove their bitter taste. Drain the greens, chop, and place in a bowl. Heat the butter in a saucepan. Add the onions and cook until transparent, then add garlic and cook again briefly. Combine with the turnip greens, cheese, eggs, cornbread crumbs or grits, herbs, Tabasco, and salt and pepper to taste.

Turkey Breast with Pecan Butter and Grapes

Serves 10–12

Fresh local Southern grapes, such as scuppernongs or muscadines, are best for this dish. If they are not available, then use any flavorful grapes. This recipe, halved, is also very nice with a whole chicken instead of turkey.

1 eight-pound turkey breast or
    11–14-pound turkey,
    at room temperature
2 cups toasted pecan pieces
1/2 cup butter
2 tablespoons rosemary,
    preferably fresh
2 cups grapes, halved and seeded

1¹/2 cups garlic-herb-flavored
    Boursin, Montrachet, or other
    soft cheese
Salt
Freshly ground black pepper
5–6 cups turkey or chicken stock (p. 320)
1 cup toasted pecan halves

Preheat the oven to 350 degrees. Ease the skin of the turkey off the meat, leaving it attached. Purée 1 cup of the pecan pieces with the butter to a very fine consistency in a food processor or blender. Continue to purée, adding the rest of the pecan pieces, rosemary, 1 cup of the grapes, and the cheese. Season with salt and pepper. Place this mixture under the skin of the turkey. If the skin tears, it may be sewn with a trussing needle and string. Reserve any leftover mixture for another time.

Place the turkey in a baking pan with stock to a depth of 1/2 inch up the sides of the turkey. Add the remaining grapes to the broth. Bake the turkey for 30 minutes, then turn the oven temperature down to 325 degrees and roast until the turkey reaches 180 degrees on a meat thermometer placed in the thigh, adding more stock when necessary. Turn the turkey so the skin is browned and crisp all over. When done, remove from the pan and let stand 30 minutes before carving. Degrease the juices. Add any remaining stock to the pan and bring to the boil, stirring the sides and bottom to deglaze the pan. Boil to reduce, tasting occasionally, until flavorful, about 20 minutes. Add the pecan halves. I prefer this sauce without further thickening, but if you wish, thicken with flour dissolved in water.

Turkey Scaloppine with Mustard and Marjoram

Serves 4

Turkey scaloppine—thin slices of boned turkey breast—are easy to prepare and make ahead, ideal for entertaining and for working people who want something

Turkey Scaloppine, continued

quick and hearty to eat when they get home from the office. It's always been a favorite of my students and may be done with chicken as well as turkey.

1/4 cup butter
4–6 turkey scaloppine

❁ ❁ ❁

Sauce:

1 tablespoon butter
2 shallots, finely chopped
1/2 cup white wine or 1/4 cup lemon juice
1 cup chicken stock (p. 320)
2 cloves garlic, chopped
1 cup heavy cream

2–3 teaspoons Dijon mustard
1 teaspoon finely chopped fresh or dried marjoram or oregano
1 teaspoon finely chopped fresh parsley
Salt to taste
Freshly ground black pepper to taste

Preheat the oven to 400 degrees. Melt the butter in a large ovenproof sauté pan. Add the turkey scaloppine and brown lightly. Cover the pan with its lid and bake 5–8 minutes, or cook on top of the stove until done, checking occasionally to be sure the scaloppine are not burning. Remove to a serving dish and keep warm. The scaloppine may be refrigerated or frozen at this point.

To make the sauce, add butter to the same pan and heat until sizzling. Add the shallots and cook until soft. Add wine, chicken stock, and garlic, and bring to a rolling boil. Boil until reduced to 1/3 cup. Add cream and mustard, stirring until the sauce returns to the boil. Boil until the sauce is nicely thickened. Season well with marjoram or oregano, parsley, salt, and pepper. Add the scaloppine and reheat until warmed through.

Grilled Duck with Muscadine Sauce

Serves 2–4

Jimmy Bentley told me a story of an old-time political friend who would have him and his wife over every hunting season for a wonderful dinner of duck, muscadine wine, rice, and black-eyed peas. In this recipe we substitute muscadine preserves for the wine.

**1 duck, cut down either side of
    backbone, backbone removed**

**1½ cups muscadine preserves
    or red currant jelly**

To grill, place the duck, skin side down, without pricking, on a slow to medium grill. Keep a spray bottle of water handy for any flare-ups. Cook until the skin is browned and crisp, then turn and cook on the other side. Brush occasionally with ½ cup of the muscadine preserves. Allow 45 minutes for the duck to cook over medium heat. If you can avoid flare-ups and keep the lid of your grill on, you may cover the grill and the duck will cook faster. Test for doneness by cutting into the leg. I like mine a little pink. When the duck is done, remove from the grill to a cutting board.

To roast, preheat the oven to 400 degrees. Place the prepared duck in a roasting pan large enough to hold duck and any fat that will be rendered as the duck is cooking. Roast 1 ½-2 hours, removing excess fat as it accumulates. Brush occasionally with the preserves. Test for doneness.

To serve, wrap your writing hand with a soft tea towel and pull out the inside breast and rib bones of the duck. The only bones left will be the wing and leg bones. Serve either halved or cut in quarters. Pass the extra preserves.

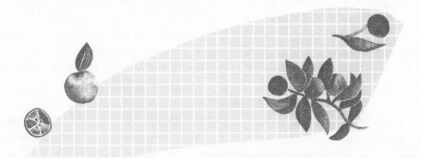

Roast Duck with Mint, Lemon, and Lime

Serves 2 or 3

Crispy duck with the flavor of mint and lemon—what a treat. Make it ahead and reheat, recrisping the skin. Chicken stock (p. 320) may be substituted for the duck stock.

Roast Duck, continued

Duck stock:

2–3 tablespoons duck fat
Giblets
1 medium brown onion, unpeeled
    and halved
Salt
1 medium carrot

Parsley stem
Bay leaf
6 peppercorns
1 teaspoon thyme
2½ cups water

✿   ✿   ✿

Duck:

2½ cups whole fresh mint sprigs
    or lemon balm leaves
Juice and grated rind of 1 lemon
Juice and grated rind of 1 lime

1 4–5½-pound duck
Salt
Freshly ground black pepper
Lemon slices for garnish

To make the duck stock, in a large saucepan heat enough duck fat to cover the bottom of a pan. Add the giblets (without the liver) and the unpeeled onion, and cook until browned. Add the remaining stock ingredients. Bring to the boil, and simmer 1 1/2–2 hours. Strain. Boil down to 1 1/2 cups.

Preheat the oven to 400 degrees. Place 2 cups of the fresh mint or lemon balm leaves and half of the grated rinds inside the cavity of the duck, and tie the legs. Place the duck in an ovenproof pan big enough to hold the duck, the stock, and the fat that will be rendered from the duck. Prick the skin well with a fork, without bruising the flesh, and pour 1/2 cup of the stock over the duck. Reserve the remaining cup of stock. Place the duck in the oven and roast 1 1/2–2 hours, turning it from side to side at 15–20-minute intervals and basting with the stock from the pan. Remove the excess fat as it accumulates. The duck is done when the skin is crisp and browned and the thigh is tender when pierced with a fork. The duck may be refrigerated at this point.

To make the sauce, remove as much fat as possible from the roasting pan. Place the pan on surface heat and add the remaining cup of stock. Add the lemon and lime juice and bring to the boil, stirring and scraping the bottom of the pan well. Season with salt and pepper, and strain. Chop the remaining mint or balm and add as desired with the rest of the grated rind. Arrange the duck on a platter with slices of lemon and spoon the sauce over it.

Serving hint: Before serving, remove the backbone by cutting down either side of the duck from the neck to the tail. Cut down the breastbone so the duck is in 2 pieces. Cool enough to pull out the breastbone and rib cage so the duck is easier to eat. To serve, reheat for 15 minutes under the broiler until hot and crispy.

Menus

A Ladies Lunch
Cheese Straws
Tomato, Pepper, Garlic, and Onion Soup
Sally Lunn with Herbs
Grilled Tuna Steak
Frozen Fruit Salad
Lucile Hill Walker's Tested Divinity Candy

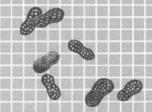

Picnic or Buffet, Hot or Cold
Crab Pie
Flank Steak Stuffed with Greens and Chorizos
Grated Beet Salad
Peaches and Cream Pie

Neighborhood Winter Pot Luck
Fried Spicy Cheese Grit Pieces
Sweet Potato and Bourbon Soup
Meat Loaf
or
Chili
White Loaf Bread
English Peas with Green Onions and Thyme or Mint
Peanut Butter Cake

A Fast Herb-Flavored Summer Family Meal
Iced Cucumber and Mint Soup
Grilled Lemon and Herb Chicken
White Loaf Bread
Basil and Garlic Grits
Ginger Tomatoes
Grated Zucchini
Liberty Cobbler

A Company Meal from the Freezer
Cream of Carrot Soup
Cooked Zucchini Salad
Chicken with Pecans
or
Beef Stew with Fennel and Pecans
Chocolate Checkerboard Cheesecake

A Cold Night's Family Meal
Rabbit Stew
Pepper Pasta
Limed Carrots and Parsnips over Red Slaw
Kate's Sweet-Milk Biscuits
Miss Mary's Date and Soda Cracker Pie

A Spring Meal
Crab Stew
Marinated Roast Leg of Lamb with Spicy Peanut Sauce
Grits with Yogurt and Herbs
Poke Sallet or Asparagus
Brandy Pecan Pie

Cocktail Party
Cold Shrimp Paste Spread on Toast Points
Marinated Beef
Buttered and Salted Pecans
Pork and Peanut Hors d'Oeuvres
Ham Pinwheels
Crispy Cheese Wafers
Eggplant Relish
Marinated Vegetables
Beaten Biscuits with Country Ham and Hot Pepper Jelly

New Year's Day
Hopping John
Greens and "Pot Likker," Old Style
Cornbread
Grilled Fresh Ham
Ambrosia
Georgia Fruitcake
Moravian Cookies

Christmas Eve
Butter Bean and Champagne Soup
Orange and Lemon Garlic Pork
or
Bourbon-Flamed Rib Roast
Grated and Sautéed Turnips
Green Beans and New Potatoes
Butter Braid Bread

A Holiday Late Breakfast
Delicate Cheese Soufflés with Crabmeat Sauce
Anne Haselden Foster's Hot Fruit
Homemade Country Sausage
Beaten Biscuits
or
Pecan Popovers
Toasted Sour Cream Pound Cake
Peach Butter

A Smashing Dinner Party
Broiled Oysters with Georgetown Caviar
Sweetbreads and Turnip Greens with Tomato-Lime Sauce
Flower Fennel Loaf
Jalousie with Peach Butter

On the Grill in the Spring
Barbecued Quail
Grilled Baby Goat with Hot Peppers
or
Butterflied Leg of Lamb
Red Lettuce and Mushroom Salad
Onion Flowers with Pecans
Marinated Vegetables
White Loaf Bread
Pecan Tart with Caramel Cream Sauce

Fourth of July Barbecue
Abercrombie Brunswick Stew
Grilled Fresh Ham
Mrs. Dull's Barbecue Sauce
Cole Slaw
Caramel Cake

A Simple Summer Meal
Pimento Soup
Vidalia Onion and Bell Pepper Salad
Sautéed Soft-Shell Crab
Pecan Tassies
Stuffed Mushrooms
Lemon Chess Pie

An Unbelievable Fall Soup Supper
Vegetable and Sausage Soup
Homemade Country Sausage
Old-Fashioned Gingerbread with Peach Sauce

An Easy, Fancy Meal
Celery and Pepper Bundles
Peanut-Roasted Pork Tenderloin
Dripping-Cooked Potatoes, Onions, and Turnips
Audrey's Pineapple Upside-Down Cake
Peach and Cream Custard with Pecan Caramel Topping

For a Special Time
Zucchini and Pecan Soup or Carrot Soup
Crown Roast of Pork with Pineapple Dressing
Green Beans and Tomato Preserves
Coconut Cake

A Winter's Meal for Friends and Family
Chicken and Pepper Dumplings
Mushroom, Pumpkin Seed, and Lettuce Salad
Pecan Roll with Chocolate Sauce

A Meal for the Boss
Barbara Persons' Caveach of
Marinated Shrimp and Scallops
Beef with Onion and Vinegar Sauce
Grated Beet Salad
Broccoli
Pecan Cookies Sandwiched with Fresh Peaches and Cream

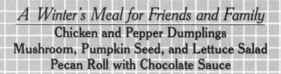

Last-Minute Meal
Quick Rainbow Trout with Pecans
Grated Turnips and Zucchini
Fennel (or Celery) and Apple Salad
Refrigerator Rolls
Banana Pudding

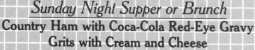

Sunday Night Supper or Brunch
Country Ham with Coca-Cola Red-Eye Gravy
Grits with Cream and Cheese
Beaten Biscuits with Hot Pepper Jelly
Apple Cobbler

An Easy Fix-Ahead Brunch
Sausage and Apple Overnight Casserole
Melon, Cucumber, and Tomato Salad
Easter Egg Bread
Hard-Cooked Egg
Lane Cake

A Fun Meal for Family or Guests
Turkey Breast with Pecan Butter and Grapes
Grits with Rosemary and Grapes
Asparagus
Pimento Muffins
Mississippi Mud Cake

A Delicious Meal for Two or Four
Grilled Duck with Muscadine Sauce (Roasted)
Black-eyed Peas with Duck Giblets
Celery and Carrots with Ginger Sauce
Brown Rice with Pecans
Kate's Sweet-Milk Biscuits
Apple Pan Dowdy

A Meal for People You Love
Pot Roast with Lemon-Lime and Tomato Sauce
English Peas with Green Onions and Thyme or Mint
LuLen's Grated Apple Pie

A Celebration of the New South
Turnip and Ginger Soup
Herb-Fried Chicken
Butter Beans with Herbs
Hot Sauce
Cornbread
Butter Pecan Cheesecake

A Quick Meal for a Hot Night
Grilled Grouper
Beets and Broccoli with Sesame Oil
Lacy Corn Fritters
Blueberries and Strawberries with Lemon Cheese Sauce

A Covered-Dish Meal or a Meal for a Crowd
Crazy Lasagna
Turnip Green Pasta
Green Salad and Herbs
Thick, Rich Custard with Caramel Top

A Buffet-Style Meal for Casual Entertaining
Iced Tea
Country Captain
Rice
Greens with Coriander Seed and Browned Butter
Fried Pies

A Family Supper
Fried Okra
Fried Watermelon Rinds
Cheese Puff and Leftover Poultry Casserole
Fresh Fruit

A Weeknight Family Supper
Chicken Breast Nuggets with Soy Sauce
Green Beans
Food Processor Biscuits
Oranges in Ginger-Caramel Sauce

A "Down Home" Supper
Fried Catfish with Creole Seasoning
Green Vegetable
Cabbage Slaw and Peanuts
Hush Puppies
Pecan-Topped Chocolate Pound Cake

A Meal for Special Friends
Turnip and Onion Soup
Carpetbag Steaks
Oven-Crisp Potatoes
Green Vegetable
Lace Cookies
Blueberries with Lemon Cheese

Sunday Dinner
Zucchini and Pecan Soup
Roast Chicken with Cornbread Dressing
Baby Glazed Carrots with Butter and Herbs
Peach Cobbler with Peach Custard Ice Cream

Lazy Cook's Meal for Family or Friends
Sautéed Sweet Potatoes with Pecans
Sautéed Pork Tenderloin
Charcoal-Broiled Vegetables
Pepper Biscuits
Pecan Shortbread

An Unusually Pleasing Meal
Chicken Pot Pie made with Rapid Puff Pastry
Cucumber and Yogurt Salad
Thick, Rich Custard with Caramel Top

A Memorable Spring or Summer Meal
Asparagus Topped with Scallops
Pecan-Smoked Pork Basted with Hot Pepper Jelly Sauce
White Loaf Bread
Frozen Ginger-Caramel Mousse

A Tasty Company Meal
Boiled Crawfish
Chicken with Rice and Garlic
Green Vegetable
Cream Puffs

A Great Dinner Party or Buffet
Basil and Greens Stuffed Fillet
Turnips and Cream
Chocolate Pecan Pie

MEATS

Orange and Lemon Garlic Pork

Serves 8–10

The South is a region influenced by many cuisines and cultures. This recipe in particular is influenced by our Spanish and Cuban neighbors as well as by Creole and Mexican cooking. Two very different cooks of Spanish origin, Carmen Sanders and Pat Portal, originally served this to me. One used a suckling pig of 20 pounds, the other a 100-pound pig cooked in a pit. The recipe can be doubled or halved, and if you can get the sour oranges that grow in Florida, you will love the pizazz they give the dish. You may cook this in the Grilled Fresh Ham recipe style (p. 185).

**1 suckling pig, 10–12 pounds,
or 1 eight-pound fresh pork ham**

✿ ✿ ✿

Marinade:

5 or 6 cloves garlic	3 limes
1 tablespoon salt	3 grapefruit
3 sour oranges or juice oranges	3 tablespoons crushed rosemary

✿ ✿ ✿

¼ cup extra-virgin olive oil

✿ ✿ ✿

Orange and Lemon Garlic Pork, continued

Sauce:

6 cloves garlic	Leftover marinade
1 tablespoon salt	1 tablespoon Hot Sauce (p. 297)
1/2 cup extra-virgin	or Tabasco
olive oil	Salt
1 cup sour orange or lime juice	Freshly ground black pepper

Make several gashes in the pork so the marinade will soak into the meat, and place it in a pan that will fit in the refrigerator. Crush the garlic with the salt to make a paste. Juice the oranges, limes, and grapefruit, reserving the shells, and prepare the marinade by stirring the juices and rosemary into the garlic paste. Pour over the pork and place the shells of the fruit on top of the pork to cover. Marinate the pork, refrigerated, up to 3 days, turning occasionally. When ready to cook, remove the pork from the refrigerator, pour off the marinade, and reserve. Preheat the oven to 350 degrees. Pat the pork dry. Brush with olive oil and place in the oven. Roast about 18–22 minutes per pound, basting with the marinade occasionally and brushing with olive oil.

To make the sauce, crush the garlic with the salt to form a paste. Heat the olive oil in a skillet. Add the orange or lime juice, the leftover marinade, the crushed garlic, and Hot Sauce or Tabasco. Mix well. Lower the heat and cook 5 minutes. Remove from the heat, let stand 15 minutes, strain, and taste for seasoning. Serve with the pork.

Peanut-Roasted Pork Tenderloin

Serves 4–6

Pigs have been raised with peanuts as part of their feed since George Washington Carver developed a strong peanut industry in the South in the late 1800s. When an animal is raised with a product as part of its feed it is frequently a local custom to cook that forage with the meat, for instance, mint or rosemary with lamb, and in this case, pork with peanuts.

1 1/2 cups roasted unsalted	2 pork tenderloins, 1–1 1/2 pounds each
peanuts, skinned	Salt
2 hot red peppers	Freshly ground black pepper
4 tablespoons butter	

✿   ✿   ✿

Sauce:

6 tablespoons white wine vinegar	1 teaspoon ground cumin
Juice of 1 lemon	3/4 pound butter
Juice of 1 lime	

Preheat the oven to 400 degrees. Chop the peanuts coarse in a food processor or blender. Seed the peppers and chop fine. Toss the peppers and peanuts together. Melt the butter in a large ovenproof skillet. Add the tenderloins and brown all over. Remove the pork from the skillet and pat on some of the peanut mixture, coating lightly. Reserve the rest for the sauce. Season the pork with salt and pepper. Return the pork to the skillet and place in the oven. Roast 30–35 minutes or until a meat thermometer registers 160 degrees. Remove from the oven and let stand while finishing the sauce. To make the sauce, place the reserved peanut-and-pepper mixture in a saucepan with the vinegar, juices, and cumin. Boil down until the liquid is nearly evaporated. Add any pan juices from the skillet and boil down briefly. Whisk in the butter, piece by piece, over low heat (see directions for White Butter Sauce on p. 301).

Pork Tenderloin with Apricots

Serves 4–6

Pork tenderloin is lean and tender, small enough to cook quickly and reheat easily. You'll find them most often sold packed two in a package.

1 cup dry white wine or vermouth	2 pork tenderloins, 1–1½ pounds each
2 tablespoons orange cognac liqueur	2 tablespoons butter
1 cup dried apricots	2 tablespoons oil

✿   ✿   ✿

Sauce:

1 cup brown stock (p. 320) or
    beef bouillon
2 tablespoons cornstarch

Combine the wine and orange liqueur, and soak the apricots in the mixture, preferably overnight. When ready to use, remove and chop the apricots, reserving the liquid for the sauce. Make a deep slit from one end of each tenderloin to the other, butterflying them. Place the chopped apricots down the center of the slit, then tie or sew the tenderloins tightly so the apricots are secured and the meat is bound together.

Pork Tenderloin with Apricots, continued

Preheat the oven to 375 degrees. Heat the butter and oil together in a heavy flameproof pan. Add the meat and brown on all sides. Place the pan in the hot oven and roast 30–40 minutes, testing with a meat thermometer until it registers 160 degrees. Remove from the oven, then remove meat from the pan, reserving the juices for the sauce. Let the meat stand while making the sauce.

Add the liquid that the apricots were soaked in to the pan juices with the brown stock or beef bouillon and cornstarch. Boil down for 5 minutes. When ready to serve, slice the pork and serve with the sauce.

Pecan-Smoked Pork Basted with Hot Pepper Jelly Sauce

Serves 25 for cocktail party or luncheon buffet, 10 for main dish

This is a gem of a recipe—the pork can be served hot or cold and it doubles easily, depending on company. To serve 4 or 5 for dinner, just halve the recipe and reduce the cooking time accordingly. If you really want to go "country," smoke two rabbits instead of pork for 1 1/2 hours. Any way you choose, the results are a sensation.

1 center-cut pork loin or crown roast, 10–12 pounds with bone in, or 4 pounds if rolled

3 cups pecan shells, or 3 cups unshelled but cracked pecans, soaked in water 1/2 hour

✿   ✿   ✿

Marinade:
2 cups dry white wine or apple juice
1 cup Hot Pepper Jelly (p. 303), preferably red

✿   ✿   ✿

Glaze:
3/4 cup Hot Pepper Jelly, preferably red
1–3 cups breadcrumbs

✿   ✿   ✿

Additional sauce, if needed:
1 cup dry white wine or apple juice
1/2 cup Hot Pepper Jelly, preferably red

Make a few 1/2-inch slashes in the pork and place in a pan. To make the marinade, heat the wine or apple juice and jelly together until the jelly melts and pour over the pork. Let the pork marinate overnight or as long as possible. Prepare the grill or smoker (allow 2–4 hours' cooking time, depending on the size of the roast). Place the pork on a grill, adding pecans or shells to the coals. Pour the marinade into a small saucepan and heat until melted. Baste the pork every 30 minutes with the marinade. It is hard to predict how long the meat should cook since grills vary radically, so start checking with a meat thermometer after 1 hour. Pork is done when a meat thermometer registers 160 degrees. Give the pork a final basting and let sit 30 minutes before carving. Slice the meat thin, removing from the bone. It is easier to carve when the meat is cold.

To roast the pork in the oven, first marinate the pork overnight or as long as possible. Preheat the oven to 400 degrees. Remove the pork from the marinade, reserving the marinade, and place the pork in the oven. Roast without basting until a meat thermometer registers 160 degrees. Remove from the oven, reheat marinade to cook any pork juices, and pour the marinade over the pork. Let rest 30 minutes before slicing. Slice and glaze.

To make the glaze, mix jelly and breadcrumbs together. Coat the sliced meat with the mixture, coating evenly all over. Run under the broiler until crisp and lightly browned, about 10 minutes. To make additional sauce, reheat the marinade and boil 5 minutes, until thick. If you've used most of the marinade, add additional jelly and wine or apple juice before boiling down.

If reheating, put sliced and glazed pork, surrounded by the unreduced sauce, in a 350-degree oven for 20 minutes. When heated, remove pork and make sauce as above. Place the sauce on the dish, or in a separate serving bowl. Serve hot or cold.

Crown Roast of Pork with Pineapple Dressing

Serves 6

A crown roast of anything is spectacular. I have chosen to give you directions for preparing an inexpensive family roast from one loin—but you may cook the traditional roast made from the center rib portions of two loins this way too.

Crown Roast of Pork, continued

Cooked on a grill and served at room temperature or cold, stuffed with pineapple chunks and garnished with the top of the pineapple, it's a knockout party dish. A good meat thermometer, preferably the instant-reading kind, is a must for pork.

1 crown roast of pork, made from the ribs of a pork loin roast and tied into a crown roast

☆   ☆   ☆

Dressing:

1/3 cup red or white wine vinegar	Freshly ground black pepper
2 tablespoons Dijon mustard	4–5 tablespoons chopped fresh mint, lemon balm, or basil (optional)
1 cup vegetable or peanut oil	1 pineapple
2 cloves garlic, crushed or chopped	Fresh lemon balm or mint for garnish
Salt	(optional)

Preheat the oven to 350 degrees. Cover the bone ends of the crown roast with foil and place a wad of aluminum foil in the center of the roast to help keep its shape. Place in a shallow pan, not on a rack, and roast about 20 minutes to the pound or until the internal temperature is 160 degrees. To cook outdoors place on a prepared grill and cook, covered, until the internal temperature is 160 degrees. Let sit 1 hour before covering, or chill and serve cold.

To make the dressing, whisk together vinegar and mustard, or place vinegar and mustard in a food processor and process briefly. Add the oil, whisking continuously. Add garlic, salt and pepper to taste, and the optional chopped fresh herb. Cut off the top of the pineapple by slicing horizontally about 2 inches below the bottom of the green part. Save for a garnish. Cut the peel off the rest of the pineapple, and cut into 1-inch chunks, throwing away the core. Combine with the dressing. Chill, if desired cold.

When ready to serve, remove the string from the roast, place on a platter or round plate, fill the center with the pineapple dressing, surrounding the roast with any remaining pineapple, taking care the dressing doesn't spill over the edges of the dish. Top the roast with the reserved green top of the pineapple. Garnish with mint or lemon balm, if you wish. Slice between the ribs to serve.

To make your own crown roast, buy a whole pork loin. Have the butcher remove the vertebrae (the backbone) only. Sometimes this is called the chine bone. At the bottom of the last rib, slice the meat through the remaining backbone and remove the bottom roast. Put aside for another time, or if you are serving a crowd, this may be roasted separately, sliced, and served surrounding the crown. If this is done, you can easily serve 15 for a buffet. This won't work for a sit-down dinner, since everyone seated will expect a rib.

French the bones on the remaining rib section by cutting out a 2-inch web between each rib down to the fleshy part of the meat and scraping the bones, starting at the end of the rib furthest away from the backbone. Try to turn the meat so the rib ends face outward, in a crown. You will have to remove 1 or 2 of the tiny ribs next to the shoulder bone. Trim off any excess fat. Try turning again. To make a good turn, remove some of the flesh as well as all of the fat. Reserve any cut-off meat to make sausage or a stir-fry. Cut off the tenderloin and save for a great breakfast treat for yourself and a friend. You should have approximately 8 ribs, webbed, still joined together, with the remaining flesh attached to the ribs trimmed of excess fat. Keep turning so the end flesh meets, trimming whatever excess meat is on the bottom. When the ends meet, sew together with a trussing needle and thread, or tie securely with butcher's twine. Place a ball of aluminum foil in the center of the roast to help keep its shape.

Grilled Fresh Ham

Serves 12–15

A ham is the full hind leg of a hog, a delicious, full cut of pork. Lee Hopper, a brilliant young cook here in Atlanta, has given us his secret for grilling fresh ham in our own backyards. When cooking half of a ham, the butt (buttock) portion is the preferred and meatier part. It's moist and juicy, perfect for a large party, served hot or cold. Some of us think the crisp skin is the best part. Try this cooking method with the Orange and Lemon Garlic Pork (p. 179). The fresh ham may also be roasted in the oven.

6 cups whole pecans, cracked and   ½ fresh ham, 5–6 pounds
    soaked in water ½ hour   Kosher salt
    (optional)

Build 2 charcoal fires at each end of a rectangular grill, or build a ring fire around the circumference of a round grill. When the coals are white and hot, drain the pecans and place on the coals. Place the grill over the coals. Over the empty

Grilled Fresh Ham, continued

space between the coals, place an aluminum pan with sides at least 1 inch high, large enough to hold the ham. Set the ham in the pan and sprinkle with kosher salt. Cover the grill and open the vents just enough to keep the fire going. Check once an hour to see if more charcoal is needed. Don't let the fire die out. Baste the ham occasionally with its own juices, and cook to an internal temperature of 160 degrees. Allow 5–6 hours' cooking time for a medium to large ham.

To roast, preheat the oven to 350 degrees. Place the ham in a pan, fat side up, and rub with kosher salt. Roast to an internal temperature of 160 degrees. Allow 18–22 minutes per pound for roasting. Let both grilled and roasted fresh ham rest for 15 minutes before carving.

Beer and Lime Short Ribs with Mustard Sauce

Serves 4–6

This recipe is adapted from Phillip Schulz's book *Cooking with Fire & Smoke.* Beer and lime are a longtime Mexican drinking partnership, and the combination also makes a perfect marinade for short ribs. Serve smoky hot with a cool mustard sauce and a six-pack of beer on the side. As Phillip says, this recipe is ideal for a good ol' boy who wants to drink beer while cooking at the table.

4 pounds meaty beef ribs

       ✿   ✿   ✿

Marinade:
1 cup beer
1/2 cup lime juice

       ✿   ✿   ✿

Sauce:

3 egg yolks	**2 tablespoons chopped fresh parsley**
2 1/2 tablespoons lemon juice	**2 teaspoons finely chopped chives**
1/4 cup Dijon mustard	**Salt**
1/2 cup olive oil	**Freshly ground black pepper**

Place the ribs in a large, shallow glass or ceramic dish. Mix together the beer and lime juice and pour over the ribs. Refrigerate, covered, overnight, turning occasionally. Bring to room temperature 2 hours before cooking.

Prepare the grill. Remove the ribs from the marinade and place on 2 sheets of heavy-duty aluminum foil each large enough to make 2 packets to wrap and seal the ribs. Sprinkle 2 tablespoons of the marinade on the ribs and seal the packets. Set aside the remaining marinade. Prepare grill. Place on it the ribs in their foil packets. Cook, covered, until the ribs are tender, 1–1 1/2 hours. (When using a charcoal grill, add more hot coals after 50 minutes to sustain the heat for the 1–1 1/2 hours of cooking time.) Remove the ribs from the foil, drain, and place back on the grill. Baste once with the reserved marinade and grill over medium coals until crisp, 15–20 minutes. Serve with the chilled mustard sauce on the side.

To make the mustard sauce, in a large bowl of an electric mixer, beat the egg yolks with lemon juice and mustard until thick, about 5 minutes. Slowly add the olive oil, continuing to mix. The sauce should have the consistency of a thin mayonnaise. Add parsley and chives and season to taste with salt and pepper. Chill.

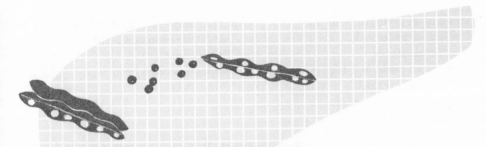

Barbecued Spareribs

Serves 4–6

The South has a multiplicity of ways of cooking ribs, and as many sauces. This method, however, is a good sure way of getting your meat done, with just a little charring around the edges.

6 pounds spareribs, cut in pieces of 5 or 6 ribs each	**2 tablespoons vinegar**
3 teaspoons salt	**1 recipe Bennie Sauce (p. 294)**

Place the ribs in a large pot. Mix the salt and vinegar with a large quantity of water and add to the pot. Bring to the boil and cover. Turn down the heat and let simmer 20 minutes. Drain. Spread the ribs out to cool and stop the cooking. Prepare Bennie Sauce. Heat the broiler or prepare the grill. Place the ribs under the broiler or on a hot grill and cook for 15 minutes, turning every 5 minutes. Baste with the sauce until browned and done.

Homemade Country Sausage

Serves 12-15

In days gone by, sausage would be made in the fall on a crisp day when the hog was killed and butchered and put in the smokehouse for several days. Everyone had a smokehouse. Now we not only use a food processor, we refrigerate homemade sausage overnight to mellow, then freeze it. To give an Italian dash, substitute ground fennel seed for the red pepper. A pork shoulder (also called pork butt) is a perfect piece of meat for making sausage and usually has the right ratio of fat to lean. Add unsalted fatback if more fat is necessary.

1 pound fresh pork fat, from the
    shoulder or fatback,
    in 1-inch pieces
2 pounds lean pork, in 1-inch pieces
1/2-1 1/2 teaspoons salt
1/2 teaspoon freshly ground
    black pepper

1 1/2 teaspoons red pepper flakes
    or 2 tablespoons ground
    fennel seed
1 teaspoon chopped fresh sage

Remove gristle from the pork and place it and the pork fat in the freezer until half frozen. Remove and place a mixture of the two in the food processor until half full. Process to grind, adding a portion of the salt, black pepper, red pepper, and herbs. Pick through for strings of fat or gristle and discard. Add more of the pork and fat mixture to the processor until all the meat has been ground. Add the remaining salt, black pepper, red pepper, and herbs. Fry up a piece and taste for seasoning. Refrigerate overnight, then shape as desired and freeze.

Zucchini and Sausage Boats

Serves 4-6

When you pick the zucchini fresh from your garden, call the neighbors in for a lovely Sunday-night supper. This dish is quite different from the Squash, Pecan, and Sausage Casserole (next recipe) in both taste and style.

6 medium zucchini
1 tablespoon butter
1 medium onion, chopped
2 cloves garlic, chopped

½ pound bulk sausage
Salt
Freshly ground black pepper
1 cup grated Swiss or Cheddar cheese

Preheat the oven to 350 degrees. To make the zucchini boats, cut the zucchini lengthwise in half and hollow out, reserving the pulp. Add the boats to a pan of boiling water and cook 5–10 minutes, depending on size, until tender but firm. Drain and set aside.

Heat the butter in a frying pan, add the onion, and cook 5 minutes. Add garlic and cook until soft. Remove and set aside. Place the sausage in the pan and brown, stirring occasionally. Add the pulp from the zucchini and toss over medium heat, breaking it up as you cook, until tender, 10–15 minutes. Return the onion and garlic to the pan and cook all together until the flavors are well married, 1–2 minutes. Taste and season with salt and pepper if necessary. Fill the zucchini boats with the sausage mixture and top with cheese. Place on a greased baking sheet and bake in the oven about 20 minutes. May be prepared ahead and baked just before serving.

Squash, Pecan, and Sausage Casserole

Serves 6–8

Southerners often serve more than one kind of meat at a meal. Historically, several meats were put out on the dinner table, family style. This practice is still observed on a daily basis in the country, but only at Sunday family dinners and holidays in city homes. This sausage casserole is served alongside the ham or turkey for brunch or a pot-luck church supper. May be made ahead and reheated. Freezes well.

Squash, Pecan, and Sausage Casserole, continued

2 pounds yellow summer squash or
   zucchini (about 5 or 6),
   sliced ½ inch thick
4 tablespoons butter
2 medium onions, sliced
2 cloves garlic, finely chopped
1 cup milk or heavy cream
1 cup fresh breadcrumbs

1 pound cooked, crumbled, and
   drained bulk sausage
5 eggs, lightly beaten
1½ cups grated sharp
   Cheddar cheese
1 cup chopped pecans
Salt to taste
Freshly ground black pepper to taste

✿   ✿   ✿

Topping:
4 tablespoons melted butter
½ cup fresh breadcrumbs

½ cup chopped pecans

Preheat the oven to 350 degrees. Grease a 2-quart casserole and set aside. Put the squash in a heavy pan and add enough water to cover. Bring to the boil, reduce the heat, and simmer for 30 minutes or until the squash is soft enough to mash. Drain, and mash with a wooden spoon, fork, or potato masher.

Melt the butter in a separate pan, add the onions and cook for 5 minutes, then add garlic and cook until soft. Combine with the drained squash. Heat the milk or heavy cream in the pan, stir in the breadcrumbs, and add this mixture to the onions and squash. Stir in the cooked sausage, eggs, cheese, pecans, salt, and pepper. Pour the combined mixture into the buttered casserole. May be made ahead to this point.

To make the topping, combine the melted butter, breadcrumbs, and pecans. Sprinkle over the casserole. Bake, uncovered, for 30 minutes. May be frozen and reheated.

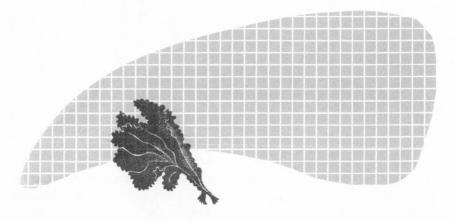

Pecan-Smoked Beef Tenderloin with Curried Peanut Sauce

Serves 10–15

This is adapted from a recipe Merle Ellis, a columnist and nationally known butcher, judged in the National Beef Cooking Contest. He created this variation in my home one night for dinner guests.

1 beef tenderloin, trimmed of excess
    fat and membranes
2 tablespoons salt

Pecans, whole or shells, crushed
    (optional)

✿   ✿   ✿

Sauce:
1 cup sour cream
1 cup mayonnaise, preferably
    homemade (p. 306)
1/2 apple, peeled, cored, and chopped

1/2 cup grated coconut
1 tablespoon curry powder
Salt to taste
Freshly ground black pepper to taste

✿   ✿   ✿

Red lettuce
1/2 cup chopped peanuts or pecans,
    tossed with curry powder
    and roasted

Place the tenderloin in a brine made of the salt and 1 quart water. Prepare the grill. Soak the pecans or shells in water for 30 minutes, then place directly on the coals or in a pan on top of the coals. Drain the tenderloin and dry. Cook, covered, approximately 3/4–1 hour. Let cool, then slice thin.

    To make the sauce, mix sour cream, mayonnaise, apple, coconut, and curry powder together. Taste for seasoning. Place the tenderloin on a bed of red lettuce leaves and top with the chopped, roasted nuts. Pass the sauce or place in a bowl and serve in the center of a platter surrounded by the tenderloin.

Carpetbag Steaks

Serves 4

The combination of steak and oysters goes back a long way, but it's also as modern as today. Originally, a tougher cut of beef was used, and the meat was slit across the top, stuffed with the oysters, sewn, then braised for a long time in the oven. The result looked like an old-time carpetbag, hence its name. Now we use tender strip steaks, and grill them briefly on each side for a rare and delicious meal.

2 New York strip steaks
   (1 1/2 pounds each)
12 ounces shelled and drained
   fresh oysters
Salt
Freshly ground black pepper

4 tablespoons lemon juice
2 tablespoons chopped fresh parsley
Creole Seasoning or Hot Sauce
   (p. 297) to taste
4 tablespoons butter, melted

Cut a horizontal slit in each steak to make a pocket. Season the oysters with salt, pepper, 2 tablespoons of the lemon juice, parsley, and Creole Seasoning or Hot Sauce. Stuff about 6 seasoned oysters into each steak. Season the steaks with more salt, pepper, and Creole Seasoning or Hot Sauce. Close with toothpicks or skewers, or sew with a trussing needle and string.

   Heat a grill or broiler and grill or broil until rare, about 6–8 minutes on each side.

   Meanwhile, in a small bowl, mix the melted butter, remaining 2 tablespoons lemon juice, and Hot Sauce or Creole Seasoning to taste. Slice the steaks diagonally across the grain and serve with the lemon-butter hot sauce.

Beef with Onion and
Vinegar Sauce

Serves 8, or 20 for a cocktail party

I don't know of a more versatile dish than this one. For a fancy cocktail party you can cook the fillet, cut it into chunks, and serve in a chafing dish with the sauce.

Or you can serve it thinly sliced for an elegant dinner party, just perfect for beef lovers. Finally, with a cup of the prepared or leftover sauce on an inexpensive roast, you can have a grand family meal. Allow 1/4–1/3 pound of trimmed fillet per person and buy accordingly. There is a large ratio of fat to meat in an untrimmed fillet. For the cheaper cuts of meat, 1/3 pound of meat is enough per person.

1 whole fillet of beef (tenderloin),
    trimmed of all fat, or 1 sirloin tip
    or chuck roast,
    4 pounds trimmed
2 tablespoons butter

☆ ☆ ☆

Basic brown sauce:
1/2 cup butter
1/2 cup flour

2 cups brown stock (p. 320) or
    canned beef bouillon

☆ ☆ ☆

Finished onion and vinegar sauce:
3 tablespoons butter
3 medium onions, sliced
1/2 cup sparkling grape juice or
    dry white wine

1/2 cup red wine vinegar
Salt
Freshly ground black pepper

Preheat the oven to 425 degrees. Rub the fillet with butter and place in the oven, uncovered, in an ovenproof dish. Roast to the desired doneness, about 35 minutes for a rare fillet.

Meanwhile, to make the vinegar sauce, first prepare a basic brown sauce by melting the butter in a large saucepan. Remove the pan from the heat and add flour to make a roux, stirring constantly. When smooth, place over moderate heat and stir until the flour and butter are browned. Remove from the heat, add stock or bouillon, and salt and pepper to taste. Place back on the heat and stir 3–4 minutes. This base sauce may be kept warm until needed for up to 30 minutes, or may be removed from the heat, cooled, and refrigerated or frozen.

Now melt the 3 tablespoons butter in a heavy frying pan and add the onions. Cook over moderately low heat about 20 minutes, stirring constantly, until a rich brown. Add grape juice or wine and vinegar. Bring to the boil and cook over high heat until the liquid has nearly evaporated, about 3 minutes.

Add the base sauce to the onion-and-vinegar mixture and bring back to the boil. Cook about 5 minutes. Season to taste with salt and pepper. If you want to remove the onions for a very smooth sauce, strain through a sieve. To serve, slice the fillet and top with some of the sauce, passing the rest at the table. For a cocktail party, cut the meat into small chunks. Place them in the sauce in a chafing

Beef with Onion and Vinegar Sauce, continued

dish, and serve from the chafing dish with small bread rolls or rounds of French bread.

To cook the chuck roast or sirloin tip, preheat the oven to 325 degrees and melt the 2 tablespoons butter in a heavy frying pan. Over high heat, brown the meat all over. Place the roast or sirloin tip on aluminum foil, with 1/2 cup of the vinegar sauce underneath and 1/2 cup on top. Wrap tightly in the foil, place in a roasting pan, and cook until tender, about 25 minutes a pound. To serve, slice and top with the remaining sauce.

Standing Rib Roast

Serves 6

The alcohol in the bourbon will flame when it comes to the boil and is ignited. It won't flame when the liquid gets too cold or when the alcohol is all cooked or burned out.

1 standing rib roast	Salt
(6–7 pounds)	Freshly ground black pepper
4 tablespoons Creole Seasoning	1/2 cup bourbon (optional)
(p. 297), optional	

Preheat the oven to 500 degrees. Rub the roast with seasoning as desired and place in a roasting pan, fat side up. Place in the oven and turn the temperature down to 400 degrees. Roast until medium rare, about 1 1/2 hours. Remove from the oven, place on a warm heatproof serving platter, and let stand 30 minutes. Carve. Pour bourbon into a saucepan. Bring to the boil and light carefully with a long fireplace-style match. Pour over the roast and serve while flaming.

Basil and Greens Stuffed Fillet

Serves 6–8

For a certain kind of company dinner, we *must* serve beef. It's all well and good to serve chicken and fish to family and close friends, but when the boss comes to dinner, we serve beef. I recommend roasting the meat, chilling it so that it may be sliced easily, and then reheating it when it's time to serve. This is a standard practice in restaurants that many home cooks have never taken advantage of.

1 beef fillet (tenderloin), trimmed of
    all fat, about 3–5 pounds
3–4 pounds fresh turnip greens
    or spinach, washed and stemmed,
    or 2 packages frozen
7 tablespoons butter
2 onions, chopped

5 cloves garlic, crushed with salt
    (see p. 315)
4 cups cooked rice
3 cups freshly grated Parmesan cheese
Salt
Freshly ground black pepper
6 tablespoons chopped fresh basil

To butterfly the fillet, make a long vertical slash down the middle of the fillet without severing into two pieces. This opens up the fillet for stuffing. Cook the greens in boiling water for 5 minutes. Drain, squeeze dry, and chop the greens. Squeeze between two plates or by hand to be sure the greens are completely drained. Meanwhile, melt 4 tablespoons of the butter, and add the onions and garlic. Cook until soft. Mix with the greens, rice, and cheese. Add the salt and pepper to taste, and the basil. Place a portion of this stuffing mixture in the split fillet. Reserve the remaining stuffing to heat separately and serve with the fillet. Close up the fillet, encasing the stuffing, and tie it with string every 3 inches or sew with a trussing needle. Rub with the remaining butter.

    Preheat the oven to 425 degrees. Roast about 30 minutes for rare, or to the desired doneness. Cool in the pan juices. Remove from the pan and chill before slicing. May be served hot or cold. When serving hot, bring the meat to room temperature, cover with foil, and heat in the oven for 15 minutes at 400 degrees. Heat up the remaining stuffing and serve surrounding the fillet.

Flank Steak Stuffed with Greens and Chorizos

Serves 4-6

Although this is wonderful served hot with a tomato sauce, it is wonderful served cold for a tailgate picnic. This is adapted from a recipe by Elise Griffin, one of my former assistants at Rich's Cooking School.

1 flank steak, 1½–2½ pounds
6 tablespoons butter
2 cloves garlic, finely chopped
2 shallots, chopped
1½ cups finely chopped and
    toasted breadcrumbs
¼ cup finely chopped fresh parsley
1½ cups blanched, chopped,
    and drained turnip greens
1 egg, beaten
½ cup freshly grated Parmesan cheese

½ cup grated Swiss cheese
Salt
Freshly ground black pepper
1 tablespoon Dijon mustard
¼ pound chorizo sausage or other
    hard, cured sausage
3 tablespoons peanut oil
½ cup red wine vinegar
12 ounces beef stock (p. 320)
2 cups Tomato Sauce (p. 299),
    optional

To butterfly the steak, make a horizontal cut the length of the flank, without severing the steak into two pieces. Open up flat like butterfly wings and place the steak between sheets of wax paper. Using a meat pounder or rolling pin pound until the meat is ¼ inch thick.

    To make the greens mixture, melt the butter, add garlic and shallots, and cook until soft but not browned. Add breadcrumbs, parsley, and the turnip greens. Stir and add the egg and cheeses. Taste and season with salt, pepper, and mustard. Cut the sausage into strips the size of your little finger. To stuff the flank steak, spread the greens mixture over the steak. Then arrange rows of the sausage strips down the length of the filling, pressing them into it. Roll up lengthwise as you would a jelly roll and tie securely with string.

    Preheat the oven to 350 degrees. Heat the oil in a large non-aluminum Dutch oven. Add the stuffed meat and brown on all sides. Remove. Combine the vinegar and stock and add to the juices in the Dutch oven, heating to the boil. Remove from the heat and add the stuffed meat. Cover and bake for 1½ hours or until the beef is tender. Remove the meat from the liquid, and freeze the liquid for another time when you make this recipe. Place the meat in a large pan and weight with a marble slab, brick, or heavy pan to press the meat together and facilitate carving. Refrigerate before slicing, then slice diagonally across the grain into 1/2-inch slices. May be served hot or cold. If reheating, place in a 350-degree oven for 15 minutes or reheat in a microwave. When serving hot, serve with Tomato Sauce.

Grilled Flank Steak

Serves 2-4

Flank steak is one of the most flavorful cuts of meat. It tends to be tough, but marinating it and carving it diagonally across the grain in thin, uniform slices help to tenderize it.

Marinade:

1/4 cup soy sauce
2 tablespoons chopped fresh ginger
1 clove garlic, crushed with salt
   (see p. 315)

1 teaspoon sesame oil
1/4 cup oil
1 tablespoon freshly ground
   black pepper

✿   ✿   ✿

1 flank steak, 11/2–21/2 pounds

To make the marinade, place the soy sauce, ginger, garlic, oils, and pepper in a food processor or blender. Blend, pour over the steak, and marinate 30 minutes or more. Prepare the grill. Remove the steak from the marinade, reserving the marinade, and place the steak on a hot grill or under a broiler. Cook for 5 minutes on each side. Slice diagonally across the grain and serve immediately. The marinade can be heated and poured over the sliced steak, if desired.

Sour Cream Swiss Steak

Serves 6

Merle Ellis, known as "The Butcher" in his nationally syndicated newspaper column and on television, is very popular in the South. His recipe for Swiss steak is a favorite among "good ol' boys" who like to have steak and potatoes every night. The sauce is the kind you "mop up" with bread.

2 pounds top round or boneless chuck steak	1/4 cup vegetable oil
2 tablespoons flour	3 tablespoons butter
1 teaspoon salt	1 medium onion, chopped
1/2 teaspoon freshly ground black pepper	1 clove garlic, chopped or crushed
1/2 teaspoon paprika	3/4 cup water
1/2 teaspoon dry mustard	3 tablespoons soy sauce
	3 tablespoons brown sugar
	3/4 cup sour cream

Preheat the oven to 300 degrees. Cut the meat into serving-size pieces. Dust with flour and pound 1/4 inch thick with a meat mallet or rolling pin or in the old traditional way with the edge of a heavy plate. Sprinkle with salt, pepper, paprika, and dry mustard. Heat the oil and butter in a flameproof casserole until it foams. Add the meat and brown on both sides. Add onion, garlic, water, soy sauce, brown sugar, and sour cream. Cover and bake 30–45 minutes, until tender. The thin sauce is delicious served with the meat or separately over potatoes.

Pot Roast with Lemon-Lime and Tomato Sauce

Serves 4-6

Everyone I know loves this recipe. Like most pot roasts and stews, it is best made ahead and refrigerated a day. And it freezes and reheats well, too.

1 three-pound chuck roast

✿ ✿ ✿

Marinade:

2 cloves garlic, chopped
Juice and grated zest (no white) of
    3 limes

Juice and grated zest (no white) of
    2 lemons

✿ ✿ ✿

4 tablespoons drippings or butter and
    oil mixed
1½ cups beef stock or canned
    beef bouillon
1 sixteen-ounce can tomatoes,
    preferably chopped
2 tablespoons flour (optional)

1 tablespoon rosemary
1 tablespoon chopped lemon balm,
    lemon grass, or lemon thyme
    (optional)
Salt and freshly ground
    black pepper to taste

Place the roast in a pan with the garlic and lime and lemon juices. Marinate several hours or overnight in the refrigerator. Remove the meat, reserving the marinade, and pat dry with a paper towel. Heat the drippings or butter and oil in a large flameproof casserole. Add the meat and brown on all sides. Pour in the stock, then the marinade, and bring to the boil. Reduce the heat to a simmer, and cook, covered, until the meat is tender, 1 1/2–2 hours.

    Remove the roast. Degrease the liquid in the casserole and add the tomatoes. Boil until thick, about 15 minutes. If the sauce has not thickened enough remove about 1/3 cup and set aside to cool. Then add the flour to the cooled sauce and mix until smooth. Pour into the unthickened sauce and bring back to a boil, stirring constantly. Slice the meat and return to the sauce. Add herbs, season to taste with salt and pepper, and heat through. Serve hot, topped with the grated zest of the limes and lemons.

Roast Beef Salad

Serves 6–8

This dish carries well for picnics, backyard parties, or a symphony in the park. Since Southerners are able to spend as much as nine months of the year outdoors, we're always thinking of possibilities for outdoor fare.

Roast Beef Salad, continued

2 pounds rare roast beef, cut into
    1/2-inch strips
1 eight-ounce can whole beets,
    drained, cut into julienne strips
1 bunch green onions, chopped

✿   ✿   ✿

Dressing:

1/3 cup red wine vinegar
2 teaspoons Dijon mustard
1 clove garlic, crushed

2/3 cup vegetable oil
Salt
Freshly ground black pepper

✿   ✿   ✿

2 six-ounce packages frozen
    snow peas or 3/4 pound
    fresh snow peas

4 tablespoons chopped fresh parsley
1 tablespoon chopped fresh oregano
    or thyme (optional)

Toss together the roast beef, beets, and onions. To make the dressing, combine the vinegar, mustard, and garlic in a small bowl. Whisk in the oil in a slow, steady stream. Season to taste with salt and pepper. Add to the beef and toss to coat. Refrigerate, covered, for 1 hour. Meanwhile, cook the peas in boiling salted water for 2 minutes. Drain. Add three-quarters of the peas to the roast beef and toss gently. Place in a serving bowl and sprinkle with the remaining peas, parsley, and oregano or thyme.

Crazy Lasagna

Serves 6–8

You don't have to worry about layering pasta squares or lasagna noodles in this dish—feel free to swirl the pasta around with the white sauce and meat sauce.

Meat sauce:

3 tablespoons peanut oil
1 onion, finely chopped
1 stalk celery, finely chopped
1 small carrot, finely chopped

1 clove garlic, crushed
1 pound country sausage, crumbled
1/4 pound fresh mushrooms, chopped
1/3 cup dry red wine vinegar
1 teaspoon chopped fresh parsley

5 tablespoons chopped herbs: oregano,
     basil, and thyme, preferably fresh
1 tablespoon rosemary, fresh or dried
Pinch nutmeg
Salt
Freshly ground black pepper

2 sixteen-ounce cans tomatoes,
     preferably Italian, peeled,
     seeded, and chopped,
     juice reserved
1 six-ounce can tomato paste
Sugar

✿   ✿   ✿

White sauce:
6 tablespoons butter
5 tablespoons flour
3 cups seasoned milk ("season" by
     bringing milk to a simmer with
     6 peppercorns, parsley stalk,
     bay leaf, small slice of celery,

small slice of carrot, small onion
     cut in half; remove from heat
     and let sit 30 minutes,
     then strain)
Salt
White pepper

✿   ✿   ✿

3/4 pound dried lasagna, or 1 recipe
     Pepper Pasta (p. 93) or Turnip
     Green Pasta (p. 95)

✿   ✿   ✿

2 cups freshly grated
     Parmesan cheese
4 tablespoons butter, melted

To make the meat sauce, heat 2 tablespoons of the oil in a large pot and add onion, celery, carrot, and garlic. Cook gently for 15 minutes, until the vegetables are soft. In a skillet, brown the sausage in the remaining tablespoon of oil. When it is well browned, drain off excess fat, add mushrooms, and sauté. Add the vinegar and cook 5 minutes, scraping the bottom of the pan to deglaze. Add the herbs, nutmeg, salt, and pepper, and cook until the liquid has completely evaporated. Remove from the heat, and add to the vegetables. Add tomatoes, tomato paste, and enough reserved tomato juice to thoroughly moisten. Bring to the boil, then simmer uncovered for 1 hour, adding more tomato juice if necessary and stirring from time to time. Taste. Season with sugar, salt, and pepper.

   To make the white sauce, melt the butter and stir in the flour. Add the seasoned milk and bring to the boil, stirring constantly until thickened. Taste and season with salt and white pepper. Remove from the heat and cover with wax paper to prevent a skin from forming.

   If using dried lasagna, break noodles into 3-inch pieces and cook al dente. Or roll out fresh pasta thin and cut into 3-inch squares. Cook 6–8 at a time in a large pot of boiling salted water. As each batch is done, remove with a slotted spoon to a bowl of cold water and cook remaining pasta. Drain and dry the pasta.

   Rather than layering, put all the pasta in a buttered 9-by-13-inch flameproof

Crazy Lasagna, continued

baking dish, then add the meat sauce, white sauce, 1 1/2 cups of the grated cheese, and the melted butter. Swirl all together and top with the remaining grated cheese. May be made ahead to this point and refrigerated.

Preheat the oven to 350 degrees and bake until very hot, 10 minutes if freshly made, longer if made ahead and refrigerated. Freezes and reheats well.

Simple Sweetbreads

Serves 6

Sweetbreads, the thymus and pancreas of a calf, are tender organs, low in calories but high in cholesterol. They are delicious done simply, as they are here.

3 pairs sweetbreads   **Salt**
Juice of 2 lemons   **Freshly ground black pepper**
6 tablespoons butter

If sweetbreads are frozen, defrost them. Soak for 1 hour in cold water and the lemon juice. Rinse and peel carefully with a sharp knife, removing the membranes. Melt the butter in a heavy frying pan. Add the sweetbreads and brown on both sides. May be made ahead to this point. About 10 minutes before serving, place under the broiler, and broil for 5 minutes on each side. Season to taste.

Sweetbreads and Turnip Greens with Tomato-Lime Sauce

Serves 2

1 pair sweetbreads
1 lemon, sliced
1/2 pound turnip greens, stemmed
and sliced 1 inch wide
4 tablespoons butter

✿   ✿   ✿

Sauce:

2 tablespoons butter
1 medium onion, chopped
1–2 cloves garlic, chopped
1 one-pound can tomatoes
Juice of 1 lime

Zest of 1 lime (no white)

2 tablespoons chopped fresh lemon
   balm or mint
1 tablespoon ground cumin seed
Salt and freshly ground black pepper

✿   ✿   ✿

Rinse the sweetbreads several times in cold water with sliced lemon added to it. Slice into 1-inch-thick pieces. This is easier to do when the sweetbreads are half frozen. Trim away the thick membrane with a sharp knife.

Bring a pot of water to the boil and add the turnip greens. Cook 2 minutes, then drain.

To make the sauce, heat 2 tablespoons butter in a saucepan and add the chopped onion. Cook until soft, about 5 minutes. Add the garlic and tomatoes and break into chunks with a wooden spoon. Add lime juice and simmer 5 minutes. Add lemon balm or mint, cumin seed, and salt and pepper to taste.

Meanwhile, heat the 4 tablespoons of butter in a frying pan. Add the sweetbreads and sauté for several minutes, until browned on both sides. Add the turnip greens and toss over heat 3–5 minutes, until the sweetbreads are done. Remove from the heat, pour tomato sauce over, and serve topped with lime zest.

Meat Loaf

Serves 8–10

Here's my mother's time-honored meat loaf recipe. Serve it hot with mashed potatoes and English peas, or cold for sandwiches.

Loaf:

2½ pounds ground beef
1¼ pounds ground pork
2 slices bread, made into crumbs
⅓ cup oatmeal
4 eggs, beaten to mix
2 teaspoons salt

1 tablespoon prepared mustard
1 cup tomato sauce
1 medium onion, chopped
1 small can evaporated milk (5 ounces)
Freshly ground black pepper

✿   ✿   ✿

Meat Loaf, continued

Sauce:
4 tablespoon dark brown sugar
1 cup tomato sauce
1/2 cup milk

4 tablespoons prepared mustard
4 tablespoons vinegar

Preheat the oven to 400 degrees. For the loaf, mix all the ingredients together, shape, and place in a greased roasting pan. Bake for 1 hour, basting occasionally with the pan juices.

To make the sauce, mix all the ingredients together in a small saucepan. Heat briefly and pour over individual slices of the meat loaf.

Marinated Roast Leg of Lamb with Spicy Peanut Sauce

Serves 8

Lamb and mutton were favorite meats of the colonial English. In areas where their descendants still live, lamb is popular. But other Southerners, for many reasons, haven't acquired a taste for lamb. Some have unpleasant wartime memories of poorly prepared mutton. But primarily the geography of the South has not fostered sheep growing. I heard about this recipe from Diana Worthington, a member of the International Association of Cooking Professionals. When lamb is marinated with wine or lemon juice, and spices like curry, its strong smell is converted to a wonderful cooking aroma. Peanut sauce, long served on ham and goat, is also good with marinated lamb. An added benefit: since the lamb is boned, the meat thickness varies and the lamb will cook rare in some areas and up to well done in others. It satisfies a range of tastes.

1 whole leg of lamb, boned,
    about 5 pounds before boning

✿   ✿   ✿

Marinade:

3 cloves garlic, crushed or chopped

3 medium shallots, chopped

1½ tablespoons Dijon mustard

¾ cup red wine vinegar

4 tablespoons curry powder

3 tablespoons chopped fresh herbs, preferably thyme and rosemary

Grated rind of 1 orange

Juice of 1 orange

Grated rind of 3 lemons

Juice of 3 lemons

Freshly ground black pepper

✿ ✿ ✿

Peanut sauce:

2 cups peanut butter

1 cup roasted and chopped peanuts

¼ cup soy sauce

1 slice ginger, chopped

8 cloves garlic, crushed or chopped

1 cup chicken stock

4 tablespoons chopped hot pepper, Hot Sauce (p. 297), or Tabasco to taste

Juice of 2 lemons

Trim the lamb of excess fat and place down flat, shaping to resemble a butterfly, in a large non-aluminum pan. Mix the marinade ingredients together and pour over the lamb. Cover and marinate 1 hour to 2 days in the refrigerator, as long as possible, turning the meat several times.

Preheat the broiler or prepare a grill. Remove the lamb from the marinade and place in a roasting pan. Place the lamb under the broiler or on the hot grill for 15 minutes. Turn. Broil or grill 15 minutes more to desired doneness. It will be burned in spots—but will taste delicious. Serve with peanut sauce.

To make the peanut sauce, combine all the ingredients in a saucepan. Whisk together until blended thoroughly. Heat gently just before serving.

Butterflied Leg of Lamb

Serves 10–12

A variation of this lamb dish appears in every Southern Junior League cookbook. Southerners are always looking for a lamb dish that doesn't taste like lamb and this one doesn't. I prefer a small leg of lamb. The large American lambs seem very flaccid and tasteless to me. If you use a large lamb, you will have to adjust the seasonings and the cooking time as it will be thicker than the one I call for.

Butterflied Leg of Lamb, continued

Marinade:

8 ounces Dijon mustard

2 tablespoons rosemary, crumbled

2 tablespoons ginger, finely chopped

2 cloves garlic, chopped

3 tablespoons soy sauce

3 tablespoons peanut oil

✿ ✿ ✿

1 whole leg of lamb, boned, about
    5 pounds before boning

To make the marinade, mix together the mustard, rosemary, ginger, garlic, soy sauce, and peanut oil. Smear over the lamb and let marinate overnight in the refrigerator.

When ready to cook, heat the broiler or prepare a grill. Place the lamb under the broiler or on the hot grill and cook 15 minutes on each side. Test for doneness. The lamb should be dark brown or black around the edges, rare inside.

Lamb with Dates and Pecans

Serves 6-8

My English friend Pat Matthews entertains beautifully. She and her husband, Tony, who was in the English army, were stationed in many parts of the world. They have brought their international palate to Southern cuisine, taking our products and adapting them. For large gatherings Pat doubles this recipe. It can be made ahead and frozen. She sometimes adds saffron, but I prefer it without.

4 pounds boneless lamb, cut in
    1½-inch pieces

¼ cup butter

2 tablespoons oil

2 medium onions, finely chopped

2 teaspoons ground cinnamon

2 cups brown stock (p. 320) or
    canned beef bouillon

1 teaspoon ground coriander seed

1 tablespoon honey

1 cup pitted dates, halved

Salt

Freshly ground black pepper

1 cup toasted pecans

2 teaspoons sesame seeds

Pat the lamb dry with a paper towel. Heat the butter and oil in a flameproof casserole. Brown the lamb in batches, turning and browning on all sides, and remove. Add the onions and cook until soft. Return the meat to the casserole. Sprinkle with 1 teaspoon of the cinnamon. Add the beef bouillon or stock and coriander seed. Bring to the boil. Reduce heat, cover, and simmer until the lamb is tender, about 1 1/2 hours. Remove the lamb and add the honey, the remaining teaspoon of cinnamon, and the dates. Simmer 5 minutes. Add salt and pepper to taste. Rewarm the lamb in the sauce and serve topped with the pecans and sesame seeds.

Grilled Baby Goat with Hot Peppers

Serves 8-10

In small towns like Social Circle, barbecues always have an array of country meats. Baby goat is frequently included, along with possum and squirrel. I don't care for possum and squirrel, but I love the little goat. Goats are available directly from farms or through wholesalers. I prefer a baby goat about 40 pounds, but I've also cooked them from 25 pounds up "on the hoof." Halve the dressed goat, splitting it down the backbone. Freeze one half and cut up the other half into a tenderloin, a shoulder, a leg, and a neck and rib rack, which I make into an Indian headdress arrangement. I also save the head. The tenderloin weighs about 1-2 pounds, the other pieces between 3 and 5 pounds each. A high heat is important to avoid a stewed taste. Save all the bones and head, and place them on the grill to brown. When folks make a fuss about my using the head, I demur. In my opinion, it is very special grilled and used in the sauce too.

Grilled Baby Goat, continued

½ baby goat, cut into pieces,
    about 20-25 pounds

✿   ✿   ✿

Marinade:

4 tablespoons chopped hot peppers
4 tablespoons chopped fresh herbs of
    your choice
1 cup red wine vinegar

2¼ cups vegetable oil,
    preferably cold-pressed virgin
    peanut oil

Place the goat in a large pan that will fit into the refrigerator. To make the marinade, combine all the ingredients. Pour over the goat and marinate 1-2 days, covered, in the refrigerator. When ready to cook, prepare the grill. Remove the goat, reserving the marinade. Total grilling time should be about 45 minutes, depending on the size of the goat, and turning once. Place the leg, head, odd bones and meat, and shoulder on the hot grill. Add the rib and neck rack after 20 minutes, and the tenderloin 10 minutes later. Remove the pieces when they are cooked. Boil the marinade with any browned bones and odd pieces of meat, strain, and serve as a sauce.

BREADS
and
BISCUITS

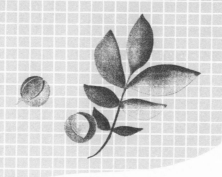

Shirley's Touch of Grace Buttermilk Biscuits

Makes 12–18

Shirley Corriher is an exceptionally gifted Southern cooking teacher who not only makes food taste extraordinary, but can explain why. She tells this story about biscuits: "My grandmother made the best biscuits in the world every day, and I would always stand right by her side watching. She made her biscuits in a large, oblong wooden bowl, called a biscuit bowl. She used only White Lily soft-wheat flour and Crisco, filling the bowl with flour, but making the biscuits at one end. She worked the shortening into the flour and then added the buttermilk, making a big wet puddle of dough in the one end of the bowl. Then she dusted her fingers with flour heavily, picked up biscuit-size pieces of the gooey wet dough, and rolled them in the flour at the other end of the bowl. She just put enough flour on the biscuits to shape them. Her biscuit was a very wet biscuit with a light skin of flour. I would use her big wooden biscuit bowl, the same flour, the same shortening, and the same buttermilk. Nanny's biscuits were light, feathery, delicate, moist. Mine were a nasty dry hard mess. I would cry out in frustration, 'Nanny, what did I do wrong?' She would wrap her arms around me and hug me and say, 'Why, Shirley, honey, you just forgot to add a touch of grace.'" By studying the technique her grandmother used in making biscuits, Shirley Corriher has duplicated her granny's biscuits. Here they are.

Buttermilk Biscuits, continued

2½ cups self-rising soft-wheat   3 tablespoons shortening
    flour (see p. 315)   ⅞ cup buttermilk
1 teaspoon salt

Preheat the oven to 500 degrees. Sift 1½ cups of the flour and the salt together into a bowl. Cut in the shortening with a pastry blender or a fork, or work it in with your fingers until the mixture resembles coarse meal. Add the buttermilk all at once, and mix with a fork until the dough holds together. Don't work it too much. It should be wet and sticky and even a little lumpy.

    Put the remaining cup of flour in another bowl. Flour your hands, then dip into the wet dough and pull off a biscuit-size hunk of dough. Roll the piece of dough lightly in the flour to coat the biscuit and make it easy to handle, then roll gently into a smooth ball in the palm of your hand. This kneads the dough, as well as smooths and shapes it. The inside should still be very wet.

    Place the biscuits, touching each other, on a lightly greased 9-inch cake pan, and give a light pat to flatten each biscuit slightly. Bake until golden brown, 8–10 minutes.

Kate's Sweet-Milk Biscuits

Makes 12–18

Like Shirley Corriher's grandmother, Kate doesn't measure her flour and is particular about using White Lily flour and Crisco. She also hand-rolls her biscuits, but I tell you how to cut them out with a biscuit cutter, a little neater and easier for novices than rolling by hand. "Sweet" milk is what the rest of the world calls whole milk—that is, not buttermilk.

2 cups self-rising soft-wheat flour   ½ cup shortening
    (see p. 315)   1 cup sweet milk

                ❖   ❖   ❖

To shape:
½–¾ cup self-rising
    soft-wheat flour

Preheat the oven to 500 degrees. Put the 2 cups of flour in a bowl and work the shortening in with your fingers or a fork until the mixture resembles coarse corn meal. Add the milk and stir together until well mixed. The dough should be soft and wet.

Spread a tea towel or a kitchen towel out on a board or table and cover with the remaining flour. Turn the wet dough out onto the center of the floured towel. Pick the dough up and turn in the flour a few times to lightly coat the outside, then place the dough to the left or right of center of the towel. Fold the floured towel over on top of the dough. With your hands or a rolling pin pat or roll the outside of the towel lightly until the dough is flattened out to 1/2 inch thick. Open the towel. The dough should be smooth, coated with flour on the outside and wet on the inside.

Cut out the biscuits with a 2 1/2-3-inch floured glass or biscuit cutter, without twisting. Place close together, sides nearly touching, on a greased baking sheet. Bake in the middle of the oven for 10 minutes or until lightly browned.

Pepper Biscuits

Makes 12-18

When you want something "hot" and different to serve, try these pepper biscuits. The basis for the biscuits is Mrs. Dull's famous recipe. The pepper addition is Elise Griffin's. For a sage biscuit, try substituting 1 tablespoon chopped fresh sage for the pepper.

2 1/2 cups all-purpose
   soft-wheat flour (see p. 314)
1 tablespoon baking powder
1/2 teaspoon salt
1 tablespoon coarsely cracked
   black pepper

1/2 teaspoon baking soda
3/4 cup shortening
1 cup buttermilk

Preheat the oven to 450-500 degrees. Sift 2 cups of the flour with the baking powder, salt, pepper, and baking soda into a bowl. Cut in the shortening with a pastry blender or fork, or work in with your fingers. Add the buttermilk to make a soft dough, mixing just until the dough holds together. Flour your hands. Pull off a piece of dough the size of a biscuit and dip the wet edge into the extra flour. Then roll or pat into a biscuit. Place, slightly touching, on a lightly greased baking sheet. Bake until golden brown, 8-10 minutes.

Beaten Biscuits

Makes 100

Beaten biscuits were developed for longtime storage. They are usually eaten at room temperature and kept in a covered jar. Traditionally, they were made by slaves who pounded the dough 1,001 times with a rolling pin or put it through a special machine that was built like a wringer washing machine. The dough would be put through the wringer until it was soft but would snap and crack, and felt like cold, smooth marble. Now, we have the food processor. Don't use a cheap one, or you'll burn out the motor. The shortening and the milk should be icy cold if possible. When using the food processor it is important to fold the dough in half before the final roll to make it easy to pull apart and fill.

6 cups all-purpose soft-wheat flour (see p. 314)	1 teaspoon baking powder
1½ teaspoons salt	1 cup shortening
1 tablespoon sugar	1 cup milk

Mix the flour, salt, sugar, and baking powder in a bowl or in a food processor fitted with a metal blade. Add the shortening and cut in or process until the mixture is the consistency of coarse meal. Pour in the milk and stir or process just until the dough holds together. If it is dry or crumbly, add more milk. If it is too wet, add more flour. Knead briefly in the food processor, then turn out onto a floured board or beat 1,001 times with a rolling pin. When it's ready, the dough should "snap" when you hit it. Fold the dough in half.

Roll out the folded dough until it is ½ inch thick. Cut with a 1 ¼-inch biscuit cutter into small rounds. Prick each round with a fork, making two parallel sets of holes in the biscuit. Keep rolling out the dough, folding before cutting, until all the scraps are gone and you have made about 100 biscuits.

Preheat the oven to 350 degrees. Place the biscuits on a lightly greased pan. Bake for 30 minutes, until crisp but not browned. They should open easily when split with a fork. They will keep for weeks tightly covered in a tin or in the freezer. Split in two before serving.

Ginger Beaten Biscuits

1 recipe Beaten Biscuits
1 tablespoon fresh ginger, grated
      or chopped

Add ginger before the shortening and proceed as with beaten biscuits.

Food Processor Biscuits

Makes 12-18

2½ cups self-rising soft-wheat flour   **½ cup shortening**
      (see p. 315)   **3/4–1 cup milk**

Preheat the oven to 500 degrees. Place 2 cups of the flour, the shortening, and 3/4 cup of milk in the food processor. Pulse quickly 2 or 3 times until the shortening is cut in and the milk is incorporated. Test the mixture and add enough flour or milk to make a soft dough. Shape as in preceding recipes. Place on a greased baking sheet and bake in the oven on the second rack for 10–12 minutes.

Cornbread

Serves 6–8

Although cornbread is good to eat on its own, we do a lot of different things with it. We put it in a cereal bowl and pour milk over it for a light supper or lunch. We split it and spread it with butter and black-eyed peas or turnip greens, then spoon their juices over this sandwich, and eat it with a fork. For crackling cornbread, add ½ cup cracklings (see p. 313).

Cornbread, continued

3 tablespoons bacon drippings or   1 egg
    peanut oil   1 cup milk
1 cup corn meal mix (see p. 310)
1/2 cup self-rising soft-wheat flour
    (see p. 315)

Preheat the oven to 500 degrees. Place the drippings or oil in a 9-inch iron skillet or 9-inch square pan and heat in the oven for 3 to 5 minutes. Meanwhile, mix together the remaining ingredients with a fork or whisk. Remove the pan from the oven and pour 1 1/2 tablespoons of the fat into the corn meal mixture. Stir. Pour the entire corn meal mixture into the hot pan and bake for 15 minutes. Remove from the pan and cut into squares or wedges and serve hot.

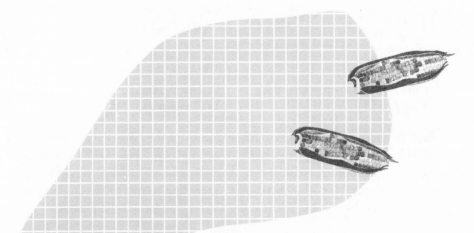

Cornbread Muffins

Makes 12

It's unthinkable to serve turnip greens without corn muffins or cornbread for dunking.

1 cup corn meal mix (see p. 310)   2 eggs
1 cup self-rising soft-wheat flour   1/4 cup shortening
    (see p. 315)   1 1/4 cups milk

Preheat the oven to 500 degrees. Mix all the ingredients together and spoon into greased muffin pans, filling each cup about two-thirds full. Bake 15 minutes.

Snacking Cornbread

Serves 6–8

Just what it says, this is an in-between-meal cornbread.

2 eggs
1/2 cup peanut oil
1 cup sour cream

1 seven-ounce can creamed corn
1 cup corn meal mix (see p. 310)

Grease an 8-inch square pan. Preheat the oven to 375 degrees. Beat together the eggs, oil, sour cream, and corn. Add the corn meal. Pour into the prepared pan and bake 30–40 minutes.

Lacy Corn Fritters (Hoe Cakes)

Makes 15 fritters, serves 2

My friends Laurie and Cicero Garner typify true Southern cooks today. Their home is fifteen minutes from downtown Atlanta, and up until two years ago they kept their own chickens and turkeys (then a neighbor's dog ran away with the turkeys). They cook traditional Southern dishes often, but usually like to prepare lighter, fresher foods. I first had these crisp lacy fritters—also called hoe cakes—in their home. It may seem that fifteen fritters is a gracious plenty, but in fact it is just enough for two. You can make these ahead and briefly reheat in a hot oven.

9 tablespoons corn meal mix
    (see p. 310)
4 1/2 tablespoons self-rising soft-wheat
    flour (see p. 315)

1–1 1/2 cups water
3–5 tablespoons vegetable oil for frying

Mix the corn meal mix, flour, and 1 cup water together until smooth. Heat a thin layer of the oil in a heavy iron skillet until very hot. Add the batter, a tablespoonful at a time, to form round fritters and fry until crisp and browned. Turn and fry briefly on the second side. Add more water to the batter to keep it thin, and more oil to the skillet if necessary. Drain on paper towels.

Hush Puppies

Makes 1 dozen

I was married in a small Methodist church on the little island of Ocracoke, North Carolina. After the wedding we all walked to the local inn and had a feast of freshly caught fried fish and hush puppies.

3/4 cup corn meal mix (see p. 310)   1 egg
1/3 cup self-rising soft-wheat flour   1/2 cup buttermilk
   (see p. 315)   Shortening
1 large onion, finely chopped

Mix all the ingredients together in a large bowl, except the shortening. Shape into 1-inch flat rounds or balls. Heat shortening in a frying pan or deep fryer to 375 degrees; there should be enough shortening to completely immerse the hush puppies. Add the rounds or balls and fry until crisp and brown. Drain on paper towels and serve hot.

Variation: Add 1 tablespoon freshly ground black pepper or a dash of Tabasco.

Food Processor Crisp Dinner Rolls

Makes 1 1/2 dozen

These rolls, soft on the inside, crisp on the outside, freeze well for reheating as you want them. What makes them crisp is the steam created by the boiling water on the rack below while they bake.

1 package active dry yeast   3-3 3/4 cups all-purpose soft-wheat
2 teaspoons sugar   or bread flour (see p. 314)
1 1/4 cups warm water   2 teaspoons salt
   (105-115 degrees)   1 tablespoon butter

☆   ☆   ☆

Glaze:
1 egg, beaten
1 tablespoon milk

Place the yeast and sugar in the warm water and let stand until dissolved. Put 3 cups of the flour in a food processor with the salt and butter. Turn on and off several times. With the machine running, add the yeast mixture slowly and beat the dough until it forms a ball in the processor. Add more flour if necessary to make a soft, slightly sticky dough. Knead by machine for 40–60 seconds.

Place in a greased bowl, and roll the dough around in the bowl to grease completely. Cover with plastic wrap and put in a warm place to rise for approximately 1 hour or until doubled in volume. Turn out onto a floured board. Pinch off a piece of dough about 2 1/2 inches in diameter and roll in your hands into a round ball. Continue making balls until all the dough is used. Place the rolls 2 inches apart on a greased baking sheet. Let rise again until double in size, about 40 minutes, uncovered.

Preheat the oven to 400 degrees. To make the glaze, beat together the egg and milk. Brush the rolls with the glaze and place on the middle rack of the oven. Place a pan of boiling water on the rack below the rolls and bake for 15 minutes. Remove from the pan and place on a rack to cool.

Pepper Rolls

Makes 2 dozen

These are especially fun for a holiday, with the colorful red and black peppers. If you want a more densely textured roll, use soft-wheat flour. For an airier texture, use bread flour.

Pepper Rolls, continued

2 packages active dry yeast
3 tablespoons sugar
1 cup warm milk (105–115 degrees)
2 eggs, beaten
1 large red bell pepper, roasted, peeled, and finely diced
3 tablespoons peanut oil

1 tablespoon thyme, preferably fresh
1 tablespoon coarsely ground black pepper
1½ teaspoons salt
3–5 cups all-purpose soft-wheat or bread flour (see p. 314)

Add the yeast and sugar to the milk and let stand until dissolved. Stir in the eggs, bell pepper, oil, thyme, black pepper, and salt. Add the flour 1 cup at a time and beat until a soft dough is formed. Turn out onto a lightly floured surface, adding more flour if necessary, and knead until the dough is smooth and bounces back when you touch it, but is not sticky. Roll the dough in a lightly oiled bowl, cover with plastic wrap, and let rise in a warm place until doubled in bulk, about 1 hour.

Pinch off a piece of dough about 2½ inches in diameter and roll in your hands into a round ball. Continue making balls until all the dough is used. Place the balls about 2 inches apart on oiled baking sheets. Let rise again, about 30 minutes. Preheat the oven to 375 degrees. Bake the rolls in the center of the oven until the tops are browned and the bottoms sound hollow when tapped with a finger, 15–20 minutes. Let cool on a rack.

Refrigerator Rolls

Makes 3 dozen

The dough lasts in the refrigerator, tightly wrapped, for 5–7 days, making it easy to have fresh rolls every night. You may use butter in place of the shortening for a richer dough.

2 packages active dry yeast
½ cup warm water (105–115 degrees)
2 cups milk
½ cup shortening, melted

½ cup sugar
1 tablespoon salt
6–8 cups soft-wheat or bread flour (see p. 314)

Stir the yeast into the warm water and let stand until it dissolves. Mix the milk, shortening, sugar, and salt in a bowl. Add the dissolved yeast and mix well. Stir in enough flour to make a soft dough. Turn out onto a lightly floured board and knead until it bounces back when touched with a finger. Place the dough in a buttered bowl, and turn to grease completely. Cover with plastic wrap and put in a warm place to rise until doubled in bulk, about 1 hour. Punch down and cover again with plastic wrap. Refrigerate, covered, until ready to bake.

Pinch off a piece of dough about 2 1/2 inches in diameter and roll in your hands into a round ball. Continue making balls until all the dough is used. Place the balls 2 inches apart on a greased baking sheet and let rise again until doubled. Preheat the oven to 400 degrees and bake in the oven 15 minutes or until done. Remove from the pan and place on a rack to cool.

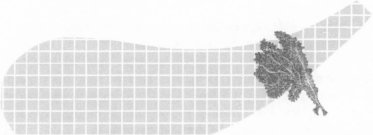

Pimento Muffins

Makes 15

These are especially decorative for a party when you are serving several varieties of muffins.

2 cups corn meal mix (see p. 310)
3/4 cup finely chopped celery
3/4 cup finely chopped onion
2 tablespoons sugar
3 tablespoons chopped pimento
    (see p. 319)
1 teaspoon thyme

Freshly ground black pepper
2 eggs, slightly beaten
1 cup milk
1/4 cup peanut oil
1 two-ounce jar sliced pimentos for
    decoration

Preheat the oven to 425 degrees. Brush 15 muffin cups with oil. Mix together the corn meal mix, celery, onion, sugar, pimento, thyme, and pepper. In another bowl combine the eggs, milk, and oil, and add to the dry ingredients, stirring only until mixed together. Fill the muffin cups two-thirds full. Decorate each muffin top with a cross made of two pimento strips. Bake 20 minutes or until golden.

Pecan Popovers

Makes 6

An interesting twist on an old favorite.

2 eggs
3/4 cup milk
1/4 cup water
1 cup all-purpose soft-wheat flour
    (see p. 314), sifted

1/2 teaspoon salt
1/3 cup chopped pecans

Preheat the oven to 450 degrees. Beat the eggs, milk, water, flour, and salt together in a mixer until smooth. Stir in the pecans.

Grease 6 custard or popover cups and fill each two-thirds full with the batter. Place on a baking sheet and bake for 35 minutes. Remove from the oven and prick with a fork or the tip of a knife at the base to let the steam escape and prevent the popovers from collapsing. Place back in the oven for 5 minutes with the door slightly ajar. The popovers should be dry and crisp on the outside, moist and tender on the inside.

Barbecue Buns

Makes 20 buns

There are two definitive ways to eat barbecue: either on sliced white loaf bread or on soft barbecue buns, with or without cracklings. No sesame seeds or whole wheat allowed! Period.

2 packages active dry yeast
2 cups warm water
    (105–115 degrees)

1/4 cup sugar
1 tablespoon salt
1/2 cup butter, at room temperature

6–8 cups all-purpose soft-wheat flour
   (see p. 314)

1/2 pound pork cracklings
   (see p. 313), optional

Dissolve the yeast in a bowl with the water, sugar, and salt. Add the butter. Stir in the flour, 1 cup at a time, to make a soft dough. Turn out onto a floured board and knead until smooth and elastic, 8–10 minutes, adding more flour if necessary. Place in a greased bowl, and turn in the bowl to grease all over. Cover with plastic wrap and let rise in a warm place until doubled in bulk, about 1 hour.

    Punch down and knead in the optional cracklings. Divide the dough in half. Roll each half into 10 three-inch balls. Place 3 inches apart on greased baking sheets and press each ball to flatten. Let rise again until doubled, about 30 minutes. Preheat the oven to 375 degrees. Bake until done, 15–20 minutes. Remove from the pan and place on a rack to cool.

White Loaf Bread

Makes 2 loaves

Homemade "loaf bread" is still a staple on the Southern table, although less so than biscuits and cornbread. I prefer using a soft-wheat flour for a denser-textured bread—it's easier to slice than a "bread flour" bread, and more flavorful.

2 packages active dry yeast
1/2 cup warm water
   (105–115 degrees)
1 1/2 tablespoons sugar
3/4 cup milk, scalded
1/2 cup butter, at room temperature

2 teaspoons salt
3 eggs, beaten to mix
6 1/2–9 cups all-purpose soft-wheat
   flour (see p. 314) or 5–7 cups
   bread flour
1/4 cup melted butter

Place the yeast in the warm water with the sugar and let stand until dissolved. In a large bowl pour the milk over the butter and salt and stir. Set aside to cool. Add the eggs, yeast, and 3 cups of the flour, beating with an electric mixer, by hand, or in a food processor until smooth. Add as much of the flour as necessary to make a soft dough that is not sticky. Turn out onto a floured board and knead until the dough bounces back when you touch it. Place in an oiled bowl, turning to coat all over. Cover with plastic wrap and a towel and let rise until doubled in bulk.

White Loaf Bread, continued

Punch down. Grease 2 9-by-5-inch loaf pans. Divide the dough in two, form into ovals approximately the length of the pans, and place one loaf in each pan. Let rise again until doubled.

Preheat the oven to 375 degrees. Brush the loaves with the melted butter. Bake 30 minutes, or until the bread comes away easily from the pans and sounds hollow when tapped on the bottom. Remove from the pans and let cool on a rack.

Sally Lunn with Herbs

Makes 1 loaf

This famous old recipe originated in England, but it's been around in the South for so long that Southerners think it's Southern. The legends vary. Some say Sally had a pastry shop in a place called Lilliput Alley in Bath, England; others that it is a corruption of the French *soleil lune,* or sun and moon cake. It was originally made with thick English cream, not butter, and was a cross between a bread and a dessert. The herb addition is a little something new and may be omitted to make the traditional recipe. To accompany a turkey meal, substitute chopped fresh sage for the basil and use half as much, since it is stronger than basil. This freezes well.

2 packages active dry yeast	10 tablespoons butter
1/2 cup sugar	3 eggs
1/4 cup warm water	3 1/2 cups bread flour
(105–115 degrees)	3 teaspoons salt
1 cup milk	1 cup chopped fresh basil

Place the yeast and sugar in the warm water and let stand until dissolved. In a separate saucepan, heat the milk and butter. Beat the eggs in an electric mixer until light. Add the yeast mixture. Sift together the flour and salt, and add to the beaten eggs, alternating with the milk mixture, beginning and ending with flour. Beat well with the mixer after each addition and at the end. The batter should be thick. Cover with plastic wrap and let rise in a warm place until doubled in volume, about 1 hour.

Butter a 10-inch tube or bundt pan. Sprinkle the dough with basil. Beat the dough down with the mixer on the lowest speed until the herbs are combined, about 30 seconds. Turn into the prepared pan. Cover with plastic wrap and allow to double again, about 30 minutes.

Preheat the oven to 350 degrees. Place the pan on a cookie sheet, then in the oven. Bake 30–40 minutes, until a toothpick comes out clean. Cool in the pan about 10 minutes, then turn out and cool on a wire rack.

Butter Braid Bread

Makes 3 loaves

This is a typical Southern yeast bread—sweet and light. Atlanta International Association of Cooking Professionals member and cook Roxanna Young made it a household favorite by making it so easily in the food processor. You may use either soft-wheat flour or bread flour, depending on your preference. It will take much more of the soft-wheat flour. The bread freezes well.

2 packages active dry yeast
1/2 cup warm water
   (105–115 degrees)
1/2 cup butter
1/3 cup sugar

2 teaspoons salt
3/4 cup scalded milk
3 eggs, beaten
5–8 cups all-purpose soft-wheat or
   bread flour (see p. 314)

☆   ☆   ☆

Glaze:
1/4 cup melted butter
1/4 cup poppy or sesame seeds

1 egg white mixed with
   1 tablespoon water

Stir the yeast and water together in a bowl and set aside to dissolve. Put the butter, sugar, and salt in a large bowl and add the hot scalded milk. Let cool to 115 degrees. Don't worry if the butter isn't melted. Add the eggs, yeast, and 3 cups of the flour. Beat until smooth by hand or portable mixer or in a food processor. Stir in more flour, 1 cup at a time, enough to make a soft dough that holds its shape and is not sticky.

Knead, adding more flour as necessary, on a lightly floured board for 8–10 minutes, or in a mixer or food processor until the dough is soft but not sticky and

Butter Braid Bread, continued

springs back when touched. Place in a greased bowl, and turn the dough to grease all over. Cover with plastic wrap and let rise about 1 hour, until doubled in bulk or until the indentations made by two fingers pushed into the edge of the dough remain.

To shape, punch down and divide the dough in thirds. Cut each third into 3 equal pieces and roll each piece into a strand about 18 inches long. Place 3 strands together on a board and pinch or press them together well at one end, tucking the pinched dough under, so the strands won't come apart. Braid the strands tightly, pinching and tucking the finished end under the loaf. Repeat for each loaf.

Place on greased baking sheets. Brush the loaves with the melted butter and sprinkle with poppy or sesame seeds. Let rise until doubled then brush with the egg-white-and-water mixture to glaze. Preheat the oven to 375 degrees. Place the loaves in the oven and bake 20 minutes, checking occasionally. When browned, remove one loaf and test for doneness by thumping the bottom to see if it sounds hollow, or running a trussing needle or skewer into the loaf to see if it comes out clean. Return to the oven until done if necessary, checking every 5–10 minutes. Remove from the pans and place on a rack to cool.

Easter Egg Bread

Serves 12

The fascinating thing about this bread is the use of uncooked eggs—they cook in the oven with the bread while it is baking.

1 recipe Butter Braid Bread
    (preceding recipe)
Grated rind of 2 lemons

12 whole eggs, uncooked and tinted
Vegetable oil for brushing

✿   ✿   ✿

Glaze:
1 egg, beaten

Follow the recipe for Butter Braid Bread, but add the lemon rind as you knead. Allow to double through the first rise. Punch down and make 2 large rings or individual rings as follows.

For large rings: Divide the dough into 4 pieces. Form each piece into a 36-inch strand. On a greased baking sheet, shape 2 of the strands into a very loosely twisted rope and form into a ring with 6 twists per ring. Each twist will be a "nest" for 1 Easter egg. Repeat this procedure with the other 2 strands of dough for the second ring. Brush oil in the twists of each ring. Arrange 6 tinted eggs in each ring, spacing them evenly.

For individual rings: Divide the dough into 12 pieces. On a greased baking sheet, twist each piece into a ring. Brush with oil and place a tinted egg in the center of each.

Cover and let rise until doubled in bulk. Brush evenly with the beaten egg. Preheat the oven to 375 degrees and bake 15 minutes for individual rings, 20 minutes for large rings, or until lightly browned. Remove to a rack to cool.

Flower Fennel Loaf

Makes 1 loaf

Fennel grows easily all over the South. A perennial, its seeds are so abundant and tasty they are a natural for yeast breads.

1 package active dry yeast
4 teaspoons sugar
1 cup warm water (105–115 degrees)
3 3/4 cups all-purpose soft-wheat
    or bread flour (see p. 314)

1 1/2 teaspoons salt
2 tablespoons soft butter
1/2 teaspoon fennel seed

✿   ✿   ✿

Glaze:
1 egg yolk
1 tablespoon milk

In a large bowl place the yeast and 1 teaspoon of the sugar in the warm water and let stand until dissolved. Stir in 3 cups of the flour, the remaining sugar, the salt, butter, and fennel seed. Turn out onto a floured board and knead, adding flour as necessary to make a soft but not sticky dough. Place the dough in a greased bowl, turning to coat all over. Cover with plastic wrap and put in a warm place to rise until doubled in bulk, about 1 hour.

Flower Fennel Loaf, continued

Punch down and shape into a smooth ball about 8 inches in diameter. Place on a greased baking sheet. Make a hole the size of a small can through the center of the dough. Oil a tube or can and place in the hole while the dough rises and bakes. Cut a circle 1/4 inch deep in the dough 1 inch from the can. With the tip of a sharp knife make slashes from the circle to the edge, scalloping the edges to form the petals of a flower. To make the glaze, lightly beat together the egg yolk and milk. Glaze the loaf with the egg wash and let rise until doubled in bulk with the can still in place.

Preheat the oven to 425 degrees. Place the loaf and can on the next to the lowest rack and remove the rack above it. Bake for 10 minutes, reduce the oven temperature to 375 degrees, and continue baking 20–25 minutes longer, covering with foil, if necessary to prevent overbrowning. When done, the loaf will be well browned and sound hollow when rapped on the bottom. Place on a rack to cool, twisting out the tube or can while warm.

SWEETS
and
PASTRY

Rapid Puff Pastry

Makes 1 1/2 pounds

Using a mixer makes this easy—but it can be done by hand as well. Don't let it fool you—it's deceptively messy to start but finishes up perfectly. The two kinds of flour help give you a tender product with a substantial rise.

1 pound bread flour (weigh, don't
    measure by cups)
1/2 pound all-purpose soft-wheat flour
    or cake flour (see p. 314)

1 teaspoon salt
1 1/2 pounds unsalted butter, cold
1 1/2 cups ice water
Flour for rolling (either kind)

Sift the flours and salt together into a large bowl. Cut the butter into 1/2-inch pieces and add to the flour. Combine the two with a knife or an electric mixer until the flour coats the butter and the butter pieces are the size of large lima or fava beans. (Don't cut in too much; if the butter pieces are small, the pastry won't rise.) Add ice water quickly and stir just until the mixture holds together.

Place some flour in a shaker or sifter, lightly dust your surface with it, and turn the dough, which will have a rough texture, out onto it. Dust the dough and a rolling pin with flour. Brush off any excess. Push or roll the dough out into a rectangle 18 inches long and about 10 inches wide. Pick up the dough to be sure it isn't sticking. Dust the surface with flour and place the dough back on it. Don't worry if the dough is crumbly. Fold over in thirds as you would a business

Rapid Puff Pastry, continued

letter—first fold the bottom up to one-third the way from the top, then fold the top down to cover it. Turn the dough so that the long open side is to your right. Sprinkle the work surface again with flour. Then roll, fold, and turn as directed above three more times. Any time the dough becomes too warm to handle, wrap in plastic wrap and refrigerate. After the fourth fold and turn, wrap in plastic wrap and let rest in the refrigerator at least 1 hour, or up to 2 days, or freeze.

Remove the dough from the refrigerator and let sit at room temperature until it is easy to roll, but not soft. Give the dough two more rolls, folds, and turns, then divide into thirds. Take one third and roll out 1/4 inch thick, while refrigerating the other two parts.

Preheat the oven to 400 degrees.

To test the thickness of the dough, cut two 3-inch squares from the rolled-out dough. Roll one square into a larger, thinner piece, 1/8 inch thick. Chill if necessary. Place both pieces on a cookie sheet in the oven. After 20 minutes turn the oven down to 350 degrees. Remove when the pastry is lightly browned. Check the height of the pastry. If the 1/8-inch square has risen 2 or more inches high, then roll the rest of the dough 1/8 inch thick for the desired shapes. If this square has risen less than 2 inches high, roll the rest of the dough 1/4 inch thick before cutting into squares or use for jalousies (see p. 242) and decorative pieces. Puff pastry may be shaped and refrigerated or frozen, or frozen before and after rolling, then defrosted overnight. Always try to place in the oven when very cold, preferably from the freezer. Bake the squares as you did the test pieces.

LuLen's Beginners' Pie Crust

Makes 1 9-inch pie shell

LuLen was a beginning cook when she moved in with me at nineteen. She made a perfect pie crust using this recipe and it was the first crust she had ever made, so I've decided it's the perfect beginners' pie crust. The filling that inspired her to try her first pie, with no help from me, was that for LuLen's Grated Apple Pie (following recipe).

1 1/4 cups all-purpose soft-wheat flour   1/2 cup shortening
   (see p. 314)   3–6 tablespoons ice water
1/2 teaspoon salt

Mix the flour and salt together in a bowl. Cut in the shortening with a pastry blender or fork until the mixture resembles corn meal. Add the ice water, a little at a time, tossing the mixture with the pastry blender or fork until it is moist and holds together. Gather into a ball and flatten. Cover and let rest a few minutes.

Flour a board or wax paper, and using a floured or stockinged rolling pin roll the pastry out 1/8 inch thick or less and at least 1 1/2–2 inches larger than your pan. Fold in quarters. Place the pastry in a 9-inch pie pan and unfold. Trim the pastry 1 inch larger than the pie pan and decorate by folding the overhanging pastry under itself, then either pressing the tines of a fork around the edge to form a pattern, or fluting, using your two thumbs to pinch the dough all around the edge so that the dough stands up where it has been pinched. Place in the freezer or chill in the refrigerator for 30 minutes before baking.

To prebake: Preheat the oven to 425 degrees. Crumple a piece of wax paper, then spread it out to the edges of the pan. To make a weight, fill the paper with raw rice or dried peas. Bake for 20 minutes. Carefully remove the paper and rice or peas. (The rice or peas may be used again the next time you prebake a pie crust.) Fill the crust with a filling and bake according to filling directions. If the filling requires no cooking, bake the pie shell 10 minutes more.

LuLen's Grated Apple Pie

Serves 6–8

This is very different from the usual apple pie. It's especially good with ice cream.

2/3 cup sugar
1 tablespoon all-purpose flour
2 teaspoons ground cinnamon
Salt
4 1/2 cups tart apples, peeled, cored, and grated coarse

1 egg, beaten
1/3 cup butter, melted
1 unbaked 9-inch pie shell (preceding recipe)
1 cup chopped pecans

Preheat the oven to 400 degrees. Mix together the sugar, flour, cinnamon, salt, and apples, then combine with the egg and butter. Spoon into the pie shell and sprinkle with pecans. Place on the top or upper middle rack of the oven, and bake for 10 minutes, then lower heat to 350 degrees, and bake for 45–50 minutes more.

Lemon Chess Pie

Serves 6–8

Lemon chess pie is a traditional Southern pie. This recipe of Atlanta International Association of Cooking Professionals member Peggy Foreman's has a slightly different twist with the use of corn meal.

Crust:

1 cup soft-wheat flour (see p. 314)	1/3 cup butter
Salt	3–4 tablespoons ice water

✿   ✿   ✿

Filling:

2 cups sugar	4 tablespoons melted butter
1 tablespoon flour	1/4 cup milk
1 tablespoon corn meal	Juice and zest of 1 lemon
3 eggs	1 teaspoon vanilla

To make the crust, mix the flour and salt together in a bowl. Cut in the butter with a pastry blender or fork until the mixture resembles corn meal. Add the water, a little at a time, tossing with a pastry blender or fork until the mixture is moist and holds together easily. Cover with a damp cloth or plastic wrap and let rest a few minutes. Flour a board or wax paper and roll out the pastry 1/8 inch thick or less, using a floured rolling pin. Place the pastry in a 9-inch pie pan. Trim the pastry 1 inch larger than the pie pan and make a decorative border by fluting the edge or folding under then pressing with the tines of a fork to create a pattern. Cover and place in the freezer or chill for 30 minutes before baking.

Preheat the oven to 425 degrees. Crumple a piece of wax paper, then spread it out to the edges of the pan. Make a weight by filling the paper with raw rice or dried peas. Bake for 20 minutes. Carefully remove the paper with the rice or peas. Discard the paper, but save the rice or peas for the next time you prebake a pie crust.

To make the filling, toss the sugar together with the flour and corn meal. Add the eggs, butter, milk, lemon juice and zest, and vanilla, and mix well. Preheat the oven to 350 degrees. Pour into the prebaked pie crust. Bake 30 minutes or until firm. If the crust browns too quickly, just cover with foil.

Blueberry and Lemon Cheese Pie

Serves 6–8

Blueberries and lemon bring out the best in each other. This pie is so delicious you'll want to use a spoon to savor every bite.

1 9-inch prebaked pie crust (p. 232)   1 recipe Lemon Cheese (p. 266)
1 pint blueberries, fresh or frozen   2 cups heavy cream, whipped

Fill the prebaked pie crust with the blueberries but save some to sprinkle on top. Mix the Lemon Cheese with the whipped cream and top the blueberries with the mixture. Garnish with the reserved berries. Serve within a few hours, or freeze.

If you use fresh berries, you can fold them into the Lemon Cheese and whipped cream mixture instead of spreading them on the bottom of the pie crust. This cannot be done with frozen berries — they will bleed into the mixture.

Peaches and Cream Pie

Serves 6–8

This is just what it sounds like — absolutely heavenly.

3/4 cup sugar   2 cups sliced fresh or frozen peaches,
1/2 cup all-purpose flour   defrosted
1 unbaked 9-inch pie shell (p. 232)   1 cup heavy cream

Preheat the oven to 350 degrees. Mix the sugar and flour together and sprinkle one-third of the mixture into the pie shell. Add the peaches and sprinkle with the remaining sugar-flour mixture. Pour the heavy cream over the top. Move the peaches around a bit with a fork so that the cream completely covers the peaches. Bake for 45 minutes. Serve hot or cool on a rack.

Peach-Pecan Pie

Serves 6-8

We tried and tried to make a peach-pecan pie better than this one adapted from *Grace Hartley's Southern Cookbook,* but there was really no sense in trying to top the best.

Peach filling:

1/4 cup soft butter	1/4 teaspoon salt
1/2 cup sugar	3 eggs
2 tablespoons flour	1 1/2 cups diced peaches
1/2 cup corn syrup	

✿   ✿   ✿

Nut crumb topping:

1/4 cup flour	3 tablespoons soft butter
1/3 cup brown sugar	1/2 cup pecans, coarsely chopped

✿   ✿   ✿

1 unbaked 9-inch pie shell (p. 232)

Preheat the oven to 375 degrees.

For the peach filling: With an electric mixer, whisk, or wooden spoon beat together the butter, sugar, and flour until light and fluffy. Add the corn syrup and salt and mix well. Beat in the eggs one at a time and add the peaches. Pour the filling into the pie shell and sprinkle with the topping (see below). Place in the oven and bake for 35 minutes or until firm in the center.

To make the topping: Combine the flour and sugar. Work in the butter with a fork until crumbly and mix in the pecans.

Buttermilk Pecan Pie

Serves 6-8

This is a very unusual twist on an old classic, buttermilk pie.

4 eggs	1 tablespoon flour
1 1/2 cups sugar	3/4 cup buttermilk

1/2 cup melted butter
1/2 teaspoon vanilla
Dash of salt

1 cup pecan halves
1 9-inch partially baked pie crust
(p. 232)

Preheat the oven to 300 degrees. Beat the eggs and sugar until mixed. Blend in the flour, buttermilk, butter, vanilla, and salt, and beat briefly until smooth. Add the pecans and pour into the pie shell. Bake until done, about 30 minutes. Serve hot or cool on a rack.

Ron's Pecan Fudge Pie

Serves 6–8

Ron was a regular listener of my radio show. He called frequently with ideas and we became close airwave friends. Because he is blind his recipes were always carefully thought out and they always worked. He made this pie with a pie crust, but I like it with a chocolate crumb crust — any chocolate wafers, like plain Oreos without the cream inside, may be used.

Crust:
1 1/2 cups chocolate wafer (cookie)
    crumbs, made by chopping in
    food processor
1/2 cup butter, at room temperature

✿　✿　✿

Filling:
12-ounce package semisweet
    chocolate chips (the real ones,
    not the chocolate-flavored chips)
4 eggs
1 cup light corn syrup

1 teaspoon vanilla
1/2 teaspoon salt
2 tablespoons butter, melted
1 1/2 cups pecan pieces, chopped

Preheat the oven to 350 degrees. To make the crust, mix the chocolate wafer crumbs and butter together with a fork or food processor until the crumbs are moistened, and press into a deep 9-inch pie dish.

For the filling: Melt the chocolate over low heat. In a bowl beat together the

Pecan Fudge Pie, continued

eggs, corn syrup, vanilla, salt, and melted butter. Rapidly stir in the melted chocolate, scraping the sides of the bowl. Fold in the nuts and pour into the pie shell. Bake 50–60 minutes. Serve warm, or cool on a rack for 1 hour, then for 3 more hours in the refrigerator, if you can wait!

Chocolate Pecan Pie

Serves 6–8

This is Ron's pecan pie with a few modifications made by Kate. My chocoholic friends are always finding ways to use chocolate in the dessert recipes we develop. This is prettiest served from a plate that has a scalloped edge.

Crust:

1 1/4 cups all-purpose soft-wheat flour (see p. 314)
1/4 teaspoon salt

1/2 cup butter
5–7 tablespoons ice water

✿   ✿   ✿

Filling:

3 eggs
1/2 cup light corn syrup
1/4 teaspoon salt
1 teaspoon vanilla

2 tablespoons butter
1 1/2 cups chocolate chips
1 cup chopped pecans

✿   ✿   ✿

Topping:

1/2 cup chopped pecans
1/2 cup chocolate chips

To make the crust, sift the flour together with the salt. Cut the butter in until it is thoroughly coated and the pieces are no larger than lima beans. Add enough water to make a dough that holds together easily. Shape into a ball, flatten to a round, and chill, wrapped in plastic, 30 minutes, or more if possible. Remove from the refrigerator to a floured surface. Roll out to fit into a 9-inch pie plate with a scalloped edge. Preheat the oven to 350 degrees.

To make the filling: Place the eggs, syrup, salt, and vanilla in a bowl, food processor, or mixer, and blend well. Melt the butter and chocolate chips over low heat and add to the filling, stirring just to mix. Fold in the pecans and pour into the pie shell. Top with chopped pecans and chocolate chips. Bake until done, about 30 minutes. Serve hot, or cool on a rack and then refrigerate until it hardens and serve cold.

Susan Rice's Chocolate Pecan Pie

Serves 6–8

A great, simple company pie.

3 eggs, slightly beaten
1 1/2 cups sugar
6 tablespoons butter, melted
    and cooled
3 teaspoons dark rum

3/4 cup flour
1 1/2 cups chocolate chips
1 3/4 cups pecans,
    chopped
1 unbaked 9-inch pie shell (p. 232)

✿ ✿ ✿

To serve:
1 cup heavy cream, whipped and
    flavored with 2 tablespoons sugar

Preheat the oven to 350 degrees. Mix well the eggs, sugar, butter, and rum in a food processor or by hand with a wooden spoon. Add the flour, chocolate chips, and pecans, and combine thoroughly. Pour into the pie shell. Place in the lower third of your oven and bake for 1 hour or a little longer, until a toothpick inserted in the center comes out clean. Serve immediately. If making ahead, bake, cool on a rack, and when ready to serve reheat in the oven for 10 minutes. Serve hot topped with whipped cream.

Brandy Pecan Pie

Serves 6–8

We never give up on pecan pie, and I think this new twist is a bit more upbeat than the traditional.

Brandy Pecan Pie, continued

1/4 cup butter
1 cup sugar
3 large eggs
1 cup light corn syrup

1/4 cup brandy
1 cup whole pecans
1 unbaked 9-inch pie shell
(p. 232)

Preheat the oven to 350 degrees. Beat the butter with an electric mixer to soften. Gradually add the sugar, then the eggs, one at a time, until well blended. Beat in the corn syrup and brandy until well blended. Pour into the pie shell and sprinkle with the pecans. Bake 45–50 minutes or until set around the edges. The filling will be puffy. Cool on a wire rack.

Miss Mary's Date and Soda Cracker Pie

Serves 6–8

This is a recipe that dates back in Georgia history. My friend Victoria (Vicky) Mooney pulled out her grandmother's handwritten receipt book to locate this recipe, and we've adapted it to today. It's unusual and you'll love it.

12 dates, chopped
1/2 cup finely chopped pecans
12 soda crackers, rolled into
    fine crumbs
1/2 teaspoon baking powder

3/4 cup sugar
3 egg whites
1 teaspoon almond extract
1 cup heavy cream, whipped

Preheat the oven to 325 degrees. Mix the dates, nuts, crackers, baking powder, and sugar. Beat the egg whites until stiff. Add the almond extract to the egg whites and fold into the date mixture. Spread into a greased 9-inch pie plate and bake 40–45 minutes. Cool and serve with whipped cream.

Fried Pies

Makes 6 pies

These little pies are a favorite dessert in my home. From my book *Cooking of the South.*

Fruit mixture:

1 seven-ounce package dried peaches or apples	1 cup water
	1/2 cup sugar

✿ ✿ ✿

Pastry:

2 cups self-rising soft-wheat flour (see p. 315)	1/4 cup shortening
	3/4 cup milk

✿ ✿ ✿

Shortening for frying

Put the fruit and water in a medium-size heavy saucepan and let stand for 1 hour or overnight. Cook over low heat until thick enough to cling to a spoon, about 45 minutes. Stir in the sugar.

To make the pastry: Place the flour in a small bowl. Cut in the shortening, using a pastry cutter or fork, until the mixture resembles coarse meal. Stir in the milk to make a soft but not sticky dough that will roll out without sticking. Add more flour to the dough if necessary. Put enough shortening in a heavy skillet to reach a depth of 1/8 inch when melted, then heat to medium hot. While the shortening is heating, prepare the pies.

Pinch off a piece of dough the size of a small egg. Place it on a well-floured surface and roll into a 5-inch circle. Place about 2 tablespoons of the fruit mixture on the bottom half of the pastry round, about 1/2 inch away from the edge. Fold the top half of the pastry over the fruit, forming a half circle. Trim to within 1/4 inch of the filling. Press the edges together with the tines of a fork, and prick the top of the pastry in several places. Fry on both sides until golden brown, adding more shortening as needed. Repeat until you've used all the pastry and fruit mixture. Serve hot.

Apple Pan Dowdy

Serves 8

"Shoo fly pie and apple pan dowdy make your eyes light up, your tummy say howdy . . . " Just what *is* apple pan dowdy? Part of a song, a tantalizing memory of days gone by? Something just plain good? Actually, a dowdy was an apple pie with a top crust only. The crust was broken into the applesauce, making it "dowdy," or messy. Once you have made your applesauce, you now have something spectacular to go with it. Try this. You'll write a song about it.

1 recipe applesauce (p. 266)
8 rounds white bread, cut to fit
    small (3-inch) ramekins or
    heatproof casseroles
8–12 tablespoons butter

Make the applesauce and distribute among 8 ramekins; set aside. Sauté the bread in the butter in a heavy frying pan until lightly browned. Place on top of the ramekins. Refrigerate or keep cool until 15 minutes before ready to serve. Preheat the oven to 350 degrees. Place the ramekins in the oven and heat through, about 15 minutes.

Jalousie with Peach Butter

Serves 8

A jalousie is a louvered blind. It keeps the sun out and the air circulating. You see them all over the South, but particularly in New Orleans and Mississippi. This pastry is made to look like one of those blinds. You might like to try filling the jalousie with Peach or Apricot and Pineapple Filling (p. 268) or with Lemon Cheese (p. 266).

1/3 recipe Rapid Puff Pastry (p. 231)

1/2 cup Peach Butter (p. 266)

Egg glaze of 1 egg and 1 tablespoon water

Water

Roll the puff pastry out into a rectangle 1/8 inch thick. Cut in half horizontally. Place one half on a baking sheet, and wrap the other half in plastic wrap and refrigerate or freeze until needed. Spread the Peach Butter over the dough, stopping 1 inch away from the edges. Fold the edges over onto the Peach Butter, and brush the edges with water.

Take the second half of the dough out of the refrigerator and unwrap. Make horizontal slices 1/4 inch apart through the dough, place over the dough covered with Peach Butter, and tuck the edges under. Brush with the egg glaze, taking care not to drip any on the baking sheet. Cover and refrigerate at least an hour, or freeze. When ready to bake, preheat the oven to 400 degrees. Place the pastry on the pan in the oven and bake 20 minutes; reduce the heat to 350 and bake until golden brown and flaky. Remove, cool on a rack, and serve.

Peach Cobbler

Serves 6–8

This is it—the best peach dessert there is. If peaches are out of season, use the very best brand of frozen peaches and cut back on the amount of sugar.

1/2 cup butter

1 cup all-purpose soft-wheat flour (see p. 314)

1 1/2 teaspoons baking powder

1/2 teaspoon salt

1 cup milk

1 cup sugar

2 cups peaches, peeled and sliced, juices reserved

Preheat the oven to 350 degrees. Put the butter in a 9-by-13-inch ovenproof serving dish and place in the oven to melt. Mix together the flour, baking powder, and salt in a bowl and stir in the milk and sugar to make a batter. Remove the hot dish with the melted butter from the oven and pour in the batter. Spoon the peaches and then the juices evenly over the batter. Place the dish back in the oven and bake until the batter is browned and has risen up and around the fruit, about 30 minutes.

Apple Cobbler

Serves 8

Cobblers are a Southerner's true love. The cooking procedure may seem unorthodox, but the self-rising flour is the trick—the baking powder in it causes the batter to rise up and around the fruit. You can, of course, make your own self-rising flour (see p. 315).

1/2 cup butter
1 cup self-rising soft-wheat flour
    (see p. 315)
1 1/2 cups milk
1 cup sugar

2 cups applesauce, preferably
    homemade (p. 266)
1 large cooking apple, peeled, cored,
    and sliced

Preheat the oven to 350 degrees. Place the butter in a 9-by-13-inch pan. Place the pan in the oven to melt the butter. To make the batter, stir together the flour, milk, and sugar in a medium-size bowl. Remove the pan of melted butter from the oven and pour the batter into the pan. Spoon the applesauce evenly over the batter and cover with apple slices. Bake until the batter has risen up around the fruit and is browned, crispy, and buttery around the edges, 30–35 minutes. The cobbler may be served plain, with whipped cream, or with rum raisin ice cream.

Liberty Cobbler

Serves 6–8

1 1/4 cups sugar
1/2 cup water
2 cups strawberries, sliced
1/2 cup butter
1 cup all-purpose soft-wheat flour
    (see p. 314)

1 1/2 teaspoons baking powder
1/2 teaspoon salt
1 cup milk

Blueberry sauce:

¼ cup water
¼ cup sugar
2 pints blueberries

1 tablespoon lemon juice
Heavy cream, whipped

Mix ¼ cup of the sugar and the water and pour over the strawberries. Set aside.

Preheat the oven to 350 degrees. Put the butter in a 9-by-13-inch ovenproof serving dish and place in the oven to melt. Mix together the flour, baking powder, and salt in a bowl, and stir in the milk and remaining sugar to make a batter. Remove the hot dish with the melted butter from the oven and pour in the batter. Spoon the strawberries evenly over the batter. Place the dish back in the oven and bake until the batter is browned and has risen up and around the fruit, about 30 minutes.

For the sauce, combine the water and sugar in a saucepan. Heat to boiling. Meanwhile, place 1 pint of the blueberries in a food processor or blender. Process, or blend, turning the machine on and off about 4 times, until the berries are coarsely puréed. Add the purée to the sugar syrup with the lemon juice, and bring back to the boil. Cook about 2 minutes more. Reserving a few whole blueberries for the topping, add the remaining whole berries to the puréed mixture. Serve the sauce over the cobbler and top with whipped cream and reserved berries.

Pecan Tassies

Makes 30

Tassies are tiny tarts frequently served at weddings and special occasions which may require a finger-food dessert treat. They freeze easily. Adapted from my *Cooking of the South.*

Pastry dough:

8 tablespoons butter, softened
1 three-ounce package cream cheese,
   softened

1 cup sifted all-purpose soft-wheat
   flour (see p. 314)

✿ ✿ ✿

Filling:

⅔ cup chopped pecans
1 egg
¾ cup brown sugar

1 tablespoon butter, softened
1 teaspoon vanilla
⅛ teaspoon salt

Pecan Tassies, continued

Preheat the oven to 325 degrees. Mix together the butter and cream cheese in a small bowl or food processor. Add the flour and blend thoroughly. Divide and shape into 30 balls. Wrap all 30 balls together in plastic wrap and chill slightly. Place each ball in a tiny ungreased fluted tart pan or muffin cup. Line the pans by pressing the dough with your fingertips against the bottoms and sides.

For the filling, place half the pecans in the dough-lined pan. Beat together the egg, sugar, butter, vanilla, and salt until all lumps are gone. Pour the egg mixture onto the pecan-topped dough. Dot with the remaining pecans. Bake for 25 minutes or until the filling is set. Cool 5 minutes on a rack and remove from the pans before they are cool, as the caramel will set.

Diana Everett's Odd Almond Tart

Serves 6–8

Diana Everett is the corporate chef for a top Atlanta firm, as well as a Delta flight attendant. She likes to dip into other cuisines and add her own interesting twists to the recipes. She adapted this from a recipe taught to her by Marcella Hazan when she attended Mrs. Hazan's cooking classes in Florence, Italy. The pasta is added uncooked, a very fascinating thing to me—it cooks in the pie!

Crust:

1 egg
1/4 cup confectioners' sugar
3/4 cup soft-wheat all-purpose flour
  (see p. 314)

7 tablespoons butter
Salt

☆ ☆ ☆

Filling:

1 cup ground almonds or pecans
3/4 cup sugar
1/2 cup chopped candied fruit

1 tablespoon cocoa
Grated rind of 1 lemon, without the
  bitter white part

☆ ☆ ☆

1/2 pound vermicelli,
  preferably fresh

1/2 cup butter
1 jigger bourbon (1 1/2 ounces)

To make the crust, combine all the ingredients in a food processor or by hand until the dough holds together and can be formed into a ball. Roll or pat out into a 9-inch pie pan. To make the filling, mix together the almonds or pecans, sugar, fruit, cocoa, and rind. Preheat the oven to 375 degrees.

Spread a layer of the filling in the unbaked crust, then add a layer of pasta (if you use dried pasta, break it up to fit into the pan). Dot with 3 tablespoons of the butter. Then continue layering until you've used all the filling, vermicelli, and butter. Finish with a layer of pasta and butter. Place in the oven and bake, uncovered, 10 minutes. Cover with foil and bake 30 minutes longer. When done, remove from the oven and sprinkle on the bourbon. Serve hot or cold. Will last in the refrigerator a long time—at least a week, maybe more.

Pecan Tart with Caramel Cream Sauce

Serves 6–8

Those with a sweet tooth will love the Caramel Cream Sauce with this! Lemon juice makes a more tender crust.

Crust:

1 cup all-purpose soft-wheat flour (see p. 314)	1/3 cup butter
	1 egg yolk
Dash of salt	1 tablespoon lemon juice
Dash of sugar	1–2 tablespoons water

✿   ✿   ✿

Filling:

3/4 cup light corn syrup	3 large eggs
1/2 cup sugar	2 tablespoons butter
1/4 cup light brown sugar	1 cup pecan halves

✿   ✿   ✿

To serve:
Caramel Cream Sauce (p. 269)

To make the pie crust, sift the flour with the salt and sugar. Cut in the butter with a fork, mixer, or food processor until the flour coats the butter and the butter pieces are the size of large lima beans. Add the egg yolk, lemon juice, and enough water

Pecan Tart, continued

to make a soft dough that holds together. Chill 30 minutes. Roll out on a floured surface into a 12-inch circle, then place the dough in a 9-inch flan ring or pie pan already on a baking sheet. Decorate by fluting the edge or by folding it under, then pressing with the tines of a fork to form a decorative pattern. Place a piece of crumpled wax paper or foil on top of the pie crust. Spread it out to the edges of the pan, then fill with rice, dried peas, or pastry weights. Chill again for 30 minutes.

Preheat the oven to 400 degrees. Place the flan ring or pie pan (on the baking sheet) in the oven and bake for 20 minutes. Remove from the oven and cool on a rack, removing the weights and paper or foil. Reduce the oven temperature to 375 degrees.

To make the filling, mix the corn syrup, sugars, and eggs together in a mixing bowl. Brown the butter and pour into the syrup mixture, beating rapidly. Pour into the prebaked pie shell and arrange the pecans on top. Place in the oven and bake 30 minutes or until firm and golden.

Serve covered with Caramel Cream Sauce.

Pecan Roll with Chocolate Sauce

Serves 6

This flawless soufflé becomes an exciting roll—easily made several days ahead, filled or unfilled, and refrigerated or frozen.

6 egg yolks
3/4 cup sugar
6 egg whites
1 1/2 cups finely chopped pecans
1 tablespoon baking powder

1/3 cup confectioners' sugar
2 cups heavy cream, whipped and
**   sweetened with 1/4 cup**
**   granulated sugar**
1 recipe Chocolate Sauce (p. 270)

Preheat the oven to 350 degrees. Oil a 10 1/2-by-15 1/2-inch jelly roll pan. Place wax paper in the pan, slightly extending over the edges. Oil the paper. Whisk the egg yolks and sugar until they are thick and light. In a clean bowl, beat the egg whites until they form stiff peaks. Add the chopped pecans and baking powder to the egg yolk mixture. With a metal spoon, fold a large spoonful of the egg whites into the pecan-egg mixture, then fold this mixture into the egg whites.

Spread over the prepared pan. Bake for 20 minutes, until puffy and light. The soufflé is done when it springs back when touched. Remove from the oven and cool slightly. Cover with a slightly damp light tea towel. This will keep the top soft. It may be refrigerated for several days in the pan.

To serve, sprinkle a sheet of wax paper with confectioners' sugar. Turn the souffle out onto the paper. Peel off the wax paper that has adhered to the soufflé. Spread the soufflé with the sweetened whipped cream and roll as you would a jelly roll. Make a final roll from the wax paper onto the platter. Cover with Chocolate Sauce.

Old-Fashioned Gingerbread with Peach Sauce

Serves 6

This is good when baked in the oven, but you can choose to do it in the fireplace on a cold winter's night. It's incredibly easy and a delightful way to end an evening with friends. Just imagine the warm glow of a fire combined with the sweet smell of baking gingerbread — and a gathering of good friends.

1/2 cup sugar
1/2 cup butter
1 egg
1 cup molasses
2 cups self-rising soft-wheat flour
  (see p. 315)
2 teaspoons ginger

1/2 teaspoon cinnamon
1/2 cup sour milk, made by adding
  1/2 teaspoon lemon juice to
  1/2 cup milk
1/2 cup brandy or apple juice
1 teaspoon brandy flavoring
1 recipe Peach Sauce (p. 268)

Preheat the oven to 350 degrees. Beat the sugar and butter together until light. Add the egg and molasses and blend well. Mix the dry ingredients together. In a separate bowl, combine the milk, brandy or juice, and flavoring. Add the dry ingredients to the batter, alternating with the milk mixture. Beat until smooth. Pour into a well-greased 9-by-13-inch pan and bake for 30 minutes.

To cook in the fireplace, use a 12-inch iron spider pot or Dutch oven with a cover. Combine the ingredients as directed above. Pour into the well-greased pot or

Gingerbread with Peach Sauce, continued

Dutch oven, cover, and place on a thin layer of coals. Add another layer of coals on top of the pot. Cook about 30 minutes or until done. Serve topped with Peach Sauce.

Southern Belle Cake

Serves 14-16

This cake is just as it sounds—light and enticing. It does not keep very long in the heat. Adapted from a recipe in Martha Meade's *Recipes from the Old South*.

2$1/4$ cups self-rising soft-wheat flour (see p. 315)
$1/2$ teaspoon mace
1 cup butter, at room temperature

1$1/2$ cups sugar
4 eggs, separated
$2/3$ cup orange juice
Grated rind of 1 orange, with no white

✿   ✿   ✿

Filling:
1 cup sugar
4 tablespoons flour
Pinch of salt
$1/2$ cup fresh orange juice

1 teaspoon lemon juice
4 tablespoons grated orange rind
2 eggs, slightly beaten
2 tablespoons butter

✿   ✿   ✿

Icing:
1$1/2$ cups heavy cream, whipped
$1/2$ teaspoon mace

Preheat the oven to 350 degrees. Grease and flour the bottoms and sides of three 9-inch cake pans. Cut out circles of wax paper and fit into each pan. Grease and flour the paper.

Sift the flour into a bowl with the mace. In a separate bowl beat the butter and sugar until light. Add the egg yolks, one at a time, beating after each addition. Add the flour, orange juice, and orange rind, and continue beating until smooth. Beat the egg whites until stiff but not dry, and fold into the batter. Pour the batter into the pans and bake 30 minutes or until a toothpick inserted in the middle comes out clean. Cool in the pans 5 minutes, then invert the cakes onto a rack and peel off the wax paper.

To make the filling, sift the sugar, flour, and salt together. Add the orange and lemon juices and the orange rind, and mix well. Add the eggs and butter and place in a heavy non-aluminum pan over low heat. Stir until thick and smooth, about 10 minutes. To finish, spread the orange filling between the layers and on top of the cake. Cover the sides with the whipped cream mixed with mace. Refrigerate the cake if you are not serving it immediately.

Mississippi Mud Cake

Serves 12–16

This wonderful dark cake is so named because it is cracked and dry-looking, like Mississippi mud in the hot, dry summer.

2 cups sugar	1/2 cup cocoa
1 cup butter	1/4 teaspoon salt
4 eggs	1 tablespoon vanilla
1 1/2 cups flour	1 cup pecans, chopped

✿　✿　✿

Icing:

1 pound confectioners' sugar	1 teaspoon vanilla
1/3 cup cocoa	1 cup pecans, chopped
1 cup butter, melted	2 tablespoons milk

To make the cake: Preheat the oven to 350 degrees and butter a 9-by-13-inch pan. Cut out a piece of wax paper to fit the bottom of the pan. Butter it. With an electric mixer, beat the sugar and butter together until light and fluffy. Add the eggs, one at a time, beating after each addition. Add the flour, cocoa, salt, vanilla, and nuts, and beat again. Turn the batter into the pan and bake for 25–30 minutes. Remove from the oven and cool on a rack. When cool, remove from pan and peel off the wax paper.

To make the icing: Sift the sugar and cocoa together. Beat in the melted butter, vanilla, pecans, and milk. When smooth, spread the icing over the cake.

Coconut Cake

Serves 10–12

This recipe of Kate's makes the moistest coconut cake I've ever tasted. Of course, I'm partial to her cooking, since she's worked for me for twelve years.

2½ cups all-purpose soft-wheat flour
   (see p. 314)
1 tablespoon baking powder
1 teaspoon salt
1½ cups sugar

¾ cup soft butter
2 large eggs
1 teaspoon vanilla
1 cup milk

✿ ✿ ✿

Icing:
3 egg whites, stiffly beaten
2 cups sugar
Meat of 1 fresh coconut, ground
   or grated

1 cup coconut milk (if needed, add
   water to make 1 cup) or
18 ounces packaged coconut plus
   ¼ cup milk and ¾ cup water

To make the cake: Preheat the oven to 350 degrees. Grease two 9-inch cake pans and dust with flour. Place circles of wax paper in the bottoms of the pans and grease and flour them.

Sift the flour, baking powder, and salt together. In a separate bowl, cream the sugar and butter, then add the eggs and vanilla and beat well. Add the dry ingredients and milk alternately, starting and ending with the dry ingredients, and beat until smooth. Pour the batter into the pans and bake 20–25 minutes. Cool on a rack, remove from the pans, and peel off the wax paper.

To make the icing: Place the beaten egg whites in a saucepan, and add sugar, coconut, and coconut milk. Over medium heat bring the mixture to a full boil, and boil 4–5 minutes. Remove from the heat, and spread on the cake while both the cake and icing are still warm.

Lane Cake

Serves 16

This is definitely a Southern cake, named after a Mrs. Lane from Alabama. It is very popular at holidays, celebrations, and church suppers.

For the batter:

3¼ cups all-purpose soft-wheat flour (see p. 314)
4½ teaspoons baking powder
1½ teaspoons salt
2¼ cups sugar

1¼ cups butter
2 teaspoons vanilla
1½ cups milk
8 egg whites

✿   ✿   ✿

Filling:

½ cup butter
1 cup sugar
⅓ cup orange juice or white grape juice
⅓ cup water
9 egg yolks, slightly beaten

1 cup raisins, finely chopped
¾ cup chopped pecans
½ cup drained and chopped canned or fresh pitted Bing cherries
½ cup flaked coconut
¾ teaspoon vanilla

✿   ✿   ✿

Icing:

1 cup sugar
⅓ cup water
¼ teaspoon cream of tartar

2 egg whites
1 teaspoon vanilla

Preheat the oven to 350 degrees. Grease and lightly flour three 9-inch round cake pans. Cut out 3 pieces of wax paper and fit into the bottom of each pan. Grease and flour the wax paper.

To make the batter, stir together the flour, baking powder, and salt. Place the sugar, butter, and vanilla in a large mixing bowl and beat with an electric mixer until light. Add the flour mixture, alternating with the milk, starting and ending with the flour, beating well after each addition. Beat the egg whites until they form stiff peaks, but do not overbeat. Fold into the batter. Divide the batter among the prepared pans. Bake until done, 20–25 minutes. Cool in the pans for 10 minutes. Then turn out onto racks to cool completely, removing the wax paper.

To prepare the filling, melt the butter with the sugar, juice, and water in a medium saucepan. Cook to the soft ball stage (240 degrees), stirring constantly to dissolve the sugar. Pour some of this hot mixture into the egg yolks, then stir and

Lane Cake, continued

combine with the entire mixture in the saucepan. Cook and stir until thickened, about 12–15 minutes more, without boiling. Remove from the heat. Stir in the raisins, nuts, cherries, coconut, and vanilla. Cover and allow to cool to room temperature. Spread between layers and on top of the cake.

To prepare the icing, place the sugar, water, and cream of tartar in a saucepan. Bring to the boil, stirring, and boil to the soft ball stage (240 degrees). Place the egg whites and vanilla in a large mixer bowl and very slowly add the hot syrup, beating constantly for 7 minutes or until stiff peaks are formed. Frost the sides and around the top edge of the cake with the icing.

Chocolate Checkerboard Cheesecake

Makes one 3-layer cake, serves 12

Absolutely lovely as a checkerboard cake, the batter may also be made into a three-layer cake, with one white layer and two layers of chocolate. If doing the checkerboard version, you will need three disposable round aluminum cake pans for the crust, to facilitate removal of the cake later. There are special checkerboard forms you can buy to make the checkerboard design.

Graham cracker crust:
8 graham cracker squares
2 tablespoons butter
1½ tablespoons sugar

Chocolate crusts:
24 chocolate wafers
6 tablespoons butter
3 tablespoons sugar

✿ ✿ ✿

Vanilla batter:
20 ounces cream cheese
1¼ cups sugar

2 eggs
1 teaspoon vanilla

✿ ✿ ✿

Chocolate batter:
3 eggs
20 ounces cream cheese
1¼ cups sugar
4 ounces semisweet chocolate, melted

1½ ounces German's sweet chocolate, chopped
1 tablespoon dark rum

✿ ✿ ✿

Icing:
1 pound milk chocolate chips
1¹/3 cups sour cream

For the graham cracker crust: Mix together all the ingredients in a blender or food processor. Pat into a 9-inch round aluminum-foil cake pan and freeze.

For the chocolate crusts: Mix together all the ingredients in a blender or food processor. Pat into two 9-inch round aluminum-foil cake pans and freeze.

When ready to use, place the foil pans inside sturdy cake pans.

For the vanilla batter: Blend all the ingredients together in a food processor or electric mixer. When smooth, pour the batter into a separate bowl.

For the chocolate batter: Blend all the ingredients in a food processor or electric mixer until smooth.

Place the checkerboard form onto one of the chocolate crusts. Pour the chocolate batter into the outside ring and the center ring of the form, filling half full. Pour the vanilla batter into the remaining ring (between the chocolate rings). Remove the form, rinse, dry, and repeat with the second chocolate crust.

Place the checkerboard form onto the graham cracker crust. Pour the vanilla batter into the outside ring and the center ring of the form, filling half full. Pour the remaining chocolate batter into the remaining ring between the vanilla rings.

Preheat the oven to 350 degrees. Place the 3 pans in the oven and bake for 50 minutes. Remove and place on racks to cool. The layers may be refrigerated or frozen at this point and removed at a later time to assemble the cake. When the layers are thoroughly chilled, melt the chocolate chips for the icing and add the sour cream, beating the mixture together until smooth. Cut the sides of one of the aluminum pans and remove one of the chocolate layers. Spread icing on top. Top it with the vanilla layer and ice again. Finish by placing the remaining chocolate layer over the vanilla layer. Ice the top, and the sides of all 3 layers. Place in the refrigerator to chill until serving time or freeze until the icing is solid, then wrap carefully. Slice and serve cold but not frozen.

Butter Pecan Cheesecake

Serves 12-14

This cheesecake can be made ahead, refrigerated or frozen, and served cold in the middle of a long hot summer.

Butter Pecan Cheesecake, continued

Crust:

1/3 cup melted butter

1 1/2 cups graham cracker crumbs

1/3 cup sugar

1/2 cup chopped pecans

✿   ✿   ✿

Cake:

3 eight-ounce packages cream cheese, softened

1 1/2 cups sugar

3 eggs

2 cups sour cream

1 teaspoon vanilla

1 teaspoon praline liqueur (optional)

1 cup chopped pecans

✿   ✿   ✿

Garnish:

1 cup toasted pecan halves
   (see p. 321)

To make the crust, mix together the butter, graham cracker crumbs, sugar, and pecans in a food processor or by hand. Press into the bottom and slightly up the sides of a 9-inch springform pan.

Preheat the oven to 475 degrees.

To make the cake: Beat together the cream cheese and sugar in a food processor or with an electric mixer. Add the eggs, one at a time, beating well after each addition. Add the sour cream, vanilla, and optional liqueur. Stir in the pecans. Pour into the springform pan and bake 10 minutes. Reduce the temperature to 300 degrees and bake 50 minutes longer. Turn off the oven, open the oven door slightly, and let sit in the oven for 1 hour. Remove from the oven. Garnish by placing the pecan halves around the outside edge of the cake. Chill and eat when cold. This freezes well for 2–3 months. Defrost in the refrigerator if possible.

Sour Cream Pound Cake

Serves 14–16

This cake freezes well. It is good slightly warm and tastes just as good toasted the next day.

3 cups all-purpose soft-wheat flour
  (see p. 314)
1/4 teaspoon salt
1/2 teaspoon baking soda
1 cup butter, at room temperature

2³/4 cups sugar
6 eggs, at room temperature
1/2 teaspoon lemon extract
1/2 teaspoon vanilla
1 cup sour cream

Preheat the oven to 350 degrees. Grease and lightly flour a 10-inch tube pan. Cut out a piece of wax paper to fit in the bottom and grease and flour the paper. Stir together the flour, salt, and soda. In a mixing bowl beat the butter until light and creamy. Gradually add the sugar, beating until light. Add the eggs, one at a time, beating for a minute after each addition; scrape the bowl often. Add the lemon extract and vanilla; beat well. Add the dry ingredients and sour cream alternately, starting and ending with flour, beating after each addition until just combined.

Pour the batter into the prepared pan. Bake about 1–1 1/2 hours or until a toothpick inserted in the cake comes out clean. Cool 15 minutes on a rack. Remove from the pan and cool. Peel off the paper.

Jewell Hoefer's Brown Sugar Pound Cake

Serves 14–16

This pound cake variation is wonderful after Sunday supper, or just any time for snacking. The icing is quite unusual.

1 pound light brown sugar
1¹/2 cups butter
7 eggs

3 cups all-purpose soft-wheat flour
  (see p. 314)

✿   ✿   ✿

Icing:
1 cup chopped pecans
1/2 cup butter
1 pound confectioners' sugar

1 teaspoon vanilla
1 small can evaporated milk

Preheat the oven to 325 degrees. Grease and lightly flour a 10-inch tube pan. Cut out a piece of wax paper to fit in the bottom of the pan, and grease and flour the paper. Beat the sugar and butter together until light. Beat in the eggs one by

Brown Sugar Pound Cake, continued

one. Fold in the flour, and pour the batter into the prepared pan. Bake 1 1/4–1 1/2 hours. Remove from the oven to a rack. Cool and remove the cake from the pan. Peel off the paper.

   To make the icing: Brown the pecans in butter in a skillet. Add the sugar and vanilla. Bring to a spreading consistency with the evaporated milk. Spread over the cake while warm.

Pecan-Topped Chocolate Pound Cake

Serves 14–16

During the taping of my television series, "New Southern Cooking," one of my assistants, Judith Tuggle, came up with this version of an old favorite. It's rich and has a strong chocolate taste. As someone once told her, "You can never have too much chocolate in anything."

1 1/2 cups butter
2 1/2 cups sugar
6 eggs
3 cups all-purpose soft-wheat flour
   (see p. 314)

1 1/2 teaspoons baking powder
1 cup milk
12 ounces chocolate chips, melted
1 cup chopped pecans

Preheat the oven to 325 degrees and grease and flour a 10-inch tube pan. Cut out a piece of wax paper to fit into the bottom and grease and flour the paper. Beat the butter in a mixer and add the sugar gradually until light and fluffy. Add the eggs one at a time, beating well. Sift the flour with the baking powder, and add to the first mixture, alternating with the milk, beginning and ending with flour. Stir in the melted chocolate, blend, and then add the pecans.

   Pour the batter into the prepared pan, and bake. Test for doneness by inserting a toothpick into the cake to see if it comes out clean after 1 1/4 hours. When the cake is done, cool in the pan for 15 minutes then remove to a rack, peel off the paper, and cool completely. For a festive look, drizzle with extra melted chocolate and sprinkle on extra pecans.

Caramel Cake

Serves 15–20

This is another one of Kate's recipes. It's traditional, it's Southern to the last bite, and it's what we crave when we are far from home. There is a grainy texture to the icing since the last batch of sugar is never dissolved.

2 cups sugar
1 1/2 cups vegetable shortening
5 eggs
3 cups all-purpose soft-wheat flour
    (see p. 314)

1/4 teaspoon salt
1/2 teaspoon baking powder
1 1/4 cups milk
1 teaspoon vanilla

✿ ✿ ✿

Caramel:
3 1/4 cups sugar
1/4 cup boiling water
1/2 cup butter

1/4 teaspoon baking soda
1 teaspoon vanilla
1 cup milk

✿ ✿ ✿

Pecan halves

Preheat the oven to 325 degrees. Grease and lightly flour four 9-inch cake pans or two 9-by-13-inch pans. Cut a piece of wax paper to fit the bottom of each of the pans and grease and flour them. Mix the sugar and shortening together and beat with an electric mixer until light. Add the eggs one at a time. Sift together the dry ingredients three times and add, alternating with the milk, to the creamed mixture. Add the vanilla and beat until smooth. Pour the batter into the cake pans and bake for 35 minutes, or until a toothpick inserted in the middle comes out clean. Remove to a wire rack to cool. Then remove from the pans and peel off paper.

    To make the caramel: Melt 1/4 cup of the sugar in an iron skillet until golden brown. Add the boiling water and cook until well blended and no lumps remain. Place the remaining 3 cups of sugar and the butter, baking soda, vanilla, and milk in a large saucepan and bring to a boil. Add a little of the milk mixture to dissolve and remove all the caramel from the pan, then pour the caramel into the boiling milk mixture. Boil rapidly, stirring constantly, to the soft ball stage — 240 degrees. Remove the pan from the heat and place in a bowl of cold water to stop the cooking. Beat until very thick and creamy. Cool and spread between the layers and on the top and sides of the cake. Decorate the top and sides with pecan halves.

Peanut Butter Cake

Serves 14–16

Kate fixes this recipe for her children and grandchildren.

1/3 cup butter
1/3 cup peanut butter
1 1/4 cups sugar
2 egg whites
2 egg yolks, beaten
2 cups all-purpose soft-wheat flour
   (see p. 314)

1 1/8 teaspoons baking powder
1 1/4 teaspoons baking soda
1 1/4 cups buttermilk
1/2 teaspoon vanilla

✿   ✿   ✿

Icing:

1 1/2 cups sugar
1/2 cup evaporated milk

1/4 cup butter
1 cup peanut butter

Preheat the oven to 350 degrees. Grease and lightly flour two 9-inch pans. Cut a piece of wax paper to fit the bottom of each pan and grease and flour the paper. To make the batter: Beat together the butter, peanut butter, and sugar. Beat the egg whites until stiff and add along with the yolks to the creamed mixture. Sift the flour, baking powder, and baking soda together and add to the creamed mixture, alternating with the buttermilk and vanilla, starting and ending with the dry ingredients. Pour the batter into the prepared pans and bake in the oven for 35 minutes. Remove to racks to cool, then remove from the pans. Peel off paper.

To make the icing, combine the sugar, milk, and butter in a saucepan, bring to the boil, and boil exactly 5 minutes. Add the peanut butter and beat until creamy. Frost the cake, working quickly because the icing hardens.

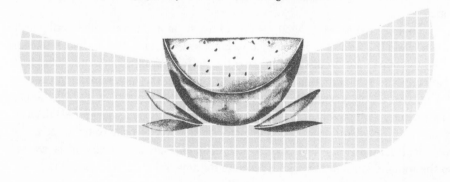

Audrey's Pineapple Upside-Down Cake

Serves 8

Audrey is my "nearly" daughter, and this was her first cake. She called me long distance to get the recipe to make it for her boyfriend.

1 can pineapple slices (8¼ ounces), with juice	2 teaspoons vanilla
⅓ cup plus 2 tablespoons butter	1 egg
½ cup brown sugar, packed	1½ cups all-purpose soft-wheat flour (see p. 314)
4 pitted cherries, halved	2½ teaspoons baking powder
¾ cup sugar	¼ teaspoon salt

Preheat the oven to 350 degrees. Drain the pineapple, reserving the juice. Melt 2 tablespoons of the butter in a 9-inch round cake pan or a 10-inch iron skillet. Stir in the brown sugar and 1 tablespoon of the pineapple juice. Add water to the remaining juice to make ⅔ cup and set aside. Arrange the pineapple slices in the pan, placing a cherry in the hole of each slice.

To make the batter: Beat the remaining ⅓ cup butter, adding the sugar and vanilla, until well blended. Add the egg and beat for a minute more. In a separate bowl, mix together the flour, baking powder, and salt. Add the flour mixture to the batter, alternating with the pineapple juice, beating after each addition. Spread the batter in the pan, place the pan on a baking sheet to catch the juices, and bake 30–40 minutes or until a toothpick inserted in the middle comes out clean. Cool 5 minutes on a rack and invert onto a plate.

Georgia Fruitcake

Makes 4 loaves

Anne Sterling is a brilliant young chef from Stone Mountain, Georgia. Her Georgia fruitcake is peaches, pecans, and pure pleasure.

Georgia Fruitcake, continued

3 pounds chopped pecans
1 pound golden raisins
2 pounds sun-dried peaches, cut in
    1/2-inch pieces
4 cups all-purpose soft-wheat
    flour (see p. 314)
1 1/2 teaspoons baking powder
1 teaspoon salt

1 teaspoon allspice
1 tablespoon cinnamon
1 pound unsalted butter
1 pound light brown sugar
10 eggs
1 cup honey
1/2 cup heavy cream
1 cup peach nectar
1 cup brandy

Oil and flour 4 9- by 5-inch loaf pans, insert a piece of wax paper in each to fit, and oil and flour again. Preheat oven to 300 degrees. Dredge the pecans, raisins, and peaches with 1 cup of the flour, tossing to coat. Set aside. Sift the remaining 3 cups of flour together with the baking powder, salt, allspice, and cinnamon. Cream the butter and sugar and beat in the eggs, one at a time. Add the honey, cream, peach nectar, and flour mixture, and beat until smooth. Combine the batter with the nut and fruit mixture and mix well. Pour evenly into the pans and bake for 1 1/2 hours. Remove and pour brandy over while still hot.

Mother's Stack Cake

Serves 8–10

My friend from Tuscaloosa, Alabama, Phyllis S. Cherry, told me the following history of the stack cake in her family. "This is my favorite winter-fall-type cake. Mother made it during the holidays like she made biscuit dough and always used apples that we dried from our green apple tree. It works with fresh apples or chunky applesauce but dried apples are better. It is good with hot spiced tea or coffee on a cool day. Traditionally, guests would each bring a layer to a wedding or church supper, and then they would put it all together to make a stack cake." A word of warning: The cake pans are turned upside down with the dough baked on the outside bottom of the pans.

6 cups all-purpose soft-wheat flour
    (see p. 314)

1 cup shortening (preferably Crisco)
1 cup sugar

2 teaspoons baking soda
2 teaspoons ginger

1/2 cup molasses
1/2 cup buttermilk

✿   ✿   ✿

Filling:
1 pound dried apples
2-3 cups sugar

3-4 teaspoons allspice

Preheat the oven to 350 degrees. With a pastry cutter or two forks, mix the flour, shortening, sugar, baking soda, and ginger together until the mixture looks like biscuit mix. Add the molasses and buttermilk and stir with a fork just until the dough holds together. Divide into 5 or 6 equal parts. Press the dough out to 3/4-inch thickness on the outside bottom of 5 or 6 greased and floured 8-inch cake pans. Bake the layers about 10 minutes, until firm. Cool slightly, remove from bottom of the pans and let cool on racks.

To make the filling: Cook the dried apples with water as directed on the package. Or place the dried apples in water to cover and cook until the apples are soft and the water nearly evaporated. Add sugar and allspice to taste. Layer the cake and applesauce until you have a 5- or 6-layer cake with the apple mixture between layers and on top. The cake is best if it sits 24 hours before cutting.

Cream Puff Dough My Way

Makes 20 puffs

This is an original method of mine. Cream puffs are a staple of small-town Southern parties. The dough may also be shaped into swans, éclairs, or a lacy filigree and placed on chocolate sauce, or into bite-sized pieces and filled with chicken. Cheese can be added and the dough made into cheese puffs or used around a cooked casserole filling for a dramatic presentation. This recipe may be halved easily.

1/2 cup butter
1 cup all-purpose soft-wheat flour (see
    p. 314), sifted with 1/2 teaspoon
    salt

1 cup water
4 eggs

✿   ✿   ✿

Glaze:
1 egg, beaten

Cream Puff Dough, continued

Melt the butter in a saucepan. Remove from the heat and stir in the flour, making a roux. Add the water and stir briefly; don't worry if it is lumpy. Return the pan to the heat and stir constantly until the mixture comes together in a paste. "Dry" over high heat 4–5 minutes by stirring until the flour is cooked and the dough does not stick to your fingers. Be careful not to burn the mixture. The bottom of the pan should have a light crust of dried dough and the dough should look like buttered mashed potatoes, with no white particles of uncooked flour.

Remove from the pan and place in a food processor bowl fitted with the metal blade, or in a mixing bowl. Add the eggs, one by one, processing after each addition in the food processor or beating well with an electric mixer. Process or beat until shiny and smooth. Now test the mixture. It should drop from a spoon like thick mayonnaise. If too much egg is added, the mixture will be too runny, causing it to collapse in baking, so add the last egg slowly, beating after each addition. (May be made in advance to this point, shaped, and cooked later as below. Any leftover dough may be kept wrapped in the refrigerator for several days, or frozen; it should be brought to room temperature or warmer before being baked.)

To make cream puffs, preheat the oven to 375 degrees and grease and flour a baking sheet. Shape the dough with two spoons or pipe through a pastry bag into small rounds of the desired size. Give each puff room to expand during baking. To glaze, brush the puffs carefully with beaten egg, being careful not to drip any on the baking sheet.

Place the baking sheet on the second rack from the top of the oven. Bake until the dough is puffed, golden, and firm. Do not underbake. The size of the puffs determines the time needed for baking, 15–20 minutes for small puffs, 25–40 minutes for medium to large puffs.

To test for doneness, remove one puff from the oven and set it aside for 1–2 minutes. If it is firm after 2 minutes and does not collapse, the puffs are done and may be removed and pricked at the side of the base with a trussing needle or fork. Place back in the oven for a few minutes to get rid of the steam and keep the pastry crisp. If not eaten the day they are made, refrigerate or freeze and recrisp briefly in the oven before filling.

For dessert puffs, the cooled puffs may be filled with sweetened, flavored whipped cream, butter cream, ice cream, or Lemon Cheese (p. 266). Caramel Cream (p. 269) or Chocolate Sauce (p. 270) may be drizzled on top.

For appetizers, small puffs may be filled with chicken or meat salad, mixed grated cheeses, cream cheese and chives, or any leftovers.

To make cheese puffs, add grated cheese to the dough. Shape and bake as directed above.

Filigrees with Chocolate Sauce and Whipped Cream

Serves 4

This delicate dessert can also be made from leftover Cream Puff Dough.

1/3 recipe **Cream Puff Dough** (preceding recipe)	1/2 recipe **Chocolate Sauce (p. 270)** 1 cup heavy cream, whipped

Preheat the oven to 375 degrees. Take a dessert-sized paper doily, place a piece of buttered and floured wax paper over it, and pipe the dough onto the paper following the doily pattern. Place the wax paper on a baking sheet. Repeat to make 3 more filigrees. Place in the oven and bake about 15 minutes, until browned. Remove from pan and cool on a rack. When ready to serve, coat plates with Chocolate Sauce and place the filigrees on it. Pipe or spoon a dollop of whipped cream into the holes of the filigrees.

Peach Butter

Makes 4 pints

This is wonderful as a spread for buttered toast and croissants or baked inside puff pastry. It is also a good sandwich filling for small meringues or butter cookies.

5 pounds peaches (about 14) 1 cup water 3 1/2 cups sugar	2 tablespoons orange liqueur or peach brandy (optional) 1 tablespoon candied ginger (optional)

Simmer the peaches in the water until the skin is easy to remove. Peel and pit the peaches, saving the cooking liquid. Purée the peaches (you will have about 8 cups) and place with the liquid (about 1/2 cup) and the sugar in a pot and cook over low heat, stirring occasionally, until thick, about 3 hours. Taste and add

Peach Butter, continued

optional liqueur or brandy and cook a few minutes more. Add the ginger if desired. Remove from the heat and cool. Place in a container in the refrigerator and keep refrigerated or freeze until ready to use.

Applesauce

Makes 4 cups

Homemade applesauce is 100 percent better than store-bought. It's good by itself but is also useful in many other recipes. I urge you to cook it, filling your house with good smells and earning great praise from your loved ones.

4 pounds tart apples, peeled, cored, and sliced
Dash freshly grated nutmeg
1/2 cup water

1/4 cup rum or applejack (optional)
1 teaspoon lemon juice (optional)
Sugar (optional)

Place the apples, nutmeg, water, and optional liquor in a heavy saucepan. Bring to the boil, stirring. Reduce the heat and simmer uncovered for 30–35 minutes, stirring occasionally to prevent sticking and burning. The applesauce should be thick enough to cling to an inverted tablespoon. Remove from the heat, add lemon juice to prevent darkening, and taste for sugar, adding if desired.

Lemon Cheese

Makes 2 1/2 cups

Lemon cheese is also called "lemon curd." Because of its high acidity, it lasts indefinitely in a covered jar in the refrigerator. Lemon cheese has a variety of uses.

It can be served alone, as a topping or sauce, as a filling for pies and tarts covered with meringue or whipped cream, or as a spread on English muffins. For a light and heavenly rendition, mix with whipped cream and use as a sauce over berries or as a cream-puff filler.

1 cup sugar
1/2 cup butter
Grated rind and strained juice of
    3 lemons (3 tablespoons rind
    and 1/2 cup juice)
3 eggs, beaten to mix

Place the sugar, butter, lemon rind and juice, and eggs in a heavy saucepan, and cook gently over low heat until the mixture is thick but still falls easily from a spoon. Do not boil or let the mixture separate. Remove from the heat and cool. Store in the refrigerator in a tightly covered jar, or freeze.

Lemon Cheese Sauce

This makes a gracious plenty, so you may want to use half a recipe of Lemon Cheese and half the cream, for several pints of berries or a dozen puffs.

1 recipe Lemon Cheese
1 1/2 cups heavy cream, whipped

Add the whipped cream to Lemon Cheese when ready to serve.

Lemon Cheese and Cream Puffs   *Makes 20*

1/2 recipe Lemon Cheese
3/4 cup heavy cream, whipped
1 recipe Cream Puffs (p. 264)

When ready to use, mix 1/2 recipe of Lemon Cheese with the whipped cream and fill each cream puff.

Peach or Apricot and Pineapple Filling

Makes 4–5 cups

Try this filling cold in cream puffs or puff-pastry rectangles. It is also fabulous baked inside puff pastry.

5 peaches or apricots, fresh or dried
1/2 cup fresh or
    canned pineapple
2/3 cup sugar

5 egg yolks
1/2 cup butter
3 tablespoons peach brandy or orange
    liqueur

Peel the fresh peaches or apricots. Or, if dried, soak in water to cover, at least an hour or overnight, and drain. Place the peaches or apricots in a food processor or blender and purée, then add the pineapple, sugar, and egg yolks. Purée again. Melt the butter in a saucepan. Add the puréed mixture. Cook, stirring constantly over low heat, until thick. Add the liqueur. Cool, cover, and refrigerate.

Peach Sauce

Makes 1 1/2 cups

4 egg yolks
1/4 cup sugar
1/3 cup peach juice, peach brandy,
    or peach schnapps
1 cup heavy cream, whipped

In a heavy pan, combine the egg yolks and sugar. Heat the peach juice, brandy, or schnapps in a small saucepan and pour into the egg-yolk mixture, whisking steadily with a whisk or electric mixer. Continue whisking over low heat until thick, about 15 minutes. Cool slightly, then fold in the whipped cream. Chill. Covered, the sauce will last in the refrigerator for the period of time the cream is dated.

Caramel Cream Sauce

Makes 1 cup

Although this sauce is wonderful as is, you can also add pecans and chocolate pieces—it's fantastic for serving over ice cream.

1/2 cup sugar
2 tablespoons light corn syrup

2/3 cup heavy cream,
at room temperature

Place the sugar and corn syrup in a heavy saucepan. Cook over low heat, then turn up the heat when the sugar has dissolved and boil until the mixture is a dark golden color. Add the cream slowly, being careful that the hot mixture does not spatter. (You might want to use an oven mitt to cover your hand while adding the cream.) Bring back to a boil and cook until the caramel dissolves. Serve at room temperature or hot.

Pecan Caramel Cream

Add 1 cup toasted pecan pieces (see p. 321).

Chocolate Pecan Caramel Cream

Add 1/4 cup chocolate chips or pieces to the sauce while still hot. Stir to mix only—the chocolate should melt slightly, not completely, so that pieces of chocolate remain.

Ginger-Caramel Sauce

Makes 3 cups

This sauce is not only good in the Frozen Ginger-Caramel Mousse (p. 271), but will keep indefinitely in a covered jar in the refrigerator to be poured over ice cream

Ginger-Caramel Sauce, continued

or fruit. If it solidifies more than you like, place it in a microwave or saucepan, melt it, and add more water. Corn syrup is a wonderful stabilizer, making it much easier to cook the caramel. Fresh ginger varies radically in spiciness, so you must determine the right amount for yourself.

2 cups sugar
1¾ cups water

¼ cup light corn syrup
⅛–¼ pound fresh ginger

Place the sugar, 1 cup of the water, and the corn syrup in a large, heavy saucepan. Melt over low heat, without boiling. Meanwhile, slice the ginger thin by hand or in a food processor. When the sugar is completely dissolved, add the desired amount of ginger. Bring to the boil slowly and boil steadily for 15–20 minutes, until the syrup is a light brown color. The ginger should be the texture of a cooked carrot, soft but still firm. Shake or stir the pan occasionally to prevent the ginger from burning. When the caramel syrup is the right color, cover your hand with a pot holder and pour the remaining 3/4 cup of water slowly into the pan. Be very careful; the hot caramel may boil up and burn you. Boil a few minutes, until the caramel is redissolved in the water and a pouring consistency. If it is too hard, more water may be added to thin it to the desired consistency.

Chocolate Sauce

Makes 1 cup

Great for dipping cream puffs, Cream Puff Filigrees, or Pecan Rolls, or for spooning over ice cream, cake, or whatever comes to mind. Will keep in the refrigerator for several weeks if the cream is fresh and the sauce is kept covered.

8 ounces semisweet chocolate,
   chopped
1 cup heavy cream

Add chocolate to the cream and melt over low heat, stirring constantly. Cool until thickened. Serve hot or cold.

Frozen Ginger-Caramel Mousse

Serves 10–12

I love frozen custards and I love ginger. This original recipe took many of my students and apprentices a lot of time to develop, and we are all proud of it. It keeps for several months in the freezer if tightly wrapped.

1 recipe Ginger-Caramel Sauce   **8 egg yolks**
   (p. 269)   **3½ cups heavy cream**

Remove the ginger from the caramel sauce, saving the syrup. If the ginger is sticky, place it in the freezer and chill briefly so it will be easier to chop. Chop in a food processor or by hand.

    In a heavy saucepan, bring the syrup to a full boil. Meanwhile, beat the egg yolks in an electric mixer and add the hot syrup. Beat until very thick, about 15 minutes. In a separate bowl, whip the cream, add the egg yolk mixture and half of the chopped ginger, and beat until thoroughly combined. Taste and add ginger as needed for flavor. Pour into a large mold and place in the freezer. Stir occasionally while freezing to prevent the ginger from settling to the bottom. When nearly set, cover well and freeze. Let the mousse thaw briefly to serve. It's beautiful when frozen in a bowl the size of the Caramel Basket (p. 281), then unwrapped and placed in the Caramel Basket before serving.

Oranges in Ginger-Caramel Sauce

Serves 8

This is particularly refreshing after a rich meal.

8 large navel oranges   **Zest of 1 orange, julienned and**
½ recipe Ginger-Caramel Sauce,   **blanched in boiling water**
   strained (p. 269)

Oranges in Ginger-Caramel Sauce, continued

Skin the oranges with a serrated knife, removing all the white part. Cut each orange into 6 horizontal slices. Place in a deep glass dish. Pour the Ginger-Caramel Sauce on top, sprinkle with orange zest, and chill.

Cold Lemon-Peach Mousse

Makes 2 quarts

Although time-consuming, this dessert is worth the effort. It doubles easily and may be made a day in advance, if covered well. Buy fresh peaches, slice, and freeze them; or use store-bought frozen peaches.

4 egg yolks
1 cup sugar
1/2 cup lemon juice,
   slightly heated
3 tablespoons finely grated lemon rind
1 one-pound bag frozen peaches,
   divided and defrosted
1 tablespoon peach schnapps
   or brandy (optional)

2 envelopes gelatin, soaked in 1/4 cup
   cold water in a small pan or
   metal measuring cup
6 egg whites
1 1/4 cups heavy cream, whipped until
   light and mousse-like

✿   ✿   ✿

Decoration:
1 cup heavy cream, whipped with
   1/4 cup sugar
1 lemon, sliced and twisted, to garnish

Oil a 2-quart mold. Place the egg yolks, sugar, lemon juice, and lemon rind in a bowl. Set the bowl over a pan of simmering water, and beat until the sugar dissolves and the mixture is light and mousse-like; when you lift the beater the mixture will be thick enough to dribble down in a trail for a few seconds before it dissolves back into the base mixture. Remove the bowl from the heat and continue beating until the mixture is cool.

   Put 2 cups of the peaches in a food processor with the schnapps or brandy and process until very fine. Add to the egg yolk mixture. Coarsely chop the remaining peaches and set aside. Melt the gelatin in the water over low heat until clear and dissolved and add to the base mixture, then put the bowl in another bowl full of ice water. With a rubber spatula stir very gently until the mixture starts to thicken, being sure to keep the bottom and sides moving and free of the mixture so the gelatin doesn't set in one spot.

Whip the egg whites until stiff. Using a spatula or metal spoon, carefully fold the whipped cream into the base mixture, followed by 1 large spoonful of the beaten egg whites to soften. Pour the mixture over the beaten whites and fold all together. If you had added the cream earlier, it would have retarded the setting. Fold in the chopped peaches, and pour into the prepared dish. Refrigerate at least 1–2 hours or until set. When ready to serve, unmold and decorate with rosettes of whipped cream and sliced lemon.

Thick, Rich Custard with Caramel Top

Serves 8–10

In both the English version of this recipe, Crème Brûlée, and the Spanish, Catalonian flan, sugar is sprinkled on top of the custard, which is then placed under the broiler to brown the sugar to a crisp caramel. I've simplified this procedure by placing a crisp caramel round made from granulated sugar and butter on top of the custard.

Custard:
1 quart heavy cream
1 vanilla bean, split
8 egg yolks

Pinch of salt
1/2 cup sugar, plus sugar for sprinkling
1 teaspoon vanilla (optional)

☆　☆　☆

Caramel rounds:
1 tablespoon butter, for buttering
    8 rounds
4 teaspoons sugar

Preheat the oven to 350 degrees. In a saucepan, bring the cream to the boil with the vanilla bean. Remove and let cool slightly. Briefly beat together the egg yolks, salt, and sugar in a large mixing bowl. Add the cream slowly and taste for vanilla

Custard with Caramel Top, continued

flavoring. Add vanilla extract if desired. Strain into custard cups. Fold a clean tea towel in the bottom of a large roasting pan, add the custard cups, and pour boiling water into the pan until the water reaches halfway up the sides of the pan. Be careful not to pour water into the custard cups.

Bake, uncovered, until set, about 30 minutes. The water bath keeps the custard from overcooking. The towel keeps the bottom heat even. If the water evaporates, add more. Remove the custard when done and refrigerate until cold, preferably overnight. When completely cool and ready to serve, top with a caramel round.

To make cooking pans for the caramel rounds, cut out circles of aluminum foil 1/4 inch larger than the top of a custard cup. Mold the foil around the rims of the cups, folding up the excess foil to create rims like small tart pans. Remove the foil from the custard cups. Butter each foil pan. Sprinkle in 1/2 teaspoon sugar for each round. Place the foil pans under the broiler until the rounds are lacy and brown. Do not burn. Remove from the oven and cool. Bend back the foil and remove the hardened round. Keep in an airtight tin or container. If the rounds break, don't worry. Just sprinkle on the custard.

Banana Pudding

Serves 10

More than just a dessert, this pudding represents a way of life—a mother's touch.

1 cup sugar	1 tablespoon vanilla
1/4 cup flour	1 twelve-ounce box vanilla wafers
Pinch salt	8 bananas, sliced
3 cups milk	8 egg whites
8 egg yolks	2 tablespoons sugar

To make the custard, mix together the 1 cup of sugar, the flour, and salt in a bowl. Pour the milk into a heavy saucepan and add the dry ingredients. Heat. Beat the egg yolks. Pour some of the hot milk mixture into the egg yolks and beat briefly, then add the egg yolk mixture to the base mixture in the saucepan. Bring to the boil over low heat, stirring constantly, and cook slowly until just thick enough to coat the back of a spoon. Be careful that the mixture doesn't scorch. Add the vanilla, remove from the heat, and cover with plastic wrap to prevent a skin from forming on the top.

Line the bottom and sides of a 9½-by-12½-inch baking pan with vanilla wafers. Put a layer of bananas, then a layer of wafers in the dish until you have used all the wafers and bananas. Then pour in the custard, completely covering the bananas and wafers.

Preheat the oven to 375 degrees. Beat the egg whites until they form soft peaks. Add 2 tablespoons of sugar and beat to stiff peaks. Spread the meringue fully over the top of the pudding, then bake until browned, about 15–20 minutes.

Sweet Potato Pudding

Serves 10–12

A simple-to-make Southern favorite. A food processor makes grating the sweet potatoes a snap.

4 cups raw sweet potatoes, grated　　**1 cup chopped pecans**
¾ cup sugar　　**¾ cup coconut**
½ teaspoon nutmeg　　**1 cup milk**
½ cup light corn syrup　　**¼ cup butter**
3 eggs

Preheat the oven to 350 degrees. Mix all the ingredients together in a large bowl. Pour into a large buttered ovenproof casserole and bake 1½ hours, stirring every 15 minutes for the first 45 minutes. Serve hot or cold.

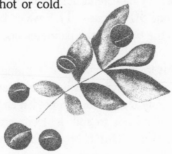

Peach and Cream Custard with Pecan Caramel Topping

Serves 6

Anne Byrne Phillips and I developed this dessert recipe to complement an all-Vidalia onion dinner we were having. The delicious topping is wonderful—it's easily doubled, made ahead, and kept in a covered jar to serve with ice cream. I've eliminated the Vidalia onion here, but if you are dying for a Vidalia recipe for dessert, add 1 1/2 teaspoons cooked onions to each custard cup.

2 cups heavy cream
4 egg yolks
2 1/2 tablespoons sugar

1 teaspoon vanilla
1/2 cup frozen or fresh peaches, puréed with 2 tablespoons sugar

✿   ✿   ✿

Caramel and pecan topping:
1 cup sugar
1/2 cup water
1 tablespoon light corn syrup

1 1/2 cups pecan pieces, browned in oven

Preheat the oven to 325 degrees. Slowly bring the cream to a boil in a heavy saucepan, being careful not to burn it. Beat the egg yolks with a mixer, adding the sugar gradually. Pour several tablespoons of cream into the egg mixture, beating well, then add the remaining cream, beating constantly. Add the vanilla and the puréed peaches, and beat until just blended. Pour into 6 small custard cups. Place a tea towel on the bottom of a large roasting pan, then place the custard cups on the towel and pour boiling water into the pan so that it reaches halfway up the sides, being careful not to get any water in the custard. Bake, uncovered, until set, about 30 minutes. This water bath keeps the custard from overcooking, as long as the water in the pan does not boil or evaporate. If it evaporates, add more water.

Meanwhile prepare the topping. In a heavy saucepan melt the sugar with water and corn syrup. When the sugar has dissolved, bring the syrup to a boil and boil steadily until it turns a golden caramel color. Remove carefully from the heat, being careful not to spill it. Pour onto a greased baking sheet and set aside to harden. When hard, chop in a food processor or by hand to make caramel crumbs. Stir in the pecan pieces and keep in a covered jar until ready to use.

Remove the pan with the custard from the oven. Sprinkle each custard with some of the topping and run under the broiler for 2–3 minutes, until the topping is browned. Remove the custard cups from the pan and refrigerate overnight. Serve cold. Pass extra caramel and pecan topping at the table.

Apples or Pears Poached in Syrup and Bourbon with Pastry Apples

Serves 8

If you do your own canning and preserving and have "put up" a lot of figs, the excess syrup is ideal in this recipe. Maple syrup is a good substitute.

6 apples or pears
1½ cups fig or maple syrup
⅓ cup bourbon
¼ cup Calvados if using apples, or
    ¼ cup pear brandy

½ recipe Rapid Puff Pastry
    (p. 231)
1 egg
1 teaspoon water

Peel, core, and slice the fruit in wedges. Add to the syrup and the bourbon and bring to a simmer in a medium-size saucepan. Poach until tender when pierced with a knife, but not mushy. Remove the fruit to a plate, reserving the syrup.

For the sauce: Place the syrup back over the heat and boil down until reduced by half. Stir in the brandy, depending on which fruit you use. Strain and refrigerate until ready to serve. At serving time, reheat.

For the pastry: Roll out the dough ⅛ inch thick. Cut out sixteen 3–4-inch circles. If you'd like the challenge of making pastry designs, make a 3–4-inch paper pattern the shape of the fruit you are using. Place the pattern on the dough and cut out 16 pieces, in the shape of your design. Make leaves from any scraps, scoring them with the tip of a knife. If the pastry becomes too soft to handle at any point, cover and chill it. Mix the egg with the water, then brush the pastry with the egg glaze, avoiding the edges. Place the leaves on the fruit-shaped dough and brush again with the egg glaze. Refrigerate at least 30 minutes or freeze.

When ready to bake, preheat the oven to 400 degrees. Place the pastry on a dampened baking sheet, and turn the temperature down to 375 degrees. Bake until

Poached Apples or Pears with Pastry, continued

the pastry is puffy and golden brown. You may bake the pastry ahead to this point and reheat, but it is best served within a few hours of being baked. Remove from the oven and place on 8 plates, two for each plate. Cover one with the poached fruit, pour a little warm sauce over it, and top with the other pastry. Serve hot.

Anne Haselden Foster's Hot Fruit

Serves 6–8

A wonderful updated version of the Southern favorite curried fruit. Curried fruit is traditionally served at buffets and church suppers and holiday feasts.

2½ cups white
    table wine
1 cup butter
1 cup brown sugar
2 tablespoons flour
1 tablespoon chopped lemon balm
1 stick cinnamon

2 or more teaspoons grated
    lemon rind
1 one-pound can mixed fruit, drained
2 Granny Smith apples, peeled, cored,
    and sliced
2 lemons, sliced
½ pound green seedless grapes

Preheat the oven to 350 degrees. Boil the wine down to 2 cups. Melt the butter in a separate saucepan and stir in the sugar and flour. Add the wine, lemon balm, cinnamon, and lemon rind. Place the canned fruit in a buttered baking dish, pour the wine sauce over, and bake 20 minutes. Remove from the oven and add the apples, lemons, and grapes and stir into the hot canned fruit.

Ambrosia

Serves 6–8

The juicy Florida oranges add a lot to this dish. It's a cross between a salad and a dessert, usually put on the table with everything else for a holiday meal, but served as dessert on ordinary occasions. Adapted from my *Cooking of the South*.

15 oranges, as juicy as possible
1½ cups shredded coconut
1 cup fresh peeled pineapple,
   in chunks

2 ounces cherries, pitted
1 banana, peeled and sliced
¼ cup orange-flavored Cognac liqueur,
   or to taste (optional)

Peel and section the oranges carefully, removing all the white and membrane and saving the juice. Mix the oranges, juice, and coconut in a bowl. Add the other fruit to the oranges, and toss lightly. Turn into an attractive glass bowl and sprinkle liqueur over just before serving.

Fruit Bowl
with Orange-Lemon Sauce

Serves 12–14

I confess I serve this sauce not only on fruit but on a salad of orange pieces and red leaf lettuce, and on chilled asparagus. It's even good without the whipped cream, served as a hot sauce over vegetables.

½ watermelon shell to use as a bowl
   (optional)

4 quarts mixed fruit of watermelon,
   blueberries, and strawberries

✿   ✿   ✿

Sauce:
⅔ cup fresh orange juice
⅓ cup fresh lemon juice
½ cup sugar

6 egg yolks, beaten together lightly
1½ cups heavy cream, whipped
Grated orange peel (optional)

Fruit Bowl with Orange-Lemon Sauce, continued

Cut the watermelon in half lengthwise, remove the pink pulp, and cut into bite-size chunks. Turn one of the shells upside down on a paper towel to drain and discard the other. Combine the watermelon chunks with the strawberries and blueberries.

To make the sauce, heat the orange and lemon juices and sugar in a heavy saucepan over low heat to dissolve the sugar. When dissolved, bring the syrup to the boil and remove from the heat. Place the egg yolks in another heavy saucepan and pour the syrup into the egg yolks in a slow, steady stream, whisking with a wire whisk or electric beater. Cook, whisking constantly, until the sauce is thick, light, and smooth. Do not let the mixture boil. Chill. Fold in the whipped cream. Put the chilled fruit into the watermelon shell or a bowl, and top with the sauce and a garnish of grated orange peel.

Frozen Fruit Salad

Serves 6–8

This dish is a summertime regular at ladies' luncheons, bridge clubs, graduation-day celebrations, bridal showers, and church suppers. My mother would make it with canned fruit cocktail, but I've spruced it up here with fresh fruit. It's sometimes a salad but most often a substitute for dessert when convenience requires a one-plate complete meal including dessert.

1 tablespoon lemon juice
1 large banana, peeled and sliced
1 cup mayonnaise
1 cup heavy cream, whipped
1 cup drained crushed pineapple
    (13¼-ounce can)
½ cup chopped pecans

½ cup chopped pitted fresh or
    canned and drained Bing cherries
¼ cup confectioners' sugar
3 tablespoons dark rum (optional)
1 teaspoon grated lemon rind
1 head lettuce, broken into leaves
    (optional)

In a large bowl, sprinkle lemon juice over the banana, and toss. In a separate bowl, fold the mayonnaise into the whipped cream, then add to the bananas. Add the pineapple, pecans, cherries, sugar, rum, and lemon rind, and mix gently. Spoon into a 9-inch pie plate and freeze until firm. Cut into wedges and serve on lettuce leaves.

Blueberries and Peaches in a Peach Sauce

Serves 6-8

This is a very pretty fruit dessert that's great for parties.

2 pints blueberries
3 cups sliced fresh peaches, or 2 packs
    frozen peaches
1 recipe Peach Sauce (p. 268)

Place the fruit in a glass bowl and pour the sauce over it just before serving.

Caramel Basket

Makes 1 basket

This impressive "nearly glass" basket freezes well, and can be pulled out for the grandest dinner party. Fill with berries or frozen caramel mousse or cream puffs. Serve from the basket, then crack the basket and eat quite grandly at the table, each person savoring a few slivers of caramel.

2 cups sugar
1 cup water

Oil a marble slab or baking sheet and the outside of a heatproof glass bowl the size of the container you envision as your caramel bowl, usually 1 1/2–2 quarts.

    Heat the sugar with the water in a heavy pan until the sugar dissolves. Do not allow to boil before the sugar dissolves or it will crystallize. Bring to the boil and boil rapidly until the syrup is a golden caramel color. Stop the boiling at once by dipping the bottom of the pan in a pan of cold water.

Caramel Basket, continued

Pour the caramel in a slow steady stream onto the oiled marble slab or baking sheet and let stand 1–2 minutes or until it begins to set. Pouring it too fast will produce little bubbles in the mixture. Turn the oiled mold or bowl upside down. When the caramel is set but still warm and pliable, loosen it with two oiled spatulas, lift it onto the mold or bowl, and gently shape the caramel with your hands. Warning: It may be very hot. Mold it to the shape of the bowl. Carefully wiggle or move the caramel every few minutes to be sure it isn't sticking to the bowl. With scissors or a knife trim the edges of the caramel while it is still warm. Let stand until hardened, about 5 minutes. Lift from the bowl onto a rack or lightly oiled plate. Wrap with plastic wrap if keeping more than a few hours. Freeze, wrapped.

Peach Custard Ice Cream

Makes 1 1/2 quarts

The sound of the ice cream churn and the aroma of fresh peaches and cream are sure signs of the Fourth of July. If you have any left over, try filling cream puffs with the ice cream.

2 cups milk	1 tablespoon flour
1 1/2 cups heavy cream	Dash salt
1 vanilla bean, split (optional)	2 cups peaches, chopped or mashed
3 eggs	2 teaspoons vanilla
1 1/4 cups sugar	

Heat the milk and cream together with the vanilla bean in a heavy pan over low heat. In a large bowl mix the eggs, sugar, flour, and salt, and stir in a little of the heated milk-cream mixture. Pour the contents of the bowl into the heavy pan with the remaining milk-cream mixture. Stir over low heat, without scorching, until thick and smooth. Remove from the heat, discard the vanilla bean, and add the peaches. Place in a hand-cranked freezer churn or an electric ice cream maker and churn until cold and thick. Let mellow 30 minutes in the freezer before serving.

Meringues

Makes 60-70

Meringues are difficult to make in humid weather, which causes them to be brown and chewy. In the South, and other humid places, therefore, a lesser amount of sugar is preferable. Ideally, they are crisp and white when done, and cooking time varies radically according to the humidity.

8 egg whites, at room temperature
1/4 teaspoon cream of tartar (optional)
1 1/4–1 1/2 cups sugar

Preheat the oven to 200 degrees. Oil a baking sheet, or line it with parchment paper. Beat the egg whites with the cream of tartar until stiff peaks form. Add half the sugar, 1 tablespoon at a time, continuing to beat until the meringue is very stiff and shiny. Fold in the remaining sugar.

To make small baskets, spoon or pipe the meringue mixture into 3-inch rounds on the prepared pan. Make a slight depression with a damp spoon or your finger in the center of each round. Bake to dry the meringues 1–3 hours. When they are completely dry, the meringues may be kept covered in an airtight container, or frozen. If frozen, dry briefly in the oven if necessary before eating. Serve with Peach Butter (p. 266) or fresh strawberries and whipped cream.

Butter Brickle Madeleines

Makes 40 madeleines

In France, madeleines traditionally are made from a very different type of batter — a butter sponge-cake batter. These diminutive tea cakes were written about, ecstatically, by Marcel Proust in *Remembrance of Things Past*. We like to use

Butter Brickle Madeleines, continued

the pretty madeleine tins for our own special batter. Use as many tins as you have and repeat until all the madeleines are baked.

2 cups all-purpose soft-wheat flour (see p. 314)
1¼ cups sugar
1 tablespoon baking powder
1 teaspoon salt

1 cup milk
½ cup shortening, at room temperature
2 teaspoons vanilla
3 egg whites

✿   ✿   ✿

Frosting:
½ cup butter
4 cups confectioners' sugar

8 tablespoons milk, heated
3 teaspoons vanilla

Oil and flour the madeleine tins. Preheat the oven to 350 degrees. Sift the flour, sugar, baking powder, and salt together in an electric mixer bowl. Pour in the milk, add the shortening and vanilla, and beat until just blended; then add the egg whites and beat another 3 minutes. Pour into the prepared madeleine tins and bake on the middle shelf of the oven for 20–30 minutes or until a toothpick inserted in the center of one comes out clean. Cool on a rack and then remove from the tins. Place on a serving platter, ribbed side up.

To make the frosting, heat the butter in a heavy saucepan until it turns golden brown. Remove from the heat and add the confectioners' sugar, milk, and vanilla. Beat for 3 minutes with an electric mixer until cool, then spread on the madeleines.

Moravian Cookies

Makes 3 pounds cookies

The best Moravian cookies in the world are made in historic Salem, North Carolina (in homes as well as cookie factories), from this 1766 recipe. These wafer-thin ginger snaps are popular at Christmas, and are fabulous with soft white cheeses, such as boucheron or Gourmandise. The dough is easier to roll out when it has mellowed for a few days—be sure to roll it out as thin as possible. The cookies will keep well in an airtight tin.

1 cup brown sugar
2 cups molasses
1/2 cup shortening or lard, melted
1/2 cup butter, melted
1 tablespoon ground cinnamon
1 1/2 teaspoons ground cloves

1 tablespoon ground ginger
1 1/2 teaspoons baking soda
4–4 1/2 cups all-purpose
    soft-wheat flour (see p. 314),
    enough to make a stiff dough,
    about 1 1/2 pounds

Combine the sugar and molasses in a large bowl and mix well. Add the melted shortening and butter. Sift the ground cinnamon, cloves, ginger, and soda with about 3 tablespoons of the flour. Stir into the molasses mixture. Continue to add flour until the dough is stiff. Cover and let stand at least overnight, but preferably several days.

Roll out very thin on a floured board or between sheets of wax paper. Grease 2 baking sheets and preheat the oven to 350 degrees. Cut the dough into shapes with cookie cutters, place on the prepared baking sheets, and bake until lightly browned, about 8 minutes. Cool on a rack. Repeat with any remaining dough.

Lace Cookies

Makes 8 dozen cookies

The trick to lace cookies is getting them off the pan while they are still warm enough to shape, but not cool enough to harden before shaping. The cookie sheets should be well seasoned or nonstick, as the cookies tend to stick to the pan otherwise.

2 cups sifted all-purpose soft-wheat
    flour (see p. 314)
2 cups finely chopped pecans
1 cup light corn syrup

1 cup unsalted butter
1 1/3 cups brown sugar,
    firmly packed

Preheat the oven to 350 degrees. Blend the flour and pecans. Place the corn syrup, butter, and brown sugar in a large, heavy saucepan over moderate heat and

Lace Cookies, continued

bring to the boil, stirring constantly. Remove from the heat, and gradually stir in the flour mixture. Cool slightly.

Oil the cookie sheets well, or use nonstick cookie sheets. Using a teaspoon, place the batter in teaspoonfuls about 3 inches apart on the cookie sheets. The cookies spread considerably.

Bake 5–6 minutes, or until the cookies are a light caramel color and the bubbling has nearly subsided. Remove from the oven. Let the cookies cool for a few minutes on the sheet until they are just cool enough to handle.

Oil the handle of a wooden spoon. While the cookies are still hot, remove them one by one by rolling around the handle of the spoon, forming a tube shape. Let harden slightly around the handle, and place on an oiled plate or rack to cool completely. If the cookies on the sheet harden, place the whole sheet back into the oven to soften slightly. Then remove from the oven and proceed as above. If one cracks, crumble it up for a topping for ice cream or pop it in your mouth! When all the cookies are baked, remove to an airtight container. May be kept a few days at room temperature, or freeze.

Pecan Cookies Sandwiched with Fresh Peaches and Cream

Makes 10–15 cookies

These cookies may be eaten plain too, of course, served as an accompaniment to the peaches and cream instead of sandwiching them. You will need a knife and fork to eat the stacked and filled cookies.

10 tablespoons unsalted butter
1/2 cup sugar
11/2 cups all-purpose soft-wheat flour
   (see p. 314)

1/3 teaspoon salt
11/4 cups toasted and finely
   chopped pecans

✿   ✿   ✿

Filling:
1–2 cups fresh peaches, or other fruit
    in season, sliced
1 cup heavy cream, whipped with
    1 teaspoon peach brandy or
    schnapps and 3 teaspoons sugar

Additional whipped cream (optional)
Confectioners' sugar (optional)

Preheat the oven to 375 degrees. Beat the butter and sugar together until light. Sift the flour with the salt, add the pecans, and stir into the creamed mixture to make an even dough. Divide into 4 pieces, placing each between 2 sheets of wax paper. Roll each piece out 1/8 inch thick. Chill 30 minutes or until firm. Remove the top sheet of wax paper, and cut the dough into 3-inch rounds with a cookie cutter. Remove to a cookie sheet. Bake 10 minutes or until the edges begin to brown. The cookies will be soft even though done and will harden as they cool. When they are nearly hard remove to racks to cool.

When cool, place in airtight container or cookie jar at room temperature, or freeze. Thirty minutes before serving, sandwich the whipped cream and peaches between 2 cookie rounds. Immediately before serving, decorate the top with additional whipped cream or sprinkle with confectioners' sugar.

Pecan Shortbread

Makes 1 dozen cookies

Not exactly Scottish shortbread, but this is great with tea anyway.

3/4 cup all-purpose soft-wheat flour
    (see p. 314)
Dash salt

1 cup pecans, finely ground
1 cup sugar
1/2 cup butter

Preheat the oven to 350 degrees. Grease and flour a 9-inch square cake pan. Combine all the ingredients together into a firm dough, using a food processor, blender, or electric mixer. Press into the prepared pan, place in the oven, and bake until lightly browned, 15–20 minutes.

Remove and quickly cut with a knife into the desired shapes—rectangles, squares, or triangles. Place the pan on a rack to cool. When cooled and hard, remove the shortbread and wrap tightly. It will keep several weeks in an airtight container.

Lucile Hill Walker's Tested Divinity Candy Recipe

Makes 1 1/2–2 pounds

Lucile Hill Walker is really known to me as Muv. She is the grandmother of LuLen, Stewart, and Savannah Walker, who happened to have stayed with me at various times when they were teenagers. During one such visit Muv sent along this recipe (which she always serves at Christmas) along with some very good cooking tips. If you don't have a candy thermometer, test for doneness by dropping bits of the mixtures into ice water. Both mixtures *must* be cooked to a very firm ball (almost hard ball) stage. If the candy begins to harden too quickly, it has been slightly overcooked.

First syrup:
2/3 cup water
1 cup light corn syrup
3 cups sugar

❀ ❀ ❀

Second syrup:
1/2 cup water
1 cup sugar

❀ ❀ ❀

3 egg whites
1/8 teaspoon cream of tartar
Pecans

To make the first syrup, mix together the water, corn syrup, and sugar. Place in a heavy saucepan and bring to the boil. Boil until the syrup reaches 250 degrees on a candy thermometer, the firm ball stage. When the syrup first begins to boil, prepare the second syrup. Place the water and sugar in a heavy pot, and cook over low heat until the sugar dissolves, then bring up to the boil. Continue to boil until the syrup reaches the firm ball stage, 250 degrees.

Meanwhile, beat the egg whites with the cream of tartar until they form stiff peaks. Pour the first syrup into the egg whites very slowly, beating all the time. Then slowly add the second syrup and continue to beat until it loses its shiny look. Drop by teaspoonfuls onto a sheet of wax paper, press a pecan on top, and let harden. This candy will stay moist and manageable for hours if kept covered.

Pecan Pralines

Makes 2 dozen

Pralines are traditionally given as Christmas gifts. Their sweetness will linger in your mouth long after the candy is gone.

2 cups sugar	2 cups pecan halves
1/2 cup light corn syrup	1/4 cup butter
1/2 cup water	1 tablespoon vanilla

Heat the sugar, syrup, water, and pecans in a heavy saucepan until the sugar is dissolved. Bring the mixture to the boil, stirring occasionally, until it reaches the soft ball stage (240 degrees). Remove the saucepan from the heat and add butter and vanilla.

Allow the candy to cool. Whip until the mixture gradually changes to an opaque color and becomes creamy. Drop by tablespoonfuls onto a buttered cookie sheet and allow to harden.

"Ma-Ma's" Peanut Brittle

Makes 1 medium tin

Rosalyn (Mrs. Jimmy) Carter contributed a similar peanut brittle recipe to the cookbook of Americus, *A Taste of Georgia*. My father-in-law was from Americus, which is next to the Carters' hometown of Plains, and this is his mother's recipe.

3 cups sugar	1 tablespoon baking soda
1/2 cup water	1/4 cup butter
1 cup light corn syrup	1 teaspoon vanilla
3 cups raw peanuts	

Place the sugar, water, and corn syrup in a heavy saucepan. Cook without boiling over moderate heat until the sugar dissolves, then add the peanuts. Now bring to

"Ma-Ma's" Peanut Brittle, continued

the boil and boil, stirring occasionally, until the mixture is golden brown and reaches 300 degrees on a candy thermometer or until a little of the hot syrup turns hard when dropped in ice water. The peanuts will "pop." Remove from the heat, add baking soda, butter, and vanilla, and stir until the butter melts and the mixture foams. Pour quickly onto 2 buttered jelly roll pans and spread out with a spatula. As the mixture begins to harden and cool, with your buttered fingers pick it up around the edges and pull and stretch it as thin as possible. When hardened, crack into bite-size pieces.

SAUCES, CONSERVES, and CONDIMENTS

Mrs. Dull's (Abercrombie's) Barbecue Sauce

Makes 3 1/2 quarts

This recipe is adapted from Mrs. S. R. Dull's classic 1928 cookbook, *Southern Cooking,* a standard by which regional cooks have been measured ever since. This book is one of the most popular Southern cookbooks still in print. Mrs. Dull was the food editor of the Atlanta *Journal* and a pioneer in establishing cooking schools and introducing modern kitchen equipment to the Southern home. The Abercrombies, an old Virginia/Georgia family, had a sauce similar to Mrs. Dull's sauce, omitting the garlic.

1/2 pound butter
2 quarts apple-cider vinegar
2 cups water
1 tablespoon Dijon mustard
1 medium onion
3/4–1 cup Worcestershire sauce
2 cups ketchup

2 cups chili sauce
Juice of 2 lemons
Rind (no white) of 1/2 lemon,
  chopped
3 cloves garlic, crushed (optional)
2 teaspoons sugar

Place all the ingredients in a large pot. Stir together and cook over medium heat for 30 minutes. Pour into sterile bottles or jars and keep refrigerated.

Bennie Sauce

Makes 3 1/2 cups

Bennie is former Georgia Governor George Busbee's friend, and this is his sauce for ribs.

1 cup lemon juice
1 cup wine vinegar
1 cup oil
1½ tablespoons salt
1½ tablespoons onion salt
1½-2 tablespoons freshly ground
    black pepper
1½ tablespoons celery salt

1 tablespoon marjoram,
    preferably fresh
1 tablespoon oregano, preferably fresh
1 tablespoon thyme, preferably fresh
1 tablespoon basil, preferably fresh
3 tablespoons soy sauce
3 tablespoons Worcestershire sauce
5 large cloves garlic

Put all the ingredients into a blender or food processor and process until well blended. Use as a basting sauce and heat any remaining sauce to serve at the table.

Poland's Original Barbecue Sauce Recipe

Makes 2 1/2 cups

Anne Poland Berg's father, who was president and owner of Poland Soap Works in Anniston, Alabama, would occasionally add an original recipe to flavor the copy in his *Bulletin,* which included reports on the economy of the country, feature stories on places he traveled to, and characters he met along the way. I've left his recipe as it was printed originally, including his tips on cleanliness, which lead into the pitch for his soap products. Only the measures have been changed—the original ingredients were measured in teacupfuls. Use this sauce for outdoor charcoal barbecuing or broiling and also for kitchen oven cooking.

2 lemons, sliced
3/4 cup white vinegar
3/4 cup water
1/2 cup Worcestershire sauce
2 tablespoons butter
2 tablespoons bacon or ham drippings

2 tablespoons salt
2 tablespoons freshly ground
    black pepper
1 tablespoon dry mustard
1 tablespoon ground red pepper

Put all the ingredients into a saucepan and bring slowly to the boil, then simmer for about 20 minutes.

Instructions for barbecuing meat:

The very best barbecue must be cooked very slowly over a fire that is not very hot. Sprinkle a very little water on the burning coals every now and then. This will make them smoke, and you need that smoke for proper flavor.

Barbecuing requires skill in handling the fire, which must be very low. Time required for spare ribs is not less than 2 hours, and they should be cooked until the fat hardly bubbles out. As long as the fat drips out, the cooking is incomplete.

For steaks, use those 2 inches thick and figure that this will take 2–3 hours cooking.

Some persons like tomato catsup on barbecue. The barbecue sauce can be strained and catsup added if wanted. Use this sauce only as a serving sauce, and never use it for cooking.

Cleanliness is always in good taste, and there is always agreement as to what constitutes good cooking.

Cleanliness is always in good taste and there is always agreement that cleanliness is attractive. When you think of cleanliness, let me tell you how to get it. . . .

Kay's Lexington Barbecue Sauce

Makes 2¹/2 cups

In Lexington, North Carolina, there are so many barbecue restaurants they hold annual barbecue-sauce contests. Kay Goldstein is from Lexington, and she taught me that barbecue sauce is best on top of cole slaw on top of barbecued pork. This is her recipe. She loves hush puppies with her barbecue and always serves the meat

Kay's Lexington Barbecue Sauce, continued

with pita bread or French bread rather than buns or store-bought "marshmallow" bread.

3 tablespoons sugar	1/8 teaspoon red pepper
1 cup apple-cider vinegar	3/4 teaspoon salt
2/3 cup ketchup	Freshly ground black pepper
1/2 cup water	Dash Tabasco

Mix together the sugar and vinegar in a small non-aluminum pan, and heat until the sugar dissolves. Add the remaining ingredients and simmer for 10 minutes, stirring occasionally. If the sauce is too thick, add more water; if too thin, boil it down a bit more. Serve over barbecue with grated cabbage or cole slaw.

Alternative Sauce for Goat

Makes 4 1/2 cups

This sauce is also wonderful served with grilled rabbit, but be sure to cut the recipe at least by half.

3 cups white wine	3 tablespoons ground hot red pepper
6 tablespoons butter	3 green onions, chopped
3 tablespoons soy sauce	
1 cup peanuts, chopped in a blender or food processor	

Mix all the ingredients together in a heavy saucepan. Bring to the boil and serve hot.

Hot Sauce

Makes 4 quarts

Many Southerners keep a jar of hot sauce on the table to sprinkle liberally on meats and vegetables alike at every meal. When I was in college, we felt our dormitory meals were inedible without it. The spiciness varies according to the amount of hot peppers, so if you like a milder sauce, use less.

1½ quarts seeded and chopped hot
    red peppers (see p. 319)
1½ quarts peeled and sliced onions

2 quarts distilled vinegar or
    apple-cider vinegar

Place the peppers, onions, and vinegar in a large pot and cook over medium heat until the peppers and onions are soft, about 30 minutes. Remove the solids and purée them in a blender or a food processor. Add the liquid and stir to blend thoroughly. Season with salt to taste and store in covered jars or bottles.

Creole Seasoning

Makes 1½ cups

Keeps indefinitely, tightly covered. If you prefer a milder version, cut the amount of black pepper and cayenne in half.

2 tablespoons oregano
⅛ cup salt
5 cloves garlic, crushed with
    1 tablespoon salt

¼ cup freshly ground black pepper
⅓ cup cayenne pepper
2 tablespoons thyme
⅓ cup paprika

Combine all the ingredients and stir to mix thoroughly. Pour into a large glass jar.

Sweet Southern Dressing

Makes 4 quarts

If you add poppy seeds, you will have a recipe popularized by the late Helen Corbitt, the famous cook for Neiman-Marcus. This dressing is fabulous on fruit salads, as well as on Fennel and Apple Salad (p. 67). It keeps indefinitely in a covered jar in the refrigerator. However, it may separate after six months or so — just pour it in the blender or food processor and reblend.

1 1/2 cups sugar
2 teaspoons Dijon mustard
2 teaspoons salt
3 tablespoons chopped onions

2/3 cup apple-cider vinegar
2 cups vegetable oil
3 tablespoons poppy seeds or
   chopped pecans

Place the sugar, mustard, salt, onions, and vinegar in a food processor or blender and blend until smooth. Pour in the oil in a steady stream, and continue to blend until thick. Add poppy seeds or pecans. Keep covered in the refrigerator.

Oyster Sauce

Makes 1/2 cup

This sauce will keep a few days in the refrigerator, and is tasty over venison, steak, and a variety of other things. A store-bought variety is available in Oriental food markets.

6 shucked oysters (see p. 318)
1/2 cup oyster liquid
1 1/2 tablespoons soy sauce

Chop the oysters and place in a pan along with their liquid. Bring to the boil and simmer, covered, for 20 minutes. Strain through a sieve and throw away the oysters. Add soy sauce and stir to blend. Store in a tightly covered jar in a cool place.

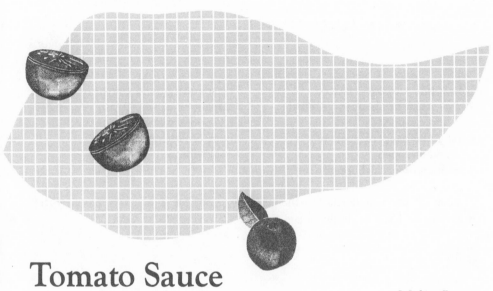

Tomato Sauce

Makes 5 cups

Ideally you make this quick tomato sauce with fresh tomatoes. I never seem to have enough of them to make both the Tomato Conserve (p. 304) and this sauce, so I use fresh tomatoes for the conserve and canned tomatoes for the sauce. A word of warning—never make sauce or conserve with those pale round things that pass for tomatoes in winter.

1/4 cup peanut oil	1/2 teaspoon oregano
2 small onions, chopped	1/2 teaspoon basil
2 cloves garlic, crushed with salt or chopped	1/2 teaspoon thyme 1 tablespoon sugar
2 one-pound cans plum tomatoes, seeded and chopped, juice saved	Salt Freshly ground black pepper
1/4 cup tomato paste	

Heat the oil in a heavy saucepan. Add the onions and cook until soft. Add garlic, cook briefly, then add the tomatoes with their juice, tomato paste, herbs, and seasonings. Bring to the boil, reduce to a simmer, and cook, partially covered, 30–45 minutes, stirring occasionally. If the sauce gets too thick, it may be thinned down with water or tomato juice. If too watery, simmer to reduce the liquid, then purée in a food processor or blender or work through a sieve.

Chili Sauce

3 quarts

1 peck ripe tomatoes, halved
4 large green bell peppers, seeded
    and chopped
6 hot green peppers, seeded
    and chopped
6 medium onions, chopped

2 teaspoons ground cinnamon
2 teaspoons cloves
2 teaspoons salt
2 cups brown sugar
5 cups vinegar

Simmer all the ingredients together in a large pot for 2 hours or more, stirring occasionally. Pack in sterilized jars and seal.

Creole Brown Fish Sauce

Makes 2¹/2 cups

This sauce is called a brown fish sauce because it calls for either a traditional brown stock like canned beef bouillon or is made from browning fish bones and vegetables, adding water and wine, and simmering. The finishing step makes it a full-bodied, glossy, rich sauce.

13 tablespoons butter, cut into pieces
5 tablespoons flour
1 cup fish stock or brown stock
    (p. 320)

2 tablespoons freshly chopped parsley
1 tablespoon Worcestershire sauce
Juice of ¹/2 lemon

Melt 5 tablespoons of the butter and cook until it turns a rich brown color. Add flour and cook again until browned. Pour in the stock and bring to the boil, stirring constantly. Reduce the heat to a simmer. To finish the sauce, whisk in the remaining butter, the parsley, and Worcestershire sauce without boiling, until the butter is completely absorbed into the sauce. Add lemon juice and whisk again until smooth.

White Butter Sauce

Makes 1 1/2 cups

This is one of my favorite sauces. It's very versatile and particularly suited to fish and vegetables, but also goes well with beef and chicken.

6 tablespoons white wine vinegar, or
   3 tablespoons vinegar and
   3 tablespoons lemon juice,
   combined
4 tablespoons dry white wine
   (optional)

2 tablespoons chopped shallots
   or scallions
1 1/2 cups butter
Salt
Freshly ground black pepper

Place all the ingredients except the butter, salt, and pepper in a saucepan and bring to the boil. Boil down until only 2 tablespoons remain. Cut the butter into 1–2-inch pieces and whisk into the sauce over low heat. If the butter separates from being too hot, remove pan and place in the refrigerator briefly, then return to heat to get the sauce back to its proper milky-white texture, whisking all the while. Taste for seasoning and add salt and pepper if necessary. May be made ahead, refrigerated, and reheated, whisking, over low heat. Strain or serve as is.

White Butter Sauce with Ginger

Add 1 tablespoon chopped fresh ginger with the shallots.

White Butter Sauce with Tomatoes and Herbs

1 tomato, peeled, seeded, and chopped
4 tablespoons chopped fresh basil or
   other fresh herbs
1 recipe White Butter Sauce

Combine the tomato, herbs, and White Butter Sauce.

White Butter Sauce with Leeks

Substitute the julienned white part of 3 leeks for the shallots.

Basil and Garlic Butter

Makes 1 pound

Just before the first frost I pick all the basil left in our garden and blend it with butter. I freeze it and use it all winter long. You can combine just the basil and butter, of course, but I frequently add garlic as well. It's wonderful as a spread for bread and as a sauce and flavoring for rice and pasta, sometimes combined with Parmesan cheese.

1 pound butter
1/3–1/2 cup chopped fresh basil
3 or 4 cloves garlic, chopped

Blend the butter and some of the basil and garlic in a food processor or blender. Taste and add more basil and garlic if desired.

Hot Onion Relish

Makes 6–8 pints

This is good on cold meats.

3 large Vidalia onions, finely chopped
12 red bell peppers, finely chopped
12 green bell peppers, finely chopped
1 hot pepper, finely chopped

1 tablespoon salt
1 cup brown sugar
1 quart white vinegar

Put the onions, bell peppers, and hot pepper into a pot of boiling water and boil for 20 minutes. Meanwhile, in a kettle bring additional water to the boil. Pour off the water in which the onions and pepper have been cooked. Then pour over enough boiling water to cover the vegetables and boil again for 15 minutes. Pour off the water again and add salt, sugar, and vinegar. Boil 10 minutes, ladle into sterilized jars, and seal.

Peach-Pimento Jelly

Makes seven 8-ounce jars

Serve with brunch, lamb, or pork dishes.

5 cups sugar
1 seven-ounce jar pimentos
4 peaches, peeled and seeded

1/2 cup white wine
2 pouches liquid pectin (see p. 318)

Place the sugar in a large pot. Purée the pimentos and peaches with the wine in a food processor or blender. Add the purée to the sugar and bring to the boil over low heat. Boil 2 minutes. Remove from the heat and stir in the pectin. Let sit 5 minutes, then skim foam off the top. Ladle into sterilized jars and seal.

Hot Pepper Jelly

Makes 4 pints

Try this on top of cream cheese spread on crackers. It is also excellent with country ham or on green beans or peas.

1/2 cup hot red pepper, seeded
    and coarsely chopped
1/2 cup hot green pepper, seeded
    and coarsely chopped

1 cup chopped onion
1 1/2 cups vinegar
5 cups sugar
2 pouches liquid pectin (see p. 318)

Place the hot peppers, onion, and vinegar in a food processor or blender. Process until very fine. Pour the sugar into a heavy non-aluminum pot. Stir in the pepper mixture, bring to the boil, and boil for 1 minute. Remove from the heat and stir in the pectin. Let sit 5 minutes and then remove the foam with a slotted spoon. Ladle into sterilized jars and seal. Turn the jars upside down occasionally to keep the peppers mixed until the jelly is cool and set.

Phyllis Cherry's Spiced Grapes

Yields 14 half pints

This recipe for spiced grapes is an old, family-prized "receipt" from a dear friend from Tuscaloosa, Alabama. It is time-consuming to make, but wonderful with venison and other game.

10 pounds Concord grapes
4½ pounds sugar
1 cup apple-cider vinegar

2½ teaspoons allspice
3½ teaspoons cinnamon
5 teaspoons ground cloves

Remove the hulls from the pulp of the grapes to a large bowl, placing the pulp in a heavy cast-iron pot. Cook the pulp over low heat until the seeds come out. Strain and throw away the seeds. Add the pulp to the bowl containing the hulls. You may stop at this point and refrigerate the grape mixture if necessary. Add the sugar, vinegar, allspice, cinnamon, and cloves, place in a heavy kettle, and bring to the boil, stirring constantly, as the mixture burns easily. Adjust the heat and boil gently about 1½ hours. The mixture will look like grape preserves. Pour into sterilized half-pint jars and seal.

Tomato Conserve (Tomato Relish or Preserves)

Makes 4 or 5 pints

This is a typical Southern relish. Serve over green beans, black-eyed peas, butter beans, or cabbage.

4 pounds fresh tomatoes, skinned and
    quartered, or 4 one-pound cans
    of tomatoes with juice, chopped
    coarse

1 cup apple-cider vinegar
½ cup sugar
Salt to taste
Freshly ground black pepper to taste

Place all the ingredients in a heavy non-aluminum saucepan. Cook slowly, stirring as necessary, until the mixture is so thick that it sticks to a spoon when you lift the spoon out of the pan, about 2 hours. Taste for seasoning, add more sugar, salt, and pepper, if needed. Put up in sterilized jars.

Grandma's Artichoke Pickle

Makes 4 quarts

This old recipe is from my family files, so I've named it in honor of my grandmother. Jerusalem artichokes are very popular in the South, easy to grow, and when pickled this way, delicious on greens.

5 pounds Jerusalem artichokes,
    well scrubbed and chopped
6 cups chopped onions
1 bunch celery, leaves removed, sliced
3 or 4 green bell peppers, chopped
1/2 cup salt (scant)
2 tablespoons mustard seed, softened
    in 1/4 cup hot water

1 pound brown sugar
1 quart apple-cider vinegar
1 1/2 teaspoons turmeric
Dash Tabasco
1/2 cup flour

Place the artichokes, onions, celery, and peppers in a large pot. Add salt, mustard seed, brown sugar, vinegar, turmeric, and Tabasco. Cover and bring to the boil, then stir in the flour. When thickened, remove from the heat and put into sterilized jars. Refrigerate only after opening.

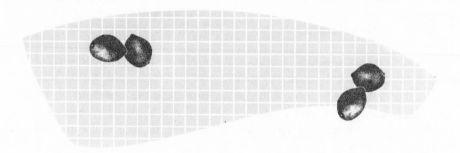

New-Style Pimento Cheese

Makes 3 cups

Try this between slices of fresh white loaf bread, or use it to top a piece of smoked turkey on a thick slice of French bread and run under the broiler a few minutes. It's also good spread on celery.

12 ounces coarsely grated
   Cheddar cheese
2 four-ounce jars diced pimentos
1 cup mayonnaise

1 small onion, grated
2 tablespoons Worcestershire sauce
Freshly ground black pepper

Combine all the ingredients in a large bowl and stir to blend thoroughly. Season to taste with lots of black pepper.

Mayonnaise

Makes 1 1/4–1 3/4 cups

Mayonnaise and hollandaise are similar sauces because they both use egg yolks to absorb the fat and to keep it in suspension. In my restaurant in Spain I made several quarts daily by hand in no more than 10 minutes. It's easy if you learn the basics.

2 whole eggs, at room temperature
Salt and pepper
1/8 teaspoon Dijon mustard

1/2–1 cup oil, at room temperature
   or warmer
2–3 tablespoons lemon juice

In a small bowl, using a small whisk, beat the eggs and 1/8 teaspoon each of salt, pepper, and mustard until thick and sticky. Add 2 tablespoons of the oil, a little at a time, then stir in 1 teaspoon of the lemon juice. Add the remaining oil, 1 tablespoon at a time, beating after each addition until it is absorbed. When all the oil has been absorbed, add the remaining lemon juice to taste and extra salt and pepper as necessary.

To thin and lighten the mayonnaise, add a little hot water. Or for a coating consistency, thin with a little cream or milk.

If the mayonnaise separates or refuses to thicken, start with a fresh yolk in a clean bowl and whisk well. Add 2 tablespoons of the curdled mixture to it very slowly and carefully drop by drop. Then add a little more quickly. When the curdled mixture is completely incorporated, more oil can be added if the mayonnaise is too thin.

Here's an alternative method: In a warm, dry mixing bowl, start with 1 teaspoon of Dijon mustard and 1 tablespoon of the "turned" mayonnaise. Beat with the whisk for several seconds, until thickened a bit. Beat in the rest of the sauce drop by drop until you can add it by tablespoons.

The mayonnaise keeps up to a week during the winter, only 2–3 days in summer if the refrigerator door is opened a lot. If it is not to be used immediately, cover it.

Peanut Butter Mayonnaise

Add 2 tablespoons peanut butter to the mayonnaise.

Notes on Ingredients

Barbecuing, see *Grilling and Barbecuing*

Caveach

This is the West Indian spelling of what is usually called "escabeche," according to Karen Hess in her edited version of *The Virginia Housewife*. In the West Indies, caveach was a very popular way of preserving fish in an acidic bath, a method that was adapted in the 1600s in England and then later in the South.

Caviar

The caviar (or eggs) from American sturgeon was once commonplace—it was even served in bars during the depression in the 1930s. Unfortunately, over the years the effects of pollution and overfishing took their toll. But gradually the American sturgeon is coming back and its roe produces a caviar to rival the Iranian and Russian. We now produce Southern caviars, such as "Georgetown" caviar named after Georgetown, South Carolina. Whether your caviar is American or imported, always place it in a small bowl, then in a larger bowl of ice and preferably eat with a non-metallic fork; second-best is a silver fork. Serve it with crisp toast rounds, chopped egg, chopped onion, and sour cream.

Chicken and Chicken Breasts
One of the hardest things to describe is a chicken breast. Every chicken has a chest, divided by a sternum bone, with a breast on each side. In France, each of these breasts is called a *suprême*. Here, however, in an attempt to be clear, we erroneously call the chest of chicken the "whole" breast. I don't like it, but I am not prepared for an all-out campaign on this issue. One-half a chicken chest (a chicken breast or *suprême*) is usually sufficient for a dinner portion. If that is not enough for your guests, you may want to prepare more for the heavier eaters. Most recipes are not affected by the addition of a chicken breast or two.

Citrus Fruits and Their Rinds
Thick-skinned citrus fruits do not contain the same amount of juice as thin-skinned. The thinner-skinned Florida citrus usually have more juice than thicker-skinned California citrus, for instance. The rinds of the California fruits are better for "zesting," however. The rind of a citrus fruit is best used when all the white, which is bitter, is removed. An easy way to do this is to peel the rind off with a potato peeler then chop it with a sharp knife. Or there are wonderful gadgets on the market that remove the zest in little slivers, without any further chopping. The rinds may also be grated, while still on the fruit, with care taken to avoid grating any of the white. I must admit I use the words zest and rind interchangeably, always meaning that the white is removed, unless stated otherwise.

Collards
Collards are a very common Southern green. Unlike some turnip greens, collards have no root vegetable. They are related to cabbage and kale. A very old vegetable, probably with African origins, they are fleshy and have a little "bite" to them. The silver-green leaves grow large and are thicker than turnip greens. They should be well washed, and the stems, ribs, and thick center vein removed before cooking. When cooked in the traditional way, they have an affinity for hot pepper sauce. Since turnip greens and collards are considered antidotes for indigestion, it is no wonder Southerners always serve them on New Year's Day. You can often substitute collards for turnip greens in recipes.

Corn Meal
Corn is divided into two general varieties, white and yellow. White corn is preferred in the Southeast and yellow corn in the West and North (except Rhode Island).

Corn meal is prepared by grinding corn to the desired degree of fineness. The bran and germ are removed in the milling process. Some Southern corn meal mixes are ground from the whole kernel, so that some of the bran and most of the germ remain. This gives a fuller corn flavor and extra nutrition. Corn meal is available to consumers as plain corn meal, self-rising corn meal, and self-rising corn meal mix (referred to in the recipes simply as "corn meal mix"). Plain corn meal is packaged as it is with essentially no added ingredients with the exception of enrichment. Self-rising corn meal includes baking powder and salt. Self-rising corn meal mixes vary as to the ingredients; generally, they are made with 1 cup corn meal, 1 cup all purpose flour, and 4 teaspoons baking powder. Sometimes you'll find a buttermilk corn meal mix.

Country Ham

Country ham—also called salted or smoked ham—is "put up" (the colloquialism for salting and curing) both at home and commercially. This was originally done to provide meat for the winter. When purchasing commercial country ham, look for those that have undergone federal inspection. As part of my television series I visited Smithfield, Virginia, to see how they cured their famous hams. I found that their hams are treated much as country hams are all over the South. After slaughtering and trimming, the usual curing process starts with hand rubbing a mixture of nitrate and salt into the country ham. After a period of refrigeration with the salt, approximately forty days, the hams are washed of their salt, then hung with string or mesh for two weeks, after which time they are oak- or hickory-smoked for ten days above ninety degrees, which kills trichinae. However, a Smithfield ham has a "long cut" that includes the loin and has the shank intact. It is salted and aged longer, a minimum of 180 days, and usually up to nine months. At one time it was required by law that pigs for Smithfield hams be fed only peanut feed. The regulation was changed in 1968, as it was no longer practical. Since an oily ham is preferred, the regulation now allows a feed mix that includes peanut oil. A corn-fed hog will shrink more than an oily hog. Most Smithfield hams come from animals that are raised in the area between Moultrie, Georgia, and Virginia.

If the federal regulations and procedures have been followed, Smithfield hams and other country hams are safe to eat with no further cooking, like a prosciutto ham. They have a moldy exterior, which needs to be scrubbed. They then may be sliced and eaten. Many people prefer to cook the ham further, although this is not necessary. My way of cooking a country ham is to slice the ham, trim off the mold and/or fat, then either fry it immediately or soak it in water for 10 minutes to an hour, changing the water if the ham is too salty, then frying it. There is no such thing as "baked country ham"—it would be nearly inedible. What's called "baked country ham" is really a boiled ham that is briefly glazed in the oven. However, I do not like this method because it tends to make the ham dry and tasteless. By the way, Betty Talmadge, of Talmadge Hams in Georgia, also prefers country ham that is sliced and fried.

If boil and bake a country ham you must, then scrub it well, and soak it overnight in water in the sink or bathtub. Change the water every few hours (if you don't you are simply creating a salt brine and you'll just rebrine your ham), then simmer the ham for 8 hours in liquid to cover—water, pineapple juice, Coca-Cola, stock, etc. The ham is done when soft enough so that a knife or skewer is easily inserted. For country hams prepared without following federal regulations, make sure the ham registers 160 degrees on a meat thermometer. (Trichinae are killed at 140 degrees.) After this simmering, the ham may be glazed and briefly baked to set the glaze.

Crabs, Hard-shell

Don't buy crabs right after a storm; they will be gritty. Only 10 to 15 percent of the hard-shell crab is edible, so the cleaning of it is truly a labor of love. The crabs must first be cooked to remove the meat. (See page 121 for cooking directions.)

To eat, twist off the claws and legs where they are attached to the body. Crack the claws and legs with a nutcracker or mallet and remove the meat. Place the crab body on its back and pull open the apron tab on its belly. This unlocks the body from the shell. Pull the shell off the body and save the shell for stuffing, if desired. Clean the crab body by removing and discarding the spongy gills (the "dead men"), the organ and mouth parts. Rinse briefly. Break the crab in half at the middle, then cut each half in two pieces. Pick out the back fin and lump meat from the body chambers. The lump meat should come out in large, white lumps; it is dear, both in price and good taste.

Crabs, Soft-shell

Completely edible, soft-shell crabs are blue crabs that have outgrown their hard outer shells. In order to continue to grow comfortably a crab must shed its shell. In their normal three-year life span, blue crabs will shed their shells as many as twenty-three times. The crabs vary in size. Measure the width between one point and the other of the crab body to determine the size—there are six sizes sold, from "small" to "whale," so how many you serve per person will be determined by that. Normally two "whales" or three "jumbos" will be sufficient for a dinner portion for one.

As crabs approach the molting stage, they're called "peelers," and develop a scarlet color on one of their claws. When crabbers see this sign they set the peelers aside in a large shallow tank of recirculating fresh saltwater, or a floating "crib." As their shells crack and they back out of them, the crabs are called "busters," or "soft-shell crabs." The defenseless "busters" need to be moved right away as the other crabs, still in their shells, occasionally will attack them. About a day or so after molting, the new shell has hardened.

There is a vast difference between fresh and frozen soft-shell crabs. Fresh soft-shell crabs have a crunch and squirt to them, as if air and water are trapped inside and released when cooked. Frozen ones are less crunchy, and don't have that wonderful flush of juiciness. Therefore, they are best battered and fried crisp. To prepare fresh soft-shell crabs for cooking, cut across the face at an upward angle with scissors to remove the eyes, sand sac, and lower mouth. Lift up the shell and remove the "dead-men" (the spongy gray gills) from either side. Pull down the apron tab and snip off the full apron.

A little sex education: Female crabs, called "sooks," have pincers with bright red tips. Male crabs, called "Jimmys," have blue-and-white pincers. The abdomen, or "tab"—it looks like the tab on a soft-drink can—also gives you a clue to the sex of the crab. The male tab is T-shaped; the female is broad and rounded. The immature female (a "Sally") has a triangular tab. Some people prefer the male, others the female. Some states do not allow you to keep the female in season.

Cracklings

Although store-bought cracklings contain the skin of the hog, country folks make their cracklings by cutting scraps of pure hog fat into small chunks. The chunks are boiled gently until the lard is rendered out of them, then fried in the lard until they are crisp.

Crawfish

Crawfish are so popular now that they are considered a second crop for Louisiana rice farmers. The crawfish are put into the rice fields in the latter part of May when the rice is eleven or twelve inches high. The females burrow down in the cool mud and remain buried until September or October, when the rice fields are reflooded. The female then emerges and releases her baby crawdads, which feed on the rice stubble and begin maturing. It takes them 90 to 120 days to reach maturity. Some are caught in December, but harvesting often continues until May.

There is a great deal of ritual to eating a crawfish. First, the crawfish is snapped in two between the head and tail. Some aficionados suck the head to remove the juicy fat inside. Others take their little fingers and scoop out the fat, licking it from their fingers. Still others avoid the head altogether and proceed to the tail. The shell of the tail is removed by peeling it off in rings. The tail is the meaty, most edible portion of the crawfish. Crawfish is available in many forms these days: whole, fresh; fresh tails, unpeeled; fresh tails, peeled and uncooked; fresh tails, peeled and cooked; and frozen tails, peeled and uncooked or cooked. Fresh are the most desirable; the frozen and cooked, the least.

Cream

First, an important distinction between heavy cream and whipping cream: heavy cream has at least 36 percent butterfat. But whipping cream by law does not need to have more than 30 percent. The higher the butterfat content the better the results, the richer the flavor, and the easier to whip. Therefore, it is important to seek out and ask for heavy cream for whipping. In cooking, the higher butterfat ratio also makes a more lustrous sauce. If you should ever need to reduce the butterfat, you could of course just add whole milk (called "sweet milk" in the South), which has 3.5 percent butterfat.

Cream has gone through many changes since colonial days. The best and the worst of it is ultra-pasteurization. Ultra-pasteurization heats to a temperature much higher than is used in regular pasteurization, and gives cream a much longer shelf life than it would have otherwise. It also makes the cream harder to whip, particularly if it has ever come to room temperature.

Eggs

I use grade A large eggs. A grade A large egg weighs two ounces. The egg white measures a bit more than an ounce, the yolk a bit under an ounce. I usually beat my egg whites by hand in a copper bowl, as a copper bowl gives nearly one-third again as much volume as beating with an electric mixer. When no copper bowl is available,

I try to use a Kitchen Aid electric mixer, as the movement of its whisk is most like the hand motion. There is a copper bowl attachment that fits this machine. If you haven't got a copper bowl you should add cream of tartar. Both the use of a copper bowl and the addition of a pinch of cream of tartar stabilize the egg whites.

Fatback

Fatback is the fat off the lower back of the hog, the preferred cut for many dishes, since it does not dissolve easily. Fatback may be fresh or salt-cured. Many people interchange fatback and streak-o'-lean.

Field Peas

The South is renowned for its flavorful field peas, which include lady peas, black-eyed peas, crowder peas (purple hulls), cowpeas, and whippoorwills. Although referred to as peas, each is technically a horticultural variety of legume, *Vigna sinensis,* which is neither a pea nor a bean. There are references to field peas in Thomas Jefferson's documented notes from the late eighteenth century.

Freshly picked, field peas require less cooking time, but they are usually used dried, and provide a valuable element of protein in our diets all winter long.

Flour

If you've ever tried to make a cake, pie crust, or bread from a recipe in a new cookbook or in a magazine article and had a flop, or if you've moved from the South to the North and can't make your favorite biscuit or cake recipe work, chances are it's because of the flour you're using. The flours sold in the North and in the South are so different because of the wheats used that it can make all the difference in a recipe.

The biscuit and cake recipes in this book depend on a soft winter-wheat flour for their success. You can try substituting a combination of one part all-purpose to one part cake flour for the soft-wheat flour I call for, but the baked goods won't be as light. Instead, I would advise using White Lily flour for these recipes; it can easily be found in markets in the South and it can be ordered by mail through the White Lily Foods Company, 218 Depot, Knoxville, Tennessee 37901.

There are many factors in the flour that affect a recipe. First, the actual difference in weight between a pure soft winter-wheat flour (a "Southern" flour) and a hard summer-wheat or blended flour (a "non-Southern" flour) can vary from 1/2 to 3/4 cup per pound of flour. A pound of "Southern" flour might average 2 3/4 or 3 cups; a pound of non-Southern all-purpose flour is about 3 1/2 cups. I'm talking about an unopened package; if the package has been opened and left on your shelf, the weight might vary even more, depending on humidity and the type of flour. In addition to the difference in weight, the flours vary in their ability to absorb liquid. Standard soft-wheat flour absorbs about 7 percent less liquid than hard wheat.

There is no accurate measure for gluten. However, sometimes the consumer can tell the difference in the gluten content of flour, if on the side of the flour package there is nutrition information. The higher the protein count (with the exception of whole-wheat flour, which cannot be included in this method of measure), the higher the gluten content is. Hence, bread flour usually has about 14 grams of protein per cup, whereas cake flour, such as Swans Down, has about 8 grams. Southern all-purpose and self-rising flours, such as White Lily, also have about 8 grams. Northern flours, or those flours distributed nationally, such as Gold Medal and Pillsbury, run about I I grams protein per cup for all-purpose, I 2 grams for unbleached all-purpose.

Self-rising flour
Self-rising flour is just all-purpose flour with baking powder and salt added to it; it is used primarily for biscuits, muffins, and other quick breads. To make self-rising flour, add 1/2 teaspoon salt and 1 1/2 teaspoons baking powder to 1 cup of all-purpose flour.

Unbleached flour
This is a flour that has not been bleached or had maturing agents added to it.

Bread flour
When you find flour labeled "bread flour" in the market, it is made of the hardest wheat flours, which are generally considered most suitable for bread baking and pasta making. However, some aficionados of homemade bread prefer soft-wheat-flour breads because they slice and hold together better in sandwiches and toast and have a fuller flavor.

Garlic
Garlic varies in size and consists of several cloves enclosed in an outer skin. The entire cluster of cloves is called a garlic "head." To peel a clove, give it a good whack with the flat side of a knife. The skin should come off easily. Chop the clove by hand with a sharp knife or in a food processor, or do as I was trained to do, crush the garlic with a little salt using the flat side of a knife. The garlic can be used right away or you might consider preparing a quantity of garlic in this way and storing it in the refrigerator. It will keep in a covered jar, if refrigerated, for several months. Please note that you might want to reduce the salt in the dish you are preparing accordingly.

Goat Cheese
The demand for this tangy white cheese has increased in recent years. First-class *chèvre*, as it is called in France, is produced in Georgia from herds of Nubian, Toggenburg, and Alpine breeds. One gallon of goat milk yields one and a half pounds of cheese. This domestic goat cheese is fresh, soft cheese, and can be combined with herbs and oil, spread on French bread, served as a filling for chicken and meats or as an accompaniment to fruits and vegetables.

Since many people do not like, or cannot get, fresh goat cheese, I have suggested substituting a soft white cheese such as an herb-flavored Boursin or Rondelé.

Green Onions, Scallions, Shallots
Who would think anything so simple could have so many names? Regional differences prevail even in this simple vegetable. Any onion bulb when planted sends out a green shoot. Scallions are the tiny immature onions plus their green shoots. They are also

called "spring onions," regardless of when they are harvested. A shallot, which is about the size of a garlic clove, is an especially flavorful member of the onion family, and tastes something like a cross between an onion and garlic. It too sends out a green shoot, and in Louisiana and some parts of Alabama the shallot is sold, when immature, as a scallion. However, in most of the South, the word used in supermarkets to describe small onions with green shoots is "green onions," not "scallions." I never knew what a scallion or a shallot was until I moved to London. I used to stand, immobilized, at the greengrocer's, trying to remember the correct word, since both started with an *s*, and both were unfamiliar to me. Scallions and shallots are quite different in flavor. However, I am not a purist in any sense. When I've specified green onions in this book, I've done so as much for color as for flavor. But you can always substitute shallots or for that matter any kind of onion, compensating for the difference in size.

Grilling and Barbecuing

Southerners have a long outdoor cooking season, owing to many months of temperate weather. Anything and everything goes on the grill. Meats, seafood, vegetables, and fruits are marinated and grilled, and served with a variety of barbecue sauces. There are several methods for grilling, but the important difference is between direct and indirect heat. Direct heat means you put the food to be grilled directly over the coals. This is the best method when you want to cook flat cuts of meat quickly. When you cook by indirect heat, you don't place your food right over the fire. Usually you shove your coals over to one side of the grill and set the food on the other. An easy way is to put a pan in the bottom of your grill and arrange your coals around it, then put your food over the pan. The time required for cooking varies with the proximity of the food to the coals, and the number of burning coals. Before putting food on the grill, always let coals heat to the point at which any lighting fluids you may have used will have burned off, or the food might taste of the fluid.

Different native woods, including hickory, pecan, oak, fruit woods, and even grapevines, are soaked in water and used for smoke and flavor. Pecans and hickory nuts are also used for their special aromas and flavors. I started using whole pecans in my grilling when my mother gave me her annual gift of unshelled pecans from her pecan trees. Every few years her trees take a rest and put out pecans that aren't quite perfect—either too small to fool around with cracking them and picking the meat out or too mealy. Rather than throw these away, I threw them on the grill in their shells, after soaking them. The result was a flavor that I thought rivaled that given by expensive mesquite.

Like mesquite, pecan "culls" are free to those who pick them, costly to those who must buy them. At any rate, pecans in their shells are a fraction of the cost of shelled pecan halves, and no more expensive than mesquite. If you can't bear to lose the meat inside, save your shells and use them instead of the whole nut, but know the flavor is not the same. I use a covered Weber grill or a smoker for my grilling. You may have to adapt times for your own setup.

Grits

Grits in their purest form are just corn ground into grist, or "grits." However, in some varieties of grits the bran and germ have been removed. In the past, grits had to be prewashed and soaked, but now, with the packaged variety, all you have to do is boil the grits in liquid for a shorter time. Yo must take care to stir frequently to avoid scorching. Southerners have grits as standard breakfast fare, served with bacon, ham, sausage, eggs, and biscuits. Grits are also a good accompaniment for fried fish and may be served as a side dish and a substitute for rice or potatoes at any meal. Leftover grits are often pressed into a tall glass, chilled, then cut into patties, dipped into cracker or corn meal, and fried in hot fat. Grits are never served as a cereal with sugar and cream. They are traditionally eaten with a pat of butter melting on top.

Grits come in many different versions, and each varies slightly as to the amount of liquid and cooking time needed. There are speckled grits, regular grits, quick grits, and instant grits, for instance. I never seem to have the right kind of grits on hand for the recipe I'm doing, so I've adapted the recipes to the grits on hand by following the package directions for cooking them, substituting liquid amounts and time for cooking. I also cook my grits in liquids other than water—whipping cream, chicken stock, yogurt, or any liquid that complements the occasion.

Herbs

Fresh herbs are now available almost year round all over the United States. Fresh parsley is available in even the smallest of towns. Local restaurants will also usually help a customer in search of a fresh herb. I grow my own. At the end of the season I wash the remaining herbs and then layer them in a jar with vegetable oil, which preserves them so I can use them all winter long. I also freeze herbs, usually chopping them first. There is no ratio for dried versus fresh herbs as far as I am concerned. A dried herb should not be kept longer than six months as it loses its flavor. The average household mistakenly keeps a dried herb for years. Therefore, you must taste to determine how much of an herb you need. I do not subscribe to the one dried to three fresh ratio—usually I use equal amounts of dried and fresh. The dried herbs are so tasteless, with a few exceptions, rosemary and tarragon primarily, that I like to use more of them.

Incidentally, I've noticed many recipes call for chopped fresh rosemary, but I find chopping it fine makes it too pungent. I sometimes crush it as you do dried rosemary. It is an herb that should be used judiciously, tasting as you add a little, rather than adding it all at once.

The stalk of parsley is stronger in flavor than the parsley leaf, and should be used in stocks, stews, etc., rather than the leaf. Parsley is a good source of iron. Remove the stalk when the stock is completed.

There are many kinds of basil, and even more varieties of thyme, so these too need to be added by taste and by using good sense. I like a medley of herbs in my recipes, picking what's fresh and available that day without a concern for ratio or type. I enjoy changing the taste of my dishes by using different herbs each day.

Madeira
Madeira is a fortified wine, meaning that brandy is added to prevent the sugar of the grapes from totally fermenting. Varieties of Madeira can taste sweet, smoky, buttery, or dry. Dry Sherry is an acceptable substitute for the dry Madeira used in these recipes.

Madeira has been popular in North America since the 1800s. It was so well liked that it was used to toast the Declaration of Independence. When the decision was made to locate the U.S. capital in Washington, D.C., Thomas Jefferson toasted the occasion with Madeira, and George Washington's Inauguration was toasted with Madeira at Fraunces Tavern. In fact, Malcolm Bell, Jr., a member of the Madeira Club of Savannah (an elite cadre of intellectuals who meet monthly), read a paper on the "Romantic Wines of Madeira," later published in the *Georgia Historical Quarterly* of December 1954, in which he stated that George Washington drank a pint of Madeira at dinner daily. Madeira parties became very popular starting in the late 1800s. They usually began at 5 p.m. and continued for 2 or 3 hours, with biscuits and nuts eaten, and six different Madeiras passed. After three wines had been served, cigars were permitted. Noël Cossart in *Madeira: The Island Vineyard,* tells us that Madeira is the only wine whose strict devotees allow smoking. He says he finds a cigarette tickles up and revives his rather jaded palate.

Muscadine and Scuppernong Grapes
These are both meaty Southern grapes, the scuppernong being a variety of the muscadine. Muscadines are thick-skinned and dull purple in color. You usually eat them whole and spit out the seeds and skins. The fragrant sweet, juicy meat is worth the trouble.

Scuppernongs are silvery and amber-green, also with thick skins. They are named after a North Carolina river. Both grapes are made into jams, jellies, and wine.

Oysters
The Georgia–South Carolina coast oysters are some of the best in the world. They are salty but unbelievably fresh-tasting owing to the freshness of the water produced by the tide change of 10 to 11 1/2 feet between Hilton Head, South Carolina, and Savannah, Georgia. They are difficult to open, however, because they have a very sharp edge. The closest easy-to-open substitute is an Appalachicola, Florida, oyster (panhandle); its plumper, rounder shell is less sharp.

Pectin, Liquid
Pectin can be bought in a box containing two separate sealed pouches of liquid, as a jellying agent. The liquid sets up faster than powdered pectin, which is also available. I much prefer the liquid. Pectin used to be sold in bottles. With today's method of packaging, two pouches equal one bottle, in case you are following an old recipe that calls for a bottle.

Peppers

Bell Peppers

There are many varieties on the market now, but the most common are green peppers, which turn red on the vine when ripe. Ripened bell peppers have a mild, sweet taste. Pimento peppers are a type of bell pepper with a pointed bottom. The tastes of a red bell pepper and of a pimento are indistinguishable except to the most discriminating palate. However, canned varieties of each vary radically according to the processing.

Hot Peppers

Hot pepper varieties abound in the South, including rooster spur, cowhorn, peter peppers, bouquet peppers, yo-yo peppers, banana peppers (which may be either a mild or hot variety), cayenne, jalapeño, and tabasco peppers. The tabasco pepper is the hot pepper from which the famous Tabasco sauce took its name. Cayenne pepper is the most available dried hot pepper, but may also be bought fresh. The hotness varies from pepper to pepper, even on the same bush. So let your own taste be your guide. Remember, you can always add more. Hot pepper sauce (see page 297), a vinegar-based sauce, is a staple on every country dinner table. It has been used since colonial days.

Seasoning Salts and Creole Seasoning

There are many seasoning mixes available in the South—Crab Boil, Old Bay Seasoning, Chef Paul Prudhomme's Louisiana Cajun Magic, and my Creole Seasoning, to name a few. They all vary in spiciness and add dash to recipes. After using them a few times judiciously, you will arrive at a degree of spiciness agreeable to you and those you cook for.

Shad and Shad Roe

In the spring, this ocean fish (a member of the herring family) migrates up the St. John's River from Jacksonville, Florida, coming inland to spawn. The shad roe season progresses northward as the flowers bloom. The fish is not as flavorful or meaty when it is carrying its roe. Each female fish produces a double roe, connected by a very thin membrane. When bought as a double roe, separate by gently removing the connective tissue into two single roes. Shad is very bony, so buy it boned when you can. It not only has backbones and ribs but an extra set of bones on each side of the backbone. One usually buys a side of boned shad, which consists of a wide center piece attached to the skin and two narrow side pieces. Both shad and shad roe freeze well when fresh.

Shrimp

There are three varieties of Gulf and Atlantic shrimp. The most common are called "brownies" but are actually gray-green in color; they come mainly from the Gulf of Mexico. White shrimp are more expensive, as they are rarer, and are usually found in South Atlantic waters. Pink shrimp are caught primarily off the coast of Key West, Florida.

Shrimp are sold in three or four sizes: small, medium, large, and jumbo. How many shrimp there are to a pound varies since there is no law governing standard market sizes. As a rule of thumb, however, jumbos should contain 16 to 20 shrimp per pound, large from 21 to 35 per pound, and medium from 36 to 50 per pound. The size I use are 30 to 35 shrimp per pound, and sometimes these are sold as medium shrimp and sometimes large. I do not usually devein shrimp, as the vein does not offend me, and I like to cook shrimp in their shells.

Stock

Stock of any kind is simply a liquid enriched and flavored by whatever has been cooked in it. Vegetable stock is usually water in which vegetables have been simmered to extract flavor and nutrients. Flavored milk is milk that has had vegetables and herbs cooked in it.

A white stock is made by adding vegetables and/or meat or poultry to water without browning them first. Chicken stock is the most common white stock. Brown stock is made by browning bones, meat, and/or vegetables first, then adding them to cold water and simmering. The bones and meat may be beef, chicken, pork, turkey, lamb, veal, or a combination of all of these.

When making brown stock, there is a skill to browning the ingredients to the right point to enhance the color and flavor without producing a charred taste. After the browned ingredients are simmered for a sufficient period of time, they may be removed. The remaining liquid is then boiled down to the desired consistency and flavor. The higher the ratio of bones and meat to water, the more gelatinous and desirable the stock. Many times the meat is not used for another purpose, in which case the stock can be cooked over low heat for days.

To make two quarts of stock:

2 onions, quartered (peeled for white stock, unpeeled for brown)
2 ribs celery, leaves removed and sliced into 1/2-inch pieces
1/2 carrot, sliced in 1/2-inch pieces

3-4 pounds chicken, meat, bones, or carcasses
Bouquet garni of 2 stalks parsley, a crumbled bay leaf
Freshly ground black pepper or 6-8 black peppercorns

To make a white stock, put about 4 quarts of cold water in a large stockpot or pan and add the stock ingredients. Bring to a boil, then reduce heat, and simmer 3–4 hours or longer, partially covered. Add more water if the liquid cooks down below a couple of quarts. Strain. Boil down the remaining liquid to a desired consistency. Cool at room temperature, then refrigerate or freeze.

To make a brown stock, place the meat bones and vegetables in a roasting pan in the oven at 350 to 400 degrees and roast until dark brown but not burned. Then place in stockpot, add water, and proceed as above.

For a fish stock, add 2 pounds of shrimp, crawfish, or lobster shells (or 2 pounds non-oily fish) and the herbs and vegetables to 4 quarts of water in a stockpot and simmer for 30 minutes without boiling.

Canned chicken stock, also called chicken broth, can be used as a substitute for homemade chicken stock. Some brands are quite salty, but Campbell's and other leading manufacturers are constantly coming up with lower-salt products, and have some good ones on the market. Canned beef bouillon is an acceptable substitute for homemade beef stock. There are also some acceptable commercial granules and dry mixes that can be used. The next time you make some stock, buy two or three commercial preparations and do a taste test to see how you need to vary your recipes when using them in place of homemade. Homemade stocks may be boiled down and frozen quite successfully. Take the time every few months to make a chicken and a meat stock. You will be very satisfied with the effort!

Streak-o'-lean
This is the fat from the belly of the pig—the same piece of side meat as household bacon with a streak of lean meat in the fat. Bacon is usually smoked and cured, whereas streak-o'-lean may be fresh fat or salt cured. Different varieties of pigs give different amounts of fat. Streak-o'-lean is frequently used as a substitute for fatback.

Thermometers
There are several types of thermometers that are handy for the home cook to have—the first is an instant thermometer, also called a "microwave thermometer." Cuisinart makes an excellent one. This type of thermometer is the most accurate. You pull the roast (or whatever you are cooking) out of the oven, insert the thermometer, and take an instant reading. It is much preferable to the type of thermometer that is jabbed in meat and left in while cooking, causing the meat to lose some of its juices. When you need to know the temperature of a liquid (for dissolving yeast, deep-fat frying, and candy making), some thermometers serve a dual function, with a gauge low enough to measure 110 degrees and high enough to test deep fat—up to 400 degrees. Others indicate specifically the temperature for candy and sugar work—hard crack stage, soft crack stage, etc.

Toasting Breadcrumbs and Nuts
Place a single layer of crumbs or nuts on a baking sheet in an oven preheated to 350 degrees. Bake 8–10 minutes, until golden brown, stirring from time to time.

Turnip Greens
Some turnip greens are attached to the round turnip that is eaten as a vegetable, while some greens are grown only for the leaf. Both varieties are cooked the same way. The leaves are a deep green color and curly. They should be well washed because they grow in sandy soil. Always stem and remove the ribs and large veins before cooking. The traditional method calls for cooking them with fatback for a long time and the odor is very strong. I cook my turnip greens a shorter time, blanching them first.

Turnips
Southern turnips are not rutabagas. The Southern turnip is distinguished as a white turnip and is even called a white turnip in the North. The rutabaga, although called a yellow turnip, is not a turnip, and should not be substituted in any of the recipes in this book. The larger the turnip, the greater the bite and the woodiness, and, therefore, the greater the need for blanching or parboiling.

Bibliography

Beard, James. *James Beard's American Cookery*. Boston: Little, Brown, 1972.

Bece, Malcolm, Jr. "Romantic Wines of Madeira." *The Georgia Historical Quarterly*, December, 1954.

Bjornskov, Elizabeth. *The Complete Book of American Fish and Shellfish Cookery*. New York: Alfred A. Knopf, 1984.

Brown, Marion. *Southern Cook Book*. Chapel Hill, N.C.: University of North Carolina Press, 1968.

Cajun Cuisine. Lafayette, La.: Beau Bayou Publishing Company, 1985.

Caldwell, Betty Rye. *From the Tennessean . . . Betty's Best Recipes!* Nashville: Favorite Recipes Press, 1982.

Child, Julia. *From Julia Child's Kitchen*. New York: Alfred A. Knopf, 1970.

Child, Julia, Simone Beck, and Louisette Bertholle. *Mastering the Art of French Cooking, Volume I*. New York: Alfred A. Knopf, 1961.

Child, Julia, and Simone Beck. *Mastering the Art of French Cooking, Volume II*. New York: Alfred A. Knopf, 1970.

Child, Lydia Maria. *The American Frugal Housewife*. Cambridge, Mass.: A George Dawson Book, 1832.

Christ Church Cook Book. Savannah, Ga.: Kennickell Printing Co., 1956.

Colonial Williamsburg Foundation. *The Williamsburg Cookbook*. Williamsburg, Va., 1971.

Corbitt, Helen. *Helen Corbitt's Cookbook.* Boston: Houghton Mifflin, 1957.

Cossart, Noël. *Madeira: The Island Vineyard.* London: Christie's Wine Publication, 1984.

Dalsass, Diana. *Miss Mary's Down-home Cooking.* New York and Scarborough, Ontario: NAL Books, 1984.

DeBolt, Margaret Wayt. *Savannah Sampler Cookbook.* Norfolk, Va.: Donning Company, 1978.

Dull, Mrs. S. R. *Southern Cooking.* New York: Grosset & Dunlap, 1928.

Dupree, Nathalie. *Cooking of the South.* New York: Irena Chalmers Cookbooks, 1982.

Ellis, Merle. *Cutting-up in the Kitchen.* San Francisco: Chronicle Books, 1975.

Episcopal Churchwomen and Friends of Christ Episcopal Church. *Pass the Plate.* New Bern, N.C., 1981.

Exum, Helen McDonald. *Helen Exum's Chattanooga Cook Book.* Chattanooga, Tenn.: Chattanooga News–Free Press, 1970.

Feibleman, Peter S. *American Cooking: Creole and Acadian.* New York: Time-Life Books, 1971.

Food Editors of *Farm Journal.* *Farm Journal's Picnic & Barbecue Cookbook.* New York: Greenwich House, 1982.

Four Great Southern Cooks. Atlanta: Dubose Publishing, 1980.

Georgia Press Association. *Georgia Receipts.* Glenn McCullough (ed.). Atlanta, 1971.

Gleaners Class. *Favorite Recipes of the Red River Valley.* Shreveport, La.: First Methodist Church, 1968.

Goldstein, Jonathan, ed. *Georgia's East Asian Connection, 1733–1983,* vol. 22. Carrollton, Ga.: West Georgia College Studies on Social Sciences, 1983.

Goolsby, Sam. *Cedar Creek Game Cookbook.* Monticello, Ga.: Cedar Creek Hunting Lodge, 1975.

Greene, Bert. *Honest American Fare.* Chicago: Contemporary Books, 1923.

Hanley, Rosemary and Peter. *America's Best Recipes, State Fair Blue Ribbon Winners.* Boston and Toronto: Little, Brown, 1983.

Hartley, Grace. *Grace Hartley's Southern Cookbook.* New York: Doubleday, 1976.

Hearn, Lafcadio. *Creole Cook Book.* New Orleans, La.: Pelican Publishing House, 1967.

Hess, John L. and Karen. *The Taste of America.* New York: Grossman Publishers, 1977.

Hooker, Richard J. *A Colonial Plantation Cookbook: The Receipt Book of Harriott Pinckney Horry, 1770.* Columbia, S.C.: University of South Carolina Press, 1984.

Houston Academy Library Committee. *Down Home in High Style.* Dothan, Ala., 1980.

Huguenin, Mary Vereen, and Anne Montague Stoney. *Charleston Receipts.* Charleston, S.C.: Walker, Evans & Cogswell Company, 1950.

Jones, Evan. *American Food: The Gastronomic Story,* 2nd ed. New York: Random House, 1981.

Junior Charity League of Monroe, Louisiana. *The Cotton Country Collection.* Memphis, Tenn., 1972.

Junior League of Augusta, Georgia. *Tea-Time at the Masters.* Augusta, Ga., 1977.

Junior League of Atlanta. *Atlanta Cooknotes.* Atlanta: Stein Printing Co., 1982.

Junior League of Charleston. *Charleston Receipts,* Charleston, S.C., 1950.

Junior League of DeKalb County, Georgia. *Puttin' on the Peachtree.* Memphis, Tenn.: Wimmer Brothers Books, 1979.

Junior League of Fayetteville. *The Carolina Collection.* Fayetteville, N.C.: Kansas City Press, 1978.

Junior League of Greenville. *300 Years of Carolina Cooking.* Greenville, S.C., 1970.

Junior League of Hampton Roads. *Virginia Hospitality.* Hampton Roads, Va., 1975.

Junior League of Jackson. *Southern Sideboards.* Jackson, Miss., 1978.

Junior League of Savannah. *Southern Style.* Savannah, Ga., 1980.

Junior League of Shreveport. *A Cook's Tour of Shreveport.* Shreveport, La., 1964.

Junior League of Tuscaloosa, Alabama. *Winning Seasons.* Tuscaloosa, Ala., 1979.

Junior Service League of Americus, Georgia. *Something Southern, A Collection of Recipes.* Americus, Ga., 1976.

Junior Women's Club of Smithfield. *The Smithfield Cookbook.* Hampton, Va.: Multi-Print, 1978.

Lewis, Edna. *The Taste of Country Cooking.* New York: Alfred A. Knopf, 1982.

Lupo, Margaret. *Southern Cooking from Mary Mac's Tea Room.* Atlanta: Marmac Publishing Co., 1983.

Marshall, Lillian Bertrom. *Cooking Across the South.* Birmingham, Ala.: Oxmoor House, 1980.

———. *Southern Living Illustrated Cookbook.* Birmingham, Ala.: Oxmoor House, 1976.

Maynard, Gloria C. *Caterin' to Charleston.* Charleston, S.C.: Merritt Publishing Co., 1981.

Meade, Martha L. *Recipes from the Old South.* New York: Holt, Rinehart & Winston, 1981.

Monroe, Betty. *Huntsville Heritage Cookbook.* Huntsville, Ala.: Grace Club Auxiliary, 1967.

Morrison, Sally. *Cross Creek Kitchens.* Gainesville, Fl.: Triad Publishing Co., 1983.

National Fisheries Institute. *Galley Greats, Fish and Seafood.* Washington, D.C., 1981.

The National Society of the Colonial Dames of America in the State of Georgia. *Georgia Heritage, Treasured Recipes.* Atlanta, 1979.

Neal, Bill. *Southern Cooking.* Chapel Hill, N.C., and London: University of North Carolina Press, 1985.

Newnan Junior Service League. *A Taste of Georgia.* Newnan, Ga., 1977.

Phillips, Anne Byrn. *Cooking in the New South.* Atlanta: Peachtree Publishers, 1984.

Prudhomme, Paul. *Chef Paul Prudhomme's Louisiana Kitchen.* New York: William Morrow & Co., 1984.

Randolph, Mary. *The Virginia House-wife.* Karen Hess (ed.). Columbia, S.C.: University of South Carolina Press, 1984.

Rawlings, Marjorie Kinnan. *Cross Creek Cookery.* New York: Charles Scribner's Sons, 1942.

Rhett, Blanche S., and Gay Lettier. *Two Hundred Years of Charleston Cooking.* Columbia, S.C.: University of South Carolina Press, 1976.

Root, Waverley. *Food.* New York: Simon & Schuster, 1980.

Rutledge, Sarah. *The South Carolina Housewife.* Columbia, S.C.: University of South Carolina Press, 1979.

Schulz, Philip Stephen. *Cooking With Fire and Smoke.* New York: Simon & Schuster, 1986.

Shell, Ella Jo and John. *Recipes from Our Front Porch.* Memphis, Tenn.: Wimmer Brothers Books, 1982.

Social Circle United Methodist Church. *Sesquicentennial Cookbook.* Social Circle, Ga.: Cookbook Publishers, 1979.

Southern Heritage Cookbook Library. Birmingham, Ala.: Oxmoor House, 1983.

Southern Living 1983 Annual Recipes. Birmingham, Ala.: Oxmoor House, 1983.

Symphony League of Jackson, Mississippi. *The Jackson Cookbook.* Jackson, Miss., 1971.

Talmadge, Betty. *Lovejoy Plantation Cookbook.* Atlanta: Peachtree Publishers, 1970.

Talmadge, Betty, Jean Robitscher, and Carolyn Carter. *How to Cook a Pig and Other Back-to-the-Farm Recipes.* New York: Simon & Schuster, 1977.

Thoroughbred Fare Cookbook of Aiken, Inc. *Thoroughbred Fare.* Aiken, S.C., 1984.

Voltz, Jeanne A. *Barbecued Ribs and Other Great Feeds.* New York: Alfred A. Knopf, 1985.

———. *The Flavor of the South.* New York: Gramercy Publishing Company, 1983.

Vashti Auxiliary. *Pines and Plantations.* Thomasville, Ga., 1976.

Walter, Eugene. *American Cooking: Southern Style,* New York: Time-Life Books, 1971.

Washington, Martha. *Martha Washington's Booke of Cookery.* Karen Hess (ed.). New York: Columbia University Press, 1981.

White Lily Foods Company. *Great Baking Begins with White Lily Flour.* Des Moines, Iowa: Meredith Corporation, 1982.

Wilson, Mrs. Henry Lumpkin. *The Atlanta Exposition Cookbook.* Athens, Ga.: University of Georgia Press, 1984.

The Women's Ministries of First Assembly of God. *Country Cookbook.* Collierville, Tenn.: Fundcraft Publishing, 1984.

Index

A NOTE ABOUT THE AUTHOR

Nathalie Dupree was born on an Army post in New Jersey but has spent more than thirty-five years in the South, dividing her time between Virginia, Texas, and Georgia. She attended Texas Western and George Washington universities and received the Advanced Certificate from the Cordon Bleu in London. Shortly thereafter she ran a restaurant in Majorca, Spain, and upon returning to the United States opened her own restaurant in Social Circle, Georgia. She was the founder of Rich's Cooking School in Atlanta and is past president of the International Association of Cooking Professionals. She is well known as radio host of a daily food-news hour and has appeared regularly on "PM Magazine" in Atlanta. Her PBS television series "New Southern Cooking with Nathalie Dupree" was launched locally in the spring of 1986 and nationwide in the fall. She is the author of *Let's Entertain* and *Cooking of the South,* for which she received a Tastemaker Award. At present, she is a food and restaurant consultant and lives in Atlanta.

A NOTE ON THE TYPE

The text of this book was set in a face called Cheltenham Old
Style, designed by the architect Bertram Grosvenor Goodhue in
collaboration with Ingalls Kimball of The Cheltenham Press of
New York. Cheltenham was introduced in the early twentieth
century, a period of remarkable achievement in type design. The
idea of creating a "family" of types by making variations on the
basic type design was originated by Goodhue and Kimball in the
design of the Cheltenham series.

Composed by Superior Type,
Champaign, Illinois

Printed and bound by
Maple-Vail Book Manufacturing Group,
Binghamton, New York

Typography and binding design by
Tasha Hall